In Quest
of Music

W. J. Henderson—*Caricature, dated 1909 (Enrico Caruso)*

In
Quest of Music
A JOURNEY IN TIME

IRVING KOLODIN

1980
Doubleday & Company, Inc.
Garden City, New York

ALSO BY IRVING KOLODIN

THE METROPOLITAN OPERA: 1883–1935

THE METROPOLITAN OPERA: 1883–1940

THE KINGDOM OF SWING
(with Benny Goodman)

A GUIDE TO RECORDED MUSIC

THE CRITICAL COMPOSER

THE NEW GUIDE TO RECORDED MUSIC

THE STORY OF THE METROPOLITAN OPERA:
1883–1950

THE GUIDE TO LONG PLAYING RECORDS:
ORCHESTRAL MUSIC

THE MUSICAL LIFE

THE METROPOLITAN OPERA: 1883–1966

THE CONTINUITY OF MUSIC

THE INTERIOR BEETHOVEN

THE OPERA OMNIBUS

Library of Congress Cataloging in Publication Data
Kolodin, Irving, 1908-
In quest of music.
Includes index.
1. Music—Addresses, essays, lectures.
2. Musicians.   I. Title.
ML60.K628   780
Library of Congress Catalog Card Number: 78-22336
ISBN: 0-385-13061-9

To
J.G.

Contents

"Music is enough for a lifetime
But a lifetime is not enough for music"

SERGEI RACHMANINOFF

Prelude
(Without Fugue)

I

All my life I have been in quest of music, even when I didn't know what it was. The violin came into my life, at five or so, because I had an older brother to whom the piano had been assigned on its arrival a few years before. I say "assigned" as though it were a football helmet or a catcher's glove, something which became his personal property. That, indeed, is what happened. Whenever the piano bench was unoccupied, and I slid in to put my hands on the inviting keyboard, I was reminded: "That's not yours."

I had nothing against the violin, save the horrid sound it gave out when rubbed the wrong way (a not infrequent happening when I was a beginner). But I was quite conscious even then that what came out of the piano was music: while the best the violin could offer was a part of music. The unaccompanied works of Bach, even as a possibility, did not come into my life until much later.

The difference between music and what was only a part of it was clearly, lastingly, established ten or so years later when, having been taken to many violin recitals and a few opera performances (holiday-type entertainment), I finally attended a piano recital. Thus my first recollections of music as a total, engrossing experience, rather than merely as a gratifying sensation, are associated with Alfred Cortot's playing of a Beethoven piano sonata (the

"Appassionata") in a high school auditorium in Newark, New Jersey, c. 1922.

I could not possibly pretend that I understood what I was hearing, or that the music conveyed more than a series of stormy impressions linked, in a curious pattern of perception, to "The Star-Spangled Banner." My schooling in the same auditorium included, almost daily, singing of the national anthem. To me, the now intensely structural part of the sonata to follow (C, A flat, F) still brings back that childish association, especially on its appearance in the major.

The experience partook of something unforgettable because of an immensely arresting visual experience that went with the aural. The rather sad, dilapidated appearance of Cortot, with a lock of hair that fell over his face as he bent over the keyboard, bore physical proof to the bodily price of becoming an Artist. Perhaps if the occasion had brought me into visual observation of the well-fed Moriz Rosenthal or the palpably powerful Harold Bauer, the result might have been quite different. But Cortot it was, locked in a desperate physical effort to prove himself worthy of a work named—or misnamed—the "Appassionata."

In another high school auditorium (this one in Montclair, New Jersey) a year or two later, I found that the symphony orchestra in concert was quite another sensation than the meager yet stirring turmoil that issued from a record player under the name of Wagner's *Rienzi* overture.

The music of the second high school auditorium experience also included Beethoven: Symphony No. 5 in C minor. But even more fateful than the knock on the door that I read about in the program notes was the tense, contorted, nearly frenzied face of the conductor. Would he, with his face nearly scarlet—charged with the flush of blood—last long enough to lead the orchestra for the first time in New York the following evening? Somehow he did: and for many, many times thereafter. I was sitting in Carnegie Hall waiting to write about it when Serge Koussevitzky conducted the Boston Symphony in New York for the last time twenty-five years later.

Childish memories are susceptible to error, we are warned. But much more important than veracity is tenacity. In these particular instances, I can guarantee both.

Nor can I pretend, or want to imagine, that my quest of music was restricted to Beethoven, the "Appassionata" or the C minor symphony. I became acquainted, at the same time, with a popular passion of the day, because it had a funny bass introduction associated with the equally funny name of "Dardanella." And I can pinpoint precisely the year, and time of year, when the older brother to whom I have referred succumbed at age seventeen to tuberculosis. When I visited him at the sanitarium in rural New Jersey in which he was being treated, a record constantly being heard and reheard was wildly popular because of the appearance, in a performance by Paul Whiteman's orchestra, of a slide whistle playing the refrain called "Whispering."

So the quest, and the music associated with it, was neither single-minded, primly restrictive in category, nor separated into compartments bearing the labels "good," "not so good," "positively terrible." Some of it, to be sure, was more difficult to search out, because it required a trip to a New York concert hall, or the Lewisohn Stadium in the summertime, as I grew older. But the most elusive of all elements, I soon found out, whether it was in the popular music all around me or the classical kind, was quality. Fortunately I had friends, slightly older and better versed than I was in both kinds, to provide the best kind of guidance, a well-bred contempt for lack of quality.

Soon enough it was clear that I was under a life sentence, to be served in concert halls and opera houses, with no time off for good behavior.

The question still to be determined, however, was—in what capacity? Onstage? Backstage? Out front? In an orchestra pit? Whatever it was going to be, some formal training might be helpful. As much as I enjoyed the new popular music of the day—and what days those were!—there was no particular place in it for me, except enjoyment. But the new abundance of interest I had found in symphonies and concertos, quartets, and sonatas, stimulated the kind of *energetic* quest that was within a teenager's reach.

I began to practice hours a day with a view to entering a musi-

cal school within a year or so. I spent the next four years practicing the violin or attending classes at the school on Morningside
Heights in New York by day,[1] and working by night in my real
finishing school—Carnegie Hall—as an usher. That was my own
formula for preparing to be I did not know what. I had, to be
sure, discovered that there were such things in the world as music
critics, and the idea of being *paid* to listen to music was so attractive an idea that finding a way to do it was beyond attainment.

The sense of *compulsion* began to gather when I came upon a
book with a London locale called *Music at Midnight*. The writer's
name was Muriel Draper, which meant little to me in 1929.

But what a cast of characters! Heading the list was an irresistible French violinist with the dashing name of Jacques Thibaud. Often associated with him in the book's pages was an elegantly turned-out Polish pianist, who—according to where he
was—could be addressed as Arthur, Artur, or perhaps Arturo Rubinstein. Also cast in a leading role of the nightly revels was a pro-
digiously facile Catalonian cellist called Pablo (Pau, to close
friends). When a pianist couldn't turn up at the needed moment
to accompany a singer, the same cellist, Casals, could fill in.

Around these suns—appropriately suitable to midnight—revolved a gaudily exclusive group of satellites. They varied from
night to night: on one, it could be Leon Goossens, master of the
oboe; on another, hornist Aubrey Brain; on a third, the eminent
English clarinetist Charles Draper. Suns though the others were,
it was the satellites to whom they had to defer nightly. Only after
public participation in a concert at Queen's Hall or an opera at
Covent Garden could the sound of the horse's hoofs bringing
them in a coach be heard and tuning for the center piece of the
evening's masterworks by Mozart or Schubert, Brahms, or whomever seriously begin.

The tide of sound at 19-19A Edith Grove, where a pair of
music-hungry Americans had joined two smallish structures to

---

[1] The building which housed the then Institute of Musical Art still stands,
adjacent to the larger structure built in the twenties for the Juilliard School,
on Claremont Avenue just beyond 120th Street. Both are now utilized by the
Manhattan School of Music.

create a music room big enough for Mendelssohn's Octet and a scattering of listeners, began to rise about the time Westminster's Big Ben was showing the final double figures for the day. Testing and tuning done, Thibaud, posed with bow in hand, would nod the downbeat when the rest of London was going to bed. Hence the title of the book.

For the avid, aurally susceptible acolyte I was, 19-19A Edith Grove was the only earthly paradise known to me. What matter if, by 1929, it all related to pre-World War London, a decade and a half in the past? Surely such a consort of heavenly voices, all of middle years, could not soon be stilled. Perhaps a new surrounding for them might be found on Grove Street in New York's Greenwich Village. If so, I would have to contrive some form of access . . .

Participation on the playing level was obviously beyond me. Qualifications of a social kind based on friendship with one of the artists would take much too long to serve any useful purpose. Perhaps a critic of a special sort—the common kind are not tolerated in such surroundings—could be given floor space (in a corner). I would be that kind of critic, hardly known then, and perhaps not even now. He would have the comprehension, likewise the compassion, to make himself sufficiently non-functional not to be intrusive, like a eunuch in a harem.

The quest by which I was then animated has brought me, among innumerable other rewards, the privilege to talk with Thibaud, with Casals, with Rubinstein, even with Leon Goossens. But I never had the opportunity to hear them in such surroundings as Muriel Draper describes in *Music at Midnight*. I have stood on Westminster Bridge as Big Ben boomed twelve, but there was, alas, no music to follow.

Given a certain amount of charity, it could be said that I made the right career decision for the wrong reason. Over decades, the quest by which I was propelled settled into a compulsion I could neither question nor control. Taken together, quest and compulsion are as good a one-two attack on career problems as I ever heard of, needed, or wanted.

Over decades, I have heard very little music at midnight, save, perhaps, on an infrequent occasion when a public performance crept, rather than ran, overtime. Most midnights have found me posed not at the keyboard of a piano played by someone else, but at a typewriter powered, alas, by myself. Such midnight rendezvous as I associate with the name of Draper relate to pleasures purveyed by sister-in-law Ruth's monologues, or by a marvelously light-footed master of the tap dance, often in company with that master of another popular art, Larry Adler, and the mouth organ. To many he was the only Paul Draper: but to his parents at 19-19A, he was Paul Draper II, son of Paul Draper, Sr., and co-host-mother-music lover Muriel.

II

The most recent mention of Edith Grove I have encountered identifies the locale as an earthly Eden of another sort. The reference appears in Arthur (not Artur or Arturo) Rubinstein's *My Young Years* (Alfred A. Knopf, 1973). Here the elegantly turned-out, sometimes turned-on pianist recalls it as the scene not only of heavenly music making, but also of a celestially secretive passion he shared with a hostess having problems with an alcoholic husband.

So what? Even the other Eden held temptations that were neither pastoral nor parochial. If the Garden of Eden could, nevertheless, typify a sense of place which has endured for eons, why not a pair of houses south of London's South Kensington, now localized as SW 10?

Over the scores of years since years and scores have become synonymous to me, the quest of music (day and night, or from dawn to midnight) has never lost even one day of fascination. Now and then the music has been the same, and the Mendelssohn Octet being played in New York's Alice Tully Hall or the smaller one in the Concertgebouw of Amsterdam can be transformed into Thibaud's London locale for his favorite string work just by closing one's eyes. If, one by one, almost all the members of this Angelic

Company have taken their final bows and made an exit, others have come to replace them.

The particular place and its musical associations persist as the enduring image for what the quest of music—and not merely chamber music—can be, given proper circumstances. Its goal is a wordless conversation among like-minded persons, a powerful stimulant for the spirit rather than the body, soul food drawn not from a pot, but from the belly of a Strad, Guarnerius, or Amati, seasoned with love, and served on wings of song.

The Grovesians, as I think of them, were hardly the founding fathers of this concept: they merely possess for me, and perhaps others, an identity preserved in print by one woman with a warm, unyielding memory. And by that memory has been preserved a singular elite of a guild which has affiliates worldwide.

They are those whom I set aside and cherish, through the quest and its consequences, as artists, not performers.

My distinction of how one differs from another may not satisfy everyone, but I tender it in faith nevertheless. The artist is primarily interested in what he or she can put into music. The performer is primarily interested in what he or she can take out of music. To be sure, the artist may take out of it a good deal of money, but also puts back into it—by deed, by example, by acts of conscience, concern, and consideration—values that defy man-made measure.

Providentially, the distinction persists from one generation to another, because music itself remains perpetual. If there is a new aspect to the part of the quest I have been allowed to pursue, it is that the range of possibilities from which such outstanding individuals may emerge is broader now than it was, say, fifty years ago: Seoul, South Korea; Christchurch, New Zealand; Johannesburg, South Africa, are as likely a possibility as Bombay, India; Budapest, Hungary; or Kalamazoo, Michigan.

The upshot, or the offshoot, is an art infinitely more diverse than at any time in human history, whose focus is far more difficult to pinpoint than when, slightly more than two hundred years ago, it could, with confidence, be specified as Paris, *or* Leipzig, *or* Milan, *or*, perhaps, one of another few cities.

Or, to quote a profound student of the subject: "To say that music was never in such estimation, or so well understood as it is at present, would be only advancing a fact as evident as that its inhabitants are now more generally civilized and refined, than they were in any other period to be found in the history of mankind."

Whether the two sides of that equation would be accepted without quibble is, in itself, a statement not beyond quibble: after all, it was written by the celebrated Dr. Charles Burney in 1773, and he was speaking wholly of Europe.

Today's quest is somewhat broader, vastly more diverse, and, I would say, at least a fraction more rewarding.

Irving Kolodin
May 1, 1980

Ernest Ansermet

One artist whom I could not possibly think of as a performer is Ernest Ansermet. The use of the present tense may confuse some who know, as I do, that Ansermet died in February 1969. But relegating Ansermet to conductors of the past would ignore the present reality which makes a contemporary, intellectually and emotionally, of any person whose art has a vital, accessible identity.

As an instance, the mere fact that Arturo Toscanini's earthly existence came to an end in 1957 did not prevent thousands of Japanese recently from subscribing to an issue unparalleled in history: an encyclopedic résumé of his hundred "best" recordings. Inasmuch as Toscanini was, during his lifetime, a remote, inaccessible paragon to the musical public of Japan, the end of his life in New York on January 16, 1957, did not in the least alter the Japanese relationship to him. He remained a remote, inaccessible paragon to whom the Japanese responded with unprecedented idolatry when the bonus, or *bonanza*, of such a collection was offered to them.

Ansermet had somewhat more reality to American audiences than Toscanini had to the Japanese, but only relatively so. Indeed, if they knew him only as a conductor, which is to say, as the guest conductor of someone else's orchestra, they knew of him only in a shadowy semblance of his true identity. He was, essentially, a *chef d'orchestre*, with all the subtle difference that the French words imply vis-à-vis any other.

More specifically, Ansermet was the *chef* of one particular *orchestre*: the Orchestre de la Suisse Romande, which was created by him in 1918, and which he continued to direct until his death more than fifty years later. That is a record which left Eugene Ormandy's astonishing forty-two years as permanent conductor of the Philadelphia Orchestra when he retired in 1980 still nearly a decade short of Ansermet's lifetime service.

As for any other recent, or present, colleague equaling Ansermet's accomplishment, that is a feat that may take even longer than half a century. As a *chef d'orchestre*, Ansermet was not only something more than a conductor, here one month, there another; he was also something more than your common variety *chef d'orchestre*, nose in the score, head in the sky. His whole life revolved around Switzerland's spacious Lac Leman, from birth in Vevey (November 11, 1883) to death in Geneva. Rather than circumscribing his activities, it concentrated them in a focused way that enabled him to build a world of his own around its two hundred and twenty-five square miles.

Both of his parents were musicians, and it was certainly a family preference that he should be, also. But they were all of the conviction that Switzerland was no place to earn a living as a composer, which he aspired to be. Clearly, however, they were also persuaded that it was more important to be a Swiss citizen earning a decent living at something else, and also composing, than to earn a decent living as a composer elsewhere than in Switzerland. His decision was to prepare himself, first at the University of Lausanne, and then at the Sorbonne, for the vocation of mathematician, and to continue his study of music as an avocation.

This worked well enough until he was twenty-seven, in 1910, with a job in hand as a teacher of math at his alma mater, the Lausanne Gymnasium. He had also worked at music and especially at conducting. Thus he was reasonably equipped when an off-season in the academic world enabled him to accept an opportunity to conduct at the Kursaal in Montreux, with two momentous outcomes. He found, in the orchestra, a lifelong attraction; and he found, in Igor Stravinsky, a friend who would help to make it a possibility.

Fresh from the success of *L'Oiseau de feu* and firmly established as a new protégé of its producer, Serge Diaghilev, the vacationing Stravinsky was ideally placed to recommend to the famous impresario any musician of whom he thought well. The recommendation was made and accepted, thus cementing what had every aspect of a lifelong friendship between conductor and composer. That was still for the future to determine. The immediate consequence was to establish a long, productive relationship between the apprentice conductor Ansermet and his senior colleague Pierre Monteux.

They spent in partnership a major part of the most exciting decade in the twentieth century's history of music. In this decade Russian ballet surged to prominence not only on the lithe bodies of Lydia Lopokova, Tamara Karsavina, and Vaslav Nijinsky, but on the veritable heartbeat in the pulse of such new scores as Stravinsky's *L'Oiseau de feu* and *Le Sacre du printemps*, Ravel's *Daphnis et Chloé* and *La Valse*, Falla's *Tricorne*, and a host of works by older composers (Tchaikovsky, Rimsky-Korsakov, Borodin, etc.) hitherto unknown to the West.

Even before the decade was out, Monteux had parted company with Diaghilev. He became conductor of the Boston Symphony Orchestra in 1919. Even before this, moreover, Ansermet found a new identity of his own as principal conductor for the first American tour of Diaghilev's Ballets Russes in 1916.

II

How much of his time in New York between April 2 and April 29 Ansermet spent elsewhere than at the Metropolitan Opera House is not fully documented. That he poked an inquisitive nose and a receptive ear into the unlikely subject of ragtime is. A few years later Ansermet wrote appreciatively of an American-born composer related in no way to Stravinsky or Ravel, Borodin or Rimsky-Korsakov:

> Some time ago I met in New York, one of the most celebrated ragtime composers, Irving Berlin. A Russian Jew by origin, he had, like César-Napoléon Gaillard,[1] been a jack of-all-trades, and

[1] The name of Gaillard is a very old one in Swiss history, with branches in the cantons of Fribourg, Genève, Valais, and Vaud stretching back to the

known all kinds of fortune, before becoming rich in writing negro music. Devoid of any musical culture, incapable of writing his notes, hardly knowing how to play the piano, he told me himself how he used to pick out the notes on the piano with one finger or whistle to a professional who noted down these melodies which entered his spirit, and how then he'd have the professional seek out the harmonies until he was satisfied. Having assimilated the negro style perfectly, it is to this style that he applies his gift of musical invention, which is indeed remarkable.[2]

If the gift of Berlin could be described as "remarkable" the receptivity of a man of Ansermet's musical qualifications was hardly less so. Its genesis may be found in an article printed in the *Revue Romande* of October 1919 (for those to whom the term may be unfamiliar, "Romande" refers to the French-speaking part of Switzerland). In it Ansermet wrote, apropos ragtime and the interest that prompted his meeting with Berlin: "I remember having traveled by railroad between Berne and Lausanne with a group of young Americans. One of them began to hum a piece of rag-time, whereupon they all joined in, marking the rhythms by beating their hands on the wooden benches . . ."[3]

The reminiscence and its consequence may well have been stimulated by an experience that came to Ansermet during a visit to London in the "season" of 1919 (July) by the Diaghilev ballet. Professionally, it was outstanding for the opportunity for Ansermet to conduct the first performance ever of Manuel de Falla's score for *Tricorne*, with Leonide Massine's choreography and the decor of Pablo Picasso. Personally, it was no less memorable for an experience that furthered his interest in ragtime. At a time when most musicians of his background regarded "jass" (or jazz)

---

fifteenth century. Felix (1847–1911), born in Lausanne, is described in the *Dictionnaire historique et biographique de la Suisse,* published in Neuchâtel, 1926, p. 306 as a "pédagogue à Lausanne" and his son Felix (1879–1920) as "directeur des tramways à Lausanne" (where, of course, Ansermet went to school and later taught). But the fame of César-Napoléon had not penetrated to this dictionary at the time it was published.

[2] This quotation and others to follow are reproduced from the French text and English translation in HOT JAZZ, Revue Internationale de la Musique de Jazz, Avril-Mai 1939.

[3] See note 2, above.

as a crude travesty of music, Ansermet was motivated to write:

> Under the name of Southern Syncopated Orchestra, there is
> an ensemble of authentic musicians of the negro race to be heard
> in London. Instrumentalists and singers, they present us pell mell
> with all sorts of manifestations of their art, the old with the new,
> the best with the worst. It's a mysterious new world which we
> were acquainted with only through its more or less distant reper-
> cussions, and which finally reaches us in its living reality. One
> can hardly imagine a more opportune manifestation, and it is to
> be hoped, for our common edification, that the British metropo-
> lis will not alone reap its benefits.

As a practitioner of an ensemble art which begins in the first instance with discipline, it is hardly remarkable that Ansermet was
drawn first of all to the orchestra as a whole:

> The first thing that strikes one about the Southern Syncopated
> Orchestra is the astonishing perfection, the superb taste and the
> fervor of its playing. I couldn't say if these artists make it a duty
> to be sincere, if they are penetrated by the idea that they have a
> "mission" to fulfill, if they are convinced of the "nobility" of
> their task, if they have that holy "audacity" and that sacred
> "valor" which our code of musical morals requires of our Euro-
> pean musicians nor indeed if they are animated by any "idea"
> whatsoever.

Having closed one door on convention with these mocking
words (worthy of a Debussy as critic) on the pretensions of much
European music making, Ansermet opens wide another on a new
vista:

> But I can see they have a very keen sense of the music they
> love, and a pleasure in making it which they communicate to the
> listener with irresistible force—a pleasure which pushes them to
> outdo themselves all the time, to constantly enrich and refine
> their medium. They play generally without notes, and even when
> they have some, it only serves to indicate the general line, for
> there are very few numbers I have heard them execute twice with
> exactly the same effect.

Has anyone ever summarized the underlying temper and character of a great jazz ensemble at work more precisely? Even without

the kind of indoctrination readily available to the neophyte of today—or, for that matter, of yesterday—from recordings, Ansermet at the dawn of (2/4) time already had its essential elements firmly in hand:

> I imagine that, knowing the voice attributed to them in the harmonic ensembles and conscious of the role their instrument is to play, they can let themselves go, in a certain direction and within certain limits, as their heart desires. They are so entirely possessed by the music they play, that they can't stop themselves from dancing inwardly to it in a way that their playing is a real show, and when they indulge in one of their favorite effects which is to take up the refrain of a dance in a tempo suddenly twice as slow and with redoubled intensity and figuration, a truly gripping thing takes place—it seems as if a great wind is passing over a forest or as if a door is suddenly opened on a wild orgy.

All of this instant analysis, evaluation, and appreciation of a folk art alien to his background qualifies Ansermet to be described as precisely what he was—a musician-logician of an extraordinary and rare order. The whole of Ansermet's prevision of jazz and what it could become is too lucid to disserve by excerpting. But two final perceptions must be mentioned. One is of the inbuilt possibility of a composer who would use the jazz idiom creatively: "Perhaps one of these days we shall see the Glinka of negro music," likening the role of such a pioneer to that of the great founding father of the Russian school of composition based on folk music. (Even as of 1919, there was, in Washington, D.C., a young pianist born Edward Kennedy Ellington [in 1899] sharpening the tools with which to carve out such a career for himself.) The other was the perpetual role in jazz of the creative soloist:

> There is in the Southern Syncopated Orchestra an extraordinary clarinet virtuoso who is, it seems to me, the first of his race to have composed perfectly formed blues on the clarinet. I've heard two of them which he had elaborated at great length, then played to his companions so that they could make up an accompaniment. Extremely different, they are equally admirable in their richness of invention, force of accent, and daring in novelty and the unexpected. Already they gave the idea of a style, and

their form was gripping, abrupt, harsh, with a brusque and pitiless ending like that of Bach's second Brandenburg Concerto.

I wish to set down the name of this artist of genius: as for myself I shall never forget it is Sidney Bechet. When one has tried to rediscover in the past one of those figures to whom we owe the advent of our art—those men of the 17th and 18th centuries, for example, who made expressive works of dance airs, clearing the way for Haydn and Mozart, not the starting point but the first milestone—what a moving thing it is to meet this very black, fat boy with white teeth and that narrow forehead, who is very glad one likes what he does, but who can say nothing of his art, save that he follows his "own way" [English in the French text] and when one thinks that this "own way" is perhaps the highway the whole world will swing along tomorrow.[4]

Of all the many words written about Bechet, born in New Orleans in 1897, of his memorable associations with Louis Armstrong, Ellington, and all the others, during his lifetime (he died in Paris in 1959), these have to be the most memorable. This "very black, fat boy with white teeth," then all of twenty-two, bore with him not only a powerful impulse of his own which was to grow and mature, decade by decade, but also a rich heritage of his Creole forebears, who had their own musical conditioning.

To review it briefly, the Creoles of New Orleans were French-descended in character and culture. In the years of the nineteenth century in which the famous French Opera flourished in New Orleans (it was destroyed by fire in 1919 and never rebuilt) Creole musicians became specialists in the playing of reed instruments and were not unknown to have advanced training in Paris, thus preparing them to play the clarinet and oboe in the orchestra of the New Orleans Opera. A predominant number of teachers of the reed instruments to the rising generation of ragtime-jazz players in New Orleans in the 1890s were French-derived: Bechet himself studied with one named Achille Bacquet.

Bechet's great career took him from a beginning with a few lessons with Bacquet to the status of world-class performer on two instruments. His mastery of the clarinet, by age twenty-two, has

[4] The French phrase is *"où le monde s'engouffrera demain."* The translation of Walter E. Schaap interpolates the "swing" catchword of the late 1930s.

been attested by a connoisseur of such matters, Ansermet himself. But Bechet also aspired to follow his "own way" on the sweetly soulful sound of the soprano saxophone (which can be distinguished from the other innovations of Adolphe Sax because it is generally straight in shape, not curved). A first try, in Chicago, by the inquisitive Bechet with an instrument he purchased in a pawnshop ended in failure because he couldn't master the fingering. A year later he bought another soprano sax and persisted to become as adept on it as he was on the clarinet.

This was, coincidentally, in London as a member of Will Marion Cook's Southern Syncopated Orchestra. As Ansermet's observation records, Bechet was still basically a performer on the clarinet. The first recorded evidence of his performance on the soprano saxophone I have found is indeed an auspicious one: as a member in 1925 of the Clarence Williams Blue Five, in which the leader-pianist was Williams, Louis Armstrong (in one of his earlier recordings) played trumpet, and Bechet played both baritone and soprano sax.[5] He was, from then, indeed on his "own way."

III

From the perceptive words written in London at thirty-six, one is tempted to wonder: what might Ansermet have discovered about jazz during his next fifty years of life had he pursued the paths that led him to Bechet? Fortunately, there were others who followed Ansermet's response to this singular Pied Piper and his gifted colleagues. No doubt at least a few were stimulated by his article of 1919, as I myself was, when it was reprinted in HOT JAZZ in 1939.

One cannot, however, think of another musician with the ability and the interest to make Switzerland the center of music that evolved after Ansermet founded the Orchestre de la Suisse Romande. He was born in Vevey, gravitated to Lausanne to find a

[5] Delaunay, Charles, HOT *Discography* (Commodore Music Shop, New York, 1940), p. 35.

vocation, and unexpectedly discovered his life purpose in Montreux: it was therefore inescapable that he should choose as the proper place for its exercise the capital city of Geneva at the other end of Lac Leman.

Already in 1918 he had conducted the premiere of *L'Histoire du soldat* so well that it earned Stravinsky's esteem nearly twenty years later when his *Chroniques de ma vie* was published:

> Among our other collaborators I had had the good fortune to discover one who later became not only a most faithful and devoted friend, but also one of the most reliable and understanding executants of my compositions: I mean Ansermet . . . I valued very highly his broad general culture, but up to that time I had not been able to form a definite opinion of him as conductor of my own works.
>
> He was frequently absent [the premiere took place in the Lausanne Theater] and it was, therefore, only rarely and by chance that I had had any opportunity of hearing him conduct my music: and the few isolated renderings I had heard, good though they were, had not been sufficient to show me what an admirable conductor he was to become, and how faithfully he could transmit my musical thought to the public, without ever falsifying it by personal or arbitrary interpretation. For, as I have already said, music should be transmitted and not be interpreted, because interpretation reveals the personality of the interpreter rather than that of the author, and who can guarantee that such an executant will reflect the author's vision without distortion?[6]

In a rare burst of laudation, Stravinsky says further of his Swiss friend: "An executant's talent lies precisely in his faculty for seeing what is actually in the score and certainly not in a determination to find what he would like to find. This is Ansermet's greatest and most precious quality, and it particularly revealed itself while we were studying the score of the *Soldat*. From that moment dates an intellectual understanding between us which time has only increased and strengthened."

The record might be extended further, were it useful, by quotations from Stravinsky's comments on Ansermet's preparation and

[6] Stravinsky, Igor, *An Autobiography* (W. W. Norton & Company, Inc., New York; first published by the Norton Library, 1962), p. 74.

production of such other new works to come as *Les Noces* (1923) and *Capriccio* (1929). The second of these marked a new departure for the dedicated Swiss, being performed with the Orchestre Symphonique de Paris (OSP), of which he was the founder in 1928. When the *Symphonie des Psaumes* (composed for the fiftieth anniversary of the Boston Symphony in 1930) was first performed in Europe, at the Palais des Beaux-Arts, Brussels, December 13, 1930, the conductor was Ansermet.

The parallel pattern thus engendered endured for years, though with some physical drift and, eventually, a spiritual rift. Ansermet's base continued to be, primarily, Geneva; Stravinsky's tended to be, more and more, a contingency of world, as well as musical, affairs. By the late thirties, it was America rather than elsewhere and, most likely, the West rather than the East Coast. When World War II settled over Europe, Stravinsky premieres were almost exclusively American events.

Ansermet's isolation in Switzerland from the bombings and distractions of war promoted one outcome that could hardly be anticipated. When London/Decca resumed record production in 1946 with new sound techniques developed in part through wartime research, the conductor to whom it turned for expert collaboration was Ansermet. The recording he produced of Stravinsky's *Petrouchka* in London's Kingsway Hall "first brought home to critics and collectors that recording techniques had taken a dramatic step forward."

The words are not mine—though I could have quoted equivalent ones—but those of Arthur Haddy, chief engineer for London/Decca, and architect of the FFRR (Full Frequency Range Recording) techniques that glorified the sound that Ansermet produced. A man whose life has been dedicated to the propagation of superior sound from 78 rpm days through the LP to stereo and beyond, Haddy is far too much a professional to permit company loyalties to qualify his judgment. His evaluation of Ansermet's competence, artistry, and engineering *aperçu* (derived, of course, from his mathematical training), written after his death in 1969,[7]

[7] Haddy, Arthur (with Thomas Heinitz), *Saturday Review*, March 29, 1969, p. 55.

is a treatise on the man, and the mind, behind the music he created.

The two came into special focus with the emergence of the long-playing system, and the creation of Decca Europe (1947) which enabled Ansermet and his own orchestra to record in the familiar home surroundings of Geneva's Victoria Hall. Reciprocally, this brought about a new standard of performance for the orchestra itself. Essentially it was a smallish ensemble, a product perhaps of the Swiss attitude that the cleanest, best-designed watches could also be the least sizable. But when the engineers demanded more bass for recording purposes, and Ansermet protested that he could produce no more from his four basses, plans were made to enlarge the personnel to equality (twelve cellos rather than six, eight basses rather than four) with Europe's finest. Needless to say, the money that Ansermet and the orchestra earned from their recordings more than paid for this expansion.

Perhaps the most illuminating of all the recordings made by Ansermet and the Orchestre de la Suisse Romande for London (they never recorded for any other label) is CSA 2101. It contains two works of Hector Berlioz (*Le Corsaire* overture and the *Symphonie fantastique*), *plus* a double-sided rehearsal record. Here the unique relationship of Ansermet to his men (and women) is vivified by his own command of language: after he tells his players that "Poor Berlioz cried a great deal—he was a hopeless romantic" (*un éperdu romantique*)—and *sings* the phrase "in his own way," they have no choice but to reproduce it to his satisfaction.

That the recording is also to the satisfaction of the most exacting Berliozian is an expression of Ansermet's attitude in another way. All his recording career, he had resisted efforts to record the *Symphonie fantastique* because, he complained, in all the reproductions he had ever heard, the bells lacked fidelity. In 1967, London's engineers produced a set of bells especially made at a German foundry, and Ansermet's objections were overcome. It is a high spot of the rehearsal recording when, in a trial of placement for the bells used in the "Witches' Sabbath" (fifth movement), they create a chaotic jangle, causing laughter in the orchestra. To this, Ansermet explains patiently: "What you hear are bells—not a xylophone. We play in tune, the bells play out of tune—that's just as it should be."

Curiously, Ansermet's final recording session (in 1969, in London) was devoted to Stravinsky's *L'Oiseau de feu*. He had been invited to fill a session with the New Philharmonia Orchestra in London's favorite recording "studio" (Kingsway Hall). "He was," remarks Haddy, "scarcely changed at all . . . his eyes were still the bluest and the most piercing I had ever encountered." And, he observes: "The new recording of the complete *Firebird* . . . was the last he made and it brought Ansermet back full circle where it had all begun with *Petrouchka* twenty-two years earlier."

IV

Cyclically, it could be said that this also fulfilled the longer arch of Ansermet's career as a conductor, which had begun in Montreux nearly sixty years before with the meeting with the composer of *Firebird*. Stravinsky's esteem for Ansermet continued in print as long as *Chroniques de ma vie* was in print (first as copyright in English by Simon & Schuster in 1936, more recently as part of the Norton Library). But it is not to be found updated in the volumes of collaboration with Robert Craft which began to appear in 1959 under the title of *Conversations with Igor Stravinsky* and the imprint of Doubleday. True to their individual endowments and pertinacity of character, both men continued to evolve. Even as Stravinsky did not feel obliged to restrict himself to the ideas and the attitudes by which he had been motivated in his early ballets, so Ansermet did not feel compelled to pretend an allegiance to consequences in which he did not believe, artistically.

So far as I can ascertain, the friendship began to erode in 1937, when, according to the composer, Ansermet "made an unauthorized cut in *Jeu de cartes*." Whether this was for concert purposes or a recording is not specified. In the same passage in *Themes and Episodes*[8] Stravinsky took issue with Ansermet for

[8] Alfred A. Knopf, Inc., New York, 1966, pp. 153, 154.

criticizing "my revisions of earlier pieces" and for decrying "my new music" and having the "temerity to express himself in a heavy but not very weighty tome on the subject."

For his own part, Ansermet used his own access to print, through interviews, to leave little doubt that, in his view, "agreement is obviously expected" by Stravinsky "for no matter what he says," and that "the composer, in person, seems to be saying the opposite of the composer in his autobiography, at any rate insofar as some of his colleagues are concerned. Thus the mention of his *Symphonies of Wind Instruments* provokes a tirade against Ansermet and his recent broadcast of it with the NBC Symphony."[9]

Clearly there were more fundamental things at work in the estrangement of old friends and close co-workers than a cut here or a disagreement there. Several years before Stravinsky made the comment in *Themes and Episodes* quoted above, Ansermet expressed in print and at length his opinions on a subject as far removed from the Southern Syncopated Orchestra as Bechet was from Berlioz.

They are to be found in two successive issues of *Recorded Sound*, Journal of the British Institute of Recorded Sound, from 1964. They are collectively titled "The Crisis of Contemporary Music," and bear the subtitles I) *The Musical Problem* (*Recorded Sound*, No. 13, January 1964) and II) *The Stravinsky Case* (*Recorded Sound*, No. 14, February 1964). They were originally delivered as lectures funded by Lady and Sir Robert Mayer in December 1963.

As he progresses on his way, Ansermet gives voice clearly to the perplexities of a man who had pondered his problem profoundly. "Having followed contemporary music closely," he says, "I have felt from the outset that this music is an aberration, but I could not show that my intuition was right. That is why I resolved to elucidate the musical phenomenon." In other words, Ansermet had called upon the part of him which was mathematician to find the answers that had eluded Ansermet the musician.

A more formidable marshaling of means to an end could hardly be imagined. Settling in to penetrate the lack of "internal form"

[9] New York *Times*, March 31, 1948.

in the compositions of those who follow the precepts of Schoenberg, Ansermet shows—with total scientific detachment—that the chordal structures of tones in Western music relate to auditory perceptions that are "logarithmic." In consequence, says Ansermet, "the musician spontaneously writes 'tonally' and this word indicates a certain organization of sounds . . . similar to the organization of words by syntax in spoken language . . ."

In tracing the successive steps by which music of the twentieth century digresses from its long preceding evolutionary process, Ansermet sets forth clearly what is abundantly evident in the great early works of Stravinsky. The ear readily accepts the *polytonality* in *Petrouchka*, *Le Sacre du printemps*, *L'Histoire du soldat*, etc. because it can sort out such complications as long as a tonal center is preserved, if only by implication (p. 171). But, says Ansermet, "if the musician does not write 'tonally' it is because he compels himself not to write tonally, and in this case his music is as incomprehensible as the speech of a man who does not comply with the syntax of his language . . ."

Why, it might be inquired, should a composer of Stravinsky's mastery, with the powers of discrimination manifest in the great works cited above, and to which many more could be added, deliberately deny everything to which he was attached? Or, in simpler terms, work with terms of his aesthetic opposite?

Simple enough, says Ansermet. "When, formerly, we used to discuss these problems, he told me that the problem of the composer was a 'how'? 'How to do it?' But then, I said, what is the 'what' of music? 'It's something,' he replied, 'which comes of itself, which is given once and for all, and with which, in consequence, there is no need to preoccupy oneself, while there devolves on the composer the task of finding the 'how.'"

Applying these recollections to the midpoint in the century at which *Agon* was born, Ansermet concludes: "It may seem paradoxical that he should have recourse to this technique [the dodecaphonic] . . . but to Stravinsky, having increasingly reduced his creative activity to a 'making' and 'how to make,' serial technique could appear as a way of making it like any other. *Agon*, for example. As a pure play of counterpoint and rhythm, and by reason of the very sure sense Stravinsky has of the ordering of musical form by melodic dialectic, by the alternation of motifs, their variations and their returns, this work can give rise to a certain aesthetic satisfaction. But the almost total absence of tonal feeling, due to the use of the series, makes voids of these forms, so that the music furnishes the ballet with no expressive substance . . ."

These two words—"expressive substance"—which come tolling back like a bell, are, in a vibrant way, a ringing affirmation of everything about Ansermet that made him the artist that he was. Neither friendship, nor convenience, nor sentiment based on a past association could bring from him an affirmative response if the experience itself did not. When he addressed himself, in the London Coliseum in 1919, to a black art in which he was all but unlettered, the intuitive reaction of his senses satisfied him immediately, enduringly. When he confronted another kind of musical experience in which he was equally unversed, the lack of stimulation, intuitive or otherwise, left him not merely lacking in response, but in a *reason* for his lack of response.

Unlike most other musicians whose own sense of response was thwarted by encounters with *Agon* and source material from which it derived, Ansermet was not lacking in the capacity to see their shortcomings as well as to hear them. By converting all of his life's experiences—non-musical as well as musical—into the production of a *non*-musical reason for rejecting that which he found to be *un*musical, Ansermet added vastly to the confidence of musical persons in their own rejection of it.

V

This curio of twentieth-century aesthetic history, in which two men who shared comprehension of as revolutionary a musical innovation as is contained in Stravinsky's early masterpieces should eventually have a falling out because of the composer's digression to another kind of revolutionary practice, may have a counterpart in arts other than music, but it does not immediately come to mind. Which was the one who adhered to artistic purpose, which the one who turned his back on it? By Ansermet's reckoning—and mine—it would have to be Stravinsky. And did he not have a possibly perverse reason for doing what the other thought beyond reason?

At the end of a long, wonderful, productive career applied to constant attention to doing that which would *épater le bourgeois* —"startle the small-minded" might be a workable translation—by writing a mass when a contra-mass might be expected, or composing a symphony without strings, or never writing another *Sacre* when one was anticipated, or inventing neoclassicism when there was no precedent for it—Stravinsky had one impossibly unlikely thing left to do: adopt the mode of procedure set in motion by his antithesis, Arnold Schoenberg, and show how well he could do that, too. Of course, he needed a deviation from the deviation, something more chic, highly stylish, as propounded by Anton Webern.

For this line of reasoning there are several contributory factors to consider: Stravinsky had finally completed that which he had always aspired to do: write an opera with an English text (*The Rake's Progress*, with W. H. Auden and Chester Kallman); Schoenberg had died on July 13, 1951; and Stravinsky had never entertained (and I think that is just the word he would have liked for something so laughable) such an idea until Robert Craft came into his life. Or, as stated in a recent survey of Craft's life, he was "instrumental in persuading Stravinsky to adopt the 12-tone method of composition."[10] To my mind, it is comparable to a man with a great capacity for language deciding to master Swahili because it had the reputation for being totally incomprehensible.

As previously mentioned (page 14), Stravinsky had an obsession with the "how" rather than the "what" of composition. It was the satisfaction of evolving an outcome, rather than communicating content, by which he was absorbed. And it was the ultimate form of demonstrating his ordination of "how" as superior to "what" that prompted him to make a twelve-person ballet of *Agon* with its twelve-note series.

[10] Baker's Biographical Dictionary of Musicians, edited by Nicolas Slonimsky (Schirmer Books, New York, Sixth Edition, 1978), p. 359.

Rhythmically it satisfies the needs of dance, which is impelled by beats and pulses (though, I have been told by one dancer who made a great success in it [Melissa Hayden], *Agon* is counted differently by its performers than by its conductor and the musicians who play it). Pictorially, it satisfies the play of textures by which rhythms are conveyed because, like the master draftsman he is, Stravinsky's choice of colors is a function of "how" rather than "what."

Should the question finally be poised: "Does the 'what' of *Agon* say anything?" the answer would have to be in the counterquestion "To whom?"

To the choreographer, such as George Balanchine, I would say it says: "Action." To the dancers: "Reaction." To the conductor: "Projection." To me, as a listener: "Dejection."

I use that term because the whole episode of Stravinsky as a "defector" from tonality, or, in some way, a renegade from his lifelong identity, is more a matter of semantics, point of view, and personalities than it is of consequences. Essentially speaking, *Agon* is an abstraction of Stravinsky's late life (he was past seventy-five when it was finished in 1957) rather than an obstruction to consideration of him as the greatest musical influence of the twentieth century.

But there is a measure of interest in what he *thought* of himself as a "serial composer" rather than what he actually was. He has stated that "The intervals of my series [the combination of intervals that takes the place of the scale in serial composition] are attracted by tonality. I compose vertically and that is, in one sense at least, to compose tonally."[11]

However, there are elaborations of these considerations that are worth listening to. "A new demand for greater in-depth listening changes time perspective. Perhaps also the operation of memory in a non-tonally developed work (tonal, but not eighteenth-century tonal system) is different. We are located in time constantly in a tonal system . . ."

Here Stravinsky has touched on two of the profound points between the vast body of music as he, and we, know it, and the part of it of recent date which has regrouped itself around other values. One is "the operation of memory"; the other is that we are "located in time" in tonal music.

Together they sum up the respects in which abstraction in the creation of music differs from abstraction in the graphic arts. All too often I hear well-meaning experts on the avant-garde of painting in this period question the rationale by which so many, otherwise open-minded people—as I would like to think I am—can see things their way in the graphic arts, but turn down what they would consider parallel freedom of choice in music.

A painting, no matter how complicated or abstract, exists in

11 *Agon*. Conducted by the composer. Columbia ML 5215.

space—within a frame, or a larger surface, such as a wall. Almost without exception, graphic art—whether painted, sculpted, or handmade of fabrics—can be seen as a *whole,* examined critically in its totality, or as a collection of component parts. It is there, fixed and immobile (except when it is, by nature, a mobile), to be scrutinized as long as the individual chooses to do so; or, if that is his preference, to be examined as a collection of details.

Everything about music differs from these conditions. No work, whether Stravinsky's *Tilim-Bom,* which may be accommodated in the thirty-seven grooves of a 78-rpm record, or Mahler's Eighth Symphony, which takes the better part of two hours to perform, is ever heard as an entity. Each is made up of a finite quantity of vibrations, one giving way to the next. It is the power of *memory* that holds the changing succession of them "located in time" into some form of pattern by which the mind produces a progressive relation between one and another, and another, *and* another.

It can be likened, to invoke another analogy, to the perpetual flicker of light which gives the eye the impression of a *moving picture,* when there is actually no such movement. Perhaps if the mode of displaying motion, as immotion, were altered in the same way as non-tonal sound has been imposed on the ear, the resulting dislocation would make that result understandable to those who are eye-, rather than ear-, minded.

The points that have been raised by Stravinsky in a few sentences could be extended into a book, without exhausting the interests they contain. But, for the moment, one particular point may bear closer scrutiny: that is the possibility that "in-depth listening," as he calls it, might produce a change in time perspective.

Long ago (now nearly twenty-five years) Stravinsky expressed his admiration for the works of Anton Webern—none of them longer than ten minutes—and the degree to which his manner of expression created "a new distance between the musical object and ourselves, and therefore . . . a new measure of musical time" (used in the inclusive sense of "duration" on the Webern scale).[12] My own summation of the same innovation of Webern is that he

[12] Stravinsky, Igor, and Craft, Robert, *Memories and Commentaries* (Doubleday & Company, Inc., Garden City, N.Y., 1960), p. 97.

created a "new factor of attention" for the listener: one derived from the utilization of *silence* as more than a lack of sound, but the basic, underlying conception of the listening experience, in which music became the interruption rather than vice versa. It was, in effect, the background to his design as canvas is to the painter.

All this hung in the realm of speculation until the appearance in 1979 of a book[13] which illuminated Webern's life, musical functioning, and career-pattern to an extent never before known. For one thing, early in life he became an enthusiastic Alpinist, and the longer he lived, the more urgent it became, periodically, to get away from Vienna, or wherever else he might be living, for what I describe as a "mountain break." There, above the timberline, he found what he craved and could not attain elsewhere—total silence.

The Moldenhauers' text also explores, at greater length and in more point-to-point specification, how Webern's activity as a conductor entered into the uneasily fragmented pattern of his life. Of particular interest is the relationship with the English-born Edward Clark. It began in Berlin in 1911 (when Clark was a student in his early twenties) and came to a particular fruition in the later twenties and into the thirties. Clark had then become an influential administrator of the British Broadcasting Corporation, and rarely allowed a year to pass without inviting Webern to conduct in London. Here he prepared programs that ranged from Haydn symphonies to one of Bruckner, but always included music of his own, invariably performed slower—by minutes!—than is considered the norm today. In another instance of the same tendency, Webern advised his idol (and teacher) Schoenberg that he was writing a work of which the first movement would last almost "a quarter of an hour." In a recording by Robert Craft, it is performed in eight minutes, fifty seconds.

All of this suggests that Webern conceived his music to be performed *substantially* slower than it is commonly heard. Much the

[13] Moldenhauer, Hans and Rosaleen, *Anton von Webern, A Chronicle of His Life and Work* (Alfred A. Knopf, New York, 1979). See pp. 325–26 on timing reference.

same could be said of some masters of the past. But in a long work, say of Schubert or Mahler or Bruckner, the fluctuation would be on the order of 5 per cent, in a work lasting an hour, rather than nearly 50 per cent faster than, in the composer's opinion, was appropriate to a work fifteen minutes in length.

How would this affect Stravinsky's belief that Webern had created "a new distance between the musical object and ourselves" or my concept of a "new factor of attention"? Only a program of Webern performed at tempos *he* considered suitable could answer: certainly the silences would be longer, the sound interruptions possibly more hypnotic. And it might support Stravinsky's contention that "in-depth listening," which I perceive to be his recommendation for understanding of non-tonal music, would alter "time perspective" to Webern's advantage.

Regrettably, the one musician-mathematician known to me who might have productively applied himself to these permutations of numerical values was Ansermet himself. But he never did.

It might have been a contribution of value to the lingering question in my mind: "What about Sidney Bechet appealed to the Stravinsky in Ansermet? What about the pre-*Agon* Igor Stravinsky appealed to the Bechet in Ansermet?"

I would appeal to Pierre Boulez for an answer; or, if he is non-disposed, or doesn't have the time, I would provide my own: "expressive substance."

Artur Schnabel

I

In a discussion of some of her notable predecessors, Maria Callas was once asked if she had ever heard a recording on which Lilli Lehmann, renowned for a career that extended from 1865 to 1909 and included such heroic roles as Norma, Fidelio, all the Brünn-hildes, and, of course, Isolde, sings Violetta's "Ah! fors' è lui" and "Sempre libera" from Verdi's *La Traviata.* "Have I heard it?" echoed Callas, adding (of a singer who retired years before she was born): "I know that voice perfectly. I can tell you every move she makes."

Somewhat the same order of vividness pervades my recol-lections of Artur Schnabel, with the added advantage of twenty-five years' exposure to his artistry live, and an uninterrupted ac-quaintance with reproductions of his playing now extending over a period more than twice as long. Mentally, I see as well as hear him full-length (or to be more specific, half-length seated at the keyboard), three-dimensionally, and with total objectivity, because Schnabel is an artist to whom I never said as much as "Pleased to meet you."

The sound of a piano struck by something resembling Schna-bel's crisp, incisive stroke preceded by several years the first oppor-tunity to hear him live. I use this rather ambiguous phraseology because the sound was not from a pallid disc of the mid-twenties but from a piano equipped to reproduce from an Ampico roll a mechanical likeness of Schnabel's performance of Bach's Con-certo in the Italian Style.

For all that the well-sounding Chickering was afflicted by the infirmities of square rhythmic definition, jerky melodic phraseology, and far from smooth dynamic transition inherent in even the best roll-operated pianos, an element of personality was conveyed. Behind the paper on the roll was the mind of a man with strong convictions about the music, and the mind of the man who had written it.

Nothing ever needed to be altered about that initial impression. All that happened thereafter, time after time, place after place, work after work, was to extend—as my perception of what he was doing improved—it in depth and breadth. I came, eventually, to comprehend that together with the strong convictions went refinement of touch, lightness of heart, or gravity of manner appropriate to what he was playing, the distance of artistic vision to see the end of the phrase in its beginnings, as well as the foresight to make the listener a partner in every shade of meaning in between.

By good fortune, I heard him at very close to his best at my first live contact. The date was April 12, 1930. The work was—blessed fortune!—the Fourth (G major) Concerto of Beethoven, with Serge Koussevitzky conducting the Boston Symphony Orchestra. The place was hardly less important: the auditorium of the Brooklyn Academy of Music, where the Boston Symphony for years played one concert each time the orchestra came to New York. For such a work as Beethoven's Fourth Concerto or any one of a dozen by Mozart, that hall still has no equal in the five boroughs of New York.

I should, I suppose, have some word of discriminating memory of the first sound of the first movement in which Schnabel pronounced Beethoven's agenda of the discussion to follow. My recollection does not go to a zeroed-in view of the bench-with-back on which Schnabel was seated at his Bechstein (one of two shipped from Germany for his use because, at that time, he would play no other piano). Rather it relates to the heavenly hush that settled over the auditorium and its human content the better to hear the whisper of confiding esteem for Schnabel's part of the dialogue which Koussevitzky coaxed from his string section.

Perhaps it was the innate urge to have something to say in print about such an experience (I was still a student) that further stimulated my immersion in *Music at Midnight* the year before, and matured into a conviction a year later. I read what I could find in the Brooklyn press (then, and for some years later, on sale in Manhattan), but did not find a suitably resonant echo of what I had heard. All I found was a recurrence, to some extent, of what I later learned was the "official" line of evaluation of Schnabel in America: good musician, yes, but his tone was unappealing, more notable for clarity than for the preferred singing sounds of a Hofmann or a Paderewski. Absent, too, was something called liquidity.

Hm. Was this Debussy that Schnabel was playing, or was it Beethoven? Liquidity, it would seem to me, would be in order for one of the fountain pieces (Liszt or Ravel), for Debussy's *La Cathédrale engloutie* or, perhaps, Iuventiun Rosas's *Sobra la olas* ("Over the Waves"). The cavil, in my view, was a tendency to confuse a major revelation with a minor reservation. A particular instance of the time, of that critical fallacy, was to minimize the merits of Ravel's music and maximize its demerits. Untrue to Shakespeare, the good in a creative artist lives on after the bad has been eroded by time.

Fortunately, Schnabel's Boston Symphony successes led to a warmer continent-wide response to his art than had followed his first American venture in 1921. This had been arranged by the late Sol Hurok at the urging, curiously, of violin virtuoso and Schnabel admirer Mischa Elman. Perhaps, in spite of the equivocal reception, Schnabel would have returned earlier, had he not been bound, for a seven-year period, to play the Knabe piano in any American performance. Eventually, in 1933, Schnabel declared Germany off limits to *all* Jewish musicians when so many others were being persecuted (even a personal appeal from Wilhelm Furtwängler could not make him change his mind). This freed Schnabel for brightening prospects in America and brought him back to a New York public which quickly became accustomed to cherishing him as one of its own.

The lapse of a decade between indifference and acceptance would suggest that Schnabel had been, finally, awarded the success that comes to a fine young artist if he is both deserving and patient. But by 1930, Schnabel was on the brink of fifty, not forty, and mature enough to be able to say what was in his mind in words as well as at the piano.

They are almost the same words which became so characteristic of Schnabel, the world-admired artist, as he grew older, grayer, and finally white-haired. They were the words that those who loved him for his art revered for the good sense they contained. But they were, as of 1930, non-conformist, intransigent, *contra mundum*, with an abrasive surface that rubbed the wrong way with most of his colleagues. By comparison with the common platitudes of others, they tended to make him sound egotistical, self-centered, single-minded to a fault, even arrogant.

The words may be found in an interview that appeared in the Boston *Transcript* during his visit of March–April 1930. Included were references to an interview with Schnabel that had appeared in the Manchester *Guardian* not long before. "It is one of my beliefs," stated Schnabel, "that the educators are always responsible, never the educated. Art, I am convinced, is the one sphere where it is the producer, and not the consumer, who counts." Asked to explain his well-known refusal to acknowledge applause by performing encores, Schnabel responded with the famous words: "The applause is the receipt, not the bill," a statement that served a useful purpose to remind a world-famous conductor of the 1970s that an encore (Ravel's *Boléro*) after Debussy's *La Mer* was, perhaps, inappropriate.[1] Sir Georg Solti stopped doing it thereafter with the Chicago Symphony (at least in New York).

In explanation of his preference for a certain, limited company of composers (which became, as his career unfolded, a contracting rather than an expanding one) Schnabel was both succinct and clear: "I have decided to play only works I consider better than they can be performed. It is a never ending task, for they are so total and universal. If I consider a piece not so good as it can be made by the performer, then it would not interest me to play it. I am living from the hope of doing my work better tomorrow than I have done it today, and if I did not I could not live as an artist . . ."

[1] Kolodin, Irving, *Saturday Review*, July 10, 1976.

II

All this is so faithful to the practices and points of view that became so characteristic of Schnabel in the last—1930–51—twenty years of his career that only one question remains: if, as Schnabel stated, "the educators are always responsible, never the educated," who was the shaper and molder of the mind which, in addition to forming the technical means to articulate Schnabel's purposes at the piano, made those purposes as enduringly worthwhile as they were?

Challenged to select (without pre-knowledge or prompting) a specific individual in the first years of this century who might qualify, an answer-seeker would probably range over Germans, Austrians, Englishmen—or some combination of all three—without coming even close to the mark. The conclusion would then have to be that some man of great merit but little celebrity found his life's objective fulfilled not only by Artur Schnabel's productive career, but also by its enduring influence after his death.

The preceding *précis* is, for a novelty, both true *and* false. The influential individual was *not* German, Austrian, or English: but he was one of the most famous piano pedagogues of his time. Even more remarkably, he earned that fame through a teacher-pupil association with a man whose name was synonymous over nearly half a century—1890–1935—for everything that Artur Schnabel was not: Ignace Jan Paderewski.

That relationship established, the individual at issue could be no one other than Theodor Leschetizky, a native of Poland, born near Lemberg on June 22, 1830. His childhood promise enabled his parents to bring him to Vienna, where he was accepted for instruction by Carl Czerny, now known primarily for his finger-breaking, patience-trying exercises. But Czerny was properly esteemed during his lifetime (he died in 1857) as a younger colleague, close associate, and frequent stand-in at the piano, of Beethoven.

Leschetizky was launched, at the age of twenty-two (1852) on a career that took him almost immediately to Russia. His musical culture as well as his pianistic capacity made him welcome not only as a performer, but also as a pedagogue. He was cherished at the court of the Grand Duchess Helen, and appointed to the faculty of the St. Petersburg Conservatory, whose director was Anton Rubinstein. The momentous association with Paderewski (then aged twenty-four) began in 1884, following Leschetizky's return to Vienna. It culminated with Paderewski's extraordinary debut in London in May 1890, and its American counterpart on November 17, 1891.

Leschetizky was no more precisely responsible for the *furore Paderewski* than Edward Burne-Jones was for the aureole that he ennobled in his celebrated painting of the pianist. Each was given something to work with, and made the most of it. The public acclaim that made Paderewski as much an embodiment of the *persona* pianist as Jascha Heifetz became of the *genre* violinist twenty years later, brought hundreds of talents to Vienna in quest of a magical transformation by Dr. Leschetizky.

In a round figure it has been estimated that those who sought such miracle from Leschetizky totaled approximately twelve hundred, or fifty per year over the quarter-century life span that followed the beginning of Paderewski's celebrity in the 1890s (Leschetizky died in November 1915). Among those who achieved sufficient worldly success for their names to retain a ring of identity years later are: Ossip Gabrilowitsch; Ignaz Friedman; two famous ladies, Fannie Bloomfield Zeisler of Chicago and Katharine Goodson of London; Benno Moiseiwitsch; Isabelle Vengerova (the piano teacher of Leonard Bernstein, among others); Frank La Forge, celebrated as an accompanist of singers from Marcella Sembrich to Marian Anderson; Martinus Sieveking, the Dutch-born master immortalized in James Hilton's *Lost Horizon*; Wassily Safonoff, more famous, eventually, as a conductor than as a pianist; and Artur Schnabel.

If there is a single factor that would bind together most of these, with Paderewski through Leschetizky, it would have been the singular kind of piano sound they produced—the shimmering, vibratory, aural essence that caused the celebrated critic-connoisseur James Huneker to whisper to a neighbor, the first time he heard Paderewski play Chopin: "Rainbows!" As it has already been noted that the Schnabel sound was more of a liability than an asset when he first performed in America, the speculation would have to be: what, then, about Leschetizky commended him to Schnabel and vice versa?

As a central, overriding element, I would say: Leschetizky was as much an artist among pedagogues as he was a pedagogue among artists. He disclaimed that he had a "method" for playing the piano, although he advocated a cupped position of the hand on the keys. The underlying essence of it all is—like Arnold Schoenberg, who also refused to teach a "method" although *he* assuredly had one—Leschetizky adapted his procedure to the character of a gifted student, rather than requiring each to form himself, or herself, in the image of the master. He rejected out of hand—and sometimes out of a lesson and into outer darkness—a student who was negligent, inattentive, or, worst sin of all, impolite. Failure to rise when an older person entered a room, rudeness in the presence of those who merited respect, discourtesy to servants were incompatible with Leschetizky's view of how a well-bred artist should behave.

Unlike most of the twelve hundred who came Leschetizky's way, Schnabel was only nine years old when the great adventure began in 1891. Reference to a present map might suggest that Schnabel's birthplace, Lipnik, was then, as now, part of Poland: however, at birth (1882) Schnabel was an Austrian (Southwest Silesia). He soon outran local pedagogy and was taken by his parents to Vienna. For a while, the boy made progress with a teacher who was a minor member of the Vienna Conservatory's faculty.

Soon the objective shifted to Leschetizky. An approach was made, and the response was encouraging, if the immediate verdict was not: the boy, however talented, would have to spend a year or two in the hands of a Leschetizky assistant. This would make the novice familiar with Leschetizky's way of working, and, when qualified, not waste the time both of teacher and pupil. A helpful introduction to the circumstances that prevailed is provided by

Ethel Newcomb,[2] an esteemed teacher of the piano in New York (1910–40), who had been one of his assistants (1904–8).[3]

The central forum of the Leschetizky Experience was the Class, a regular gathering of all those—the "fifty" or more—who were enrolled at any particular time. In addition to periodic sessions with the master—weekly or so—all were required to be present at the group meetings and to be prepared to perform the piece or pieces on which they were working. This procedure had a twofold purpose: to fortify the students for the eventual pressures of playing in public, and to enable all who were studying with Leschetizky to hear his comments on the individual student.

What might happen was recounted by Miss Newcomb, who was exposed to the Class at an early point of her studies with Leschetizky.

> I gave him the name of the three pieces I had played in my lesson that week and waited my turn to play. The first went well, and I was about to go to the second, a mazurka of his own, when he stopped me.
>
> "Wait a moment," he asked. "Can't you make a little modulation from the first piece to the second?"
>
> I told him I was afraid I could not.
>
> "Have you never studied harmony?" was the next question.
>
> "Not yet, Professor."
>
> "Not yet," he repeated, "but you have played Liszt rhapsodies: that is real American . . ."
>
> Turning to Artur Schnabel, who was then a boy of eight or nine, Leschetizky asked him to come forward and make a modulation for the lady. The use of the word "lady" made me realize in a moment that I was grown up beside this boy, who made my modulation with the greatest ease and beauty.[4]

Clearly the "boy's" command of such knowledge and skill—formerly an expected, anticipated part of a public recital by any pianist of true concert caliber, but now *passé*, along with tonality itself

2 Newcomb, Ethel, *Leschetizky As I Knew Him* (D. Appleton, New York, 1921).

3 Baker's Biographical Dictionary of Musicians, op. cit., Sixth Edition, p. 1229.

4 Newcomb, op. cit., p. 16.

—was among the factors that commended him to Leschetizky. And it was the great master's psychological stroke of singling *him* out for such a prideful demonstration of ability that commended Leschetizky to Schnabel.

However, liking was not to be misconstrued with lenience. On an occasion when the future master of the Beethoven literature omitted a few notes in one of the sonatas, Leschetizky's rebuke left the boy with tears running down his face.[5] But, recounts Mrs. Newcomb, the Leschetizky attitude was impartial. To one prize talent who cringed under similar objectivity, Leschetizky said: "If you expect me to pay you compliments here, well, you have come to the wrong address."[6]

Lest it be supposed that Leschetizky was the only molder of Schnabel's mind in this formative time of his life, it may be noted that the interview of 1930 referred not to "educator" but to "educators." The compassionate, offsetting personality to Leschetizky was Eusebius Mandyczewski, learned as well as genial, then only thirty-five. But he was, as archivist of the Gesellschaft der Musikfreunde in Vienna, already on the way to the eminence that qualified him to be editor of the complete editions of Haydn, Schubert, and Brahms. He agreed to further Schnabel's knowledge of theoretical matters, provided the boy came to him for a lesson at the only time he could offer—8 A.M.

The custom evolved of each session ending with a walk (and talk) en route to the famous building on Bösendorferstrasse where Mandyczewski's duties began at nine-fifteen. From time to time, Schnabel would be included as a junior member of a picnic party whose venerated senior might, on occasion, be Johannes Brahms. Or he might accompany Mandyczewski to the flat of the composer, with whom his "tutor" was on intimate terms.

These treasured treats would have terminated with the illness and death of Brahms in 1897. This was also the year which ended Schnabel's novitiate and saw the beginning, with his first public recital, of a professional identity. One journal reported him to be an "extraordinary talent" and predicted that "with the excellent guidance which he enjoys it is only a matter of a very short time before he will arouse wide comment . . ."[7] Prophecy could hardly have had a quicker fulfillment: by 1898 Schnabel was on his own in Berlin, preparing to establish a place in the musical community of a city that would be his home for more than thirty years.

Needless to say, there are many unanswered questions arising from the remarkable association that began with a boy of nine and a professor of sixty-one. Schnabel himself has provided some insight into his own reactions. He retained a lifelong affection for Leschetizky and realized ever more, as time passed, how special a case the older man had made of him. The only derogatory thing Schnabel had to say of Leschetizky was that he was too strict. Unlike most of the others who sought out the famous pedagogue in Vienna, there were no "Hungarian Rhapsodies" for Schnabel. This suggests to me that he discerned in Schnabel other aptitudes and another destiny: could it be a lingering recollection of his relationship with Czerny, which had not yielded as much as it might have to him, from one directly descended from Beethoven?

To those who expressed puzzlement to him on the Leschetizky-Paderewski-Schnabel paradox, Schnabel commented: "What he aimed at was truthfulness of expression, and he would not tolerate any violation or deviation from what he felt to be true. Altogether his devotion, seriousness and artistic integrity seemed incompatible with the virtuoso type he was supposed to represent."[8]

What Leschetizky thought of the art of piano playing on the level he demanded of a student may best be summarized in the words of one highly qualified to express it: himself, when the question of conducting (in which he sometimes indulged) came up: "Conducting is not difficult. It is harder to play six bars well on the pianoforte than to conduct the whole of Beethoven's Ninth Symphony."[9] The key word here is *well*—well, that was the Leschetizky standard in being.

[7] Searchinger, op. cit., p. 37.
[8] Ibid., p. 16.
[9] Grove's Dictionary of Music and Musicians, edited by Eric Blom (St. Martin's Press, New York, Fifth Edition), Vol. V, p. 144.

III

In retrospect, Leschetizky's "artistic integrity" applied also to the judgment he pronounced on the youthful Schnabel when he told him: "Artur, you will never be a pianist. *You* are a musician." This has been quoted (in his preface to Searchinger's biography) by the much admired Sir Clifford Curzon—a living link in the pianistic line from Leschetizky, as a pupil of Katharine Goodson (see page 28), who had been *his* pupil, to Schnabel, with whom he began to study in the early thirties—as a "paradox." He also cites it as proof that "great teachers are rarely great prophets where their own students are concerned."

Precisely what was in Leschetizky's mind died with him in 1915. But it is at least a possibility that what he intended was more a compliment than a condemnation: that Schnabel was too good a musician to satisfy the nineteenth-century expectation for a *pianistic* success.

But another century might bring other expectations. Between the time of Schnabel's debut in Vienna (in 1897) and death in 1951 stretched a full five decades, with the new half century's unprecedented opportunities, unexploited accessories, and unpredictable fulfillments, all descended from Thomas Edison, whose mind might permit it to be called the first century A.E. (After Edison).

Add to these physical factors the development of a world of musical possibilities in the Americas, and Leschetizky's words were more prophecy than "paradox." After all, he was the one who told Schnabel: "Schubert has written fifteen sonatas for piano which almost nobody knows. They are almost forgotten. No one ever plays them. *You* might like them."[10] Such a program of action is more than a random suggestion to any young person. It is a wise man's charter to one endowed with the rarest of attributes: *not* as a pianist able to have a career like other pianists', but as a musician capable of having a career unlike other pianists'.

[10] Searchinger, op. cit., p. 16.

The glint in the mentor's eye derived, no doubt, from the results that accrued when Leschetizky told a pupil several years' Artur's senior: "Go over your piece with Schnabel." Presumably, then, it took in too Schnabel's Berlin workweek of a class sought out by young pianists from all over the world (after 1933, it was relocated in Tremezzo on Lake Como). In both instances he was perpetuating a nineteenth-century function of the artist as teacher derived, as it happens, from Mozart and Beethoven themselves.

However, the new time brought the new opportunities previously mentioned. One path bridged time two ways: forward and backward. As Hans von Bülow, one of the first musicians to play all thirty-two sonatas of Beethoven in public, also made his own edited text for the works, so too did Schnabel (in time for publication on the centenary of the composer's death, in 1927).

From there Schnabel proceeded to expand his views on the subject in a way that Bülow could not: by making the first recording of the cycle, followed by the great variations (especially those of opus 35 and opus 120). In this way, Schnabel provided a ground plan of the text itself, supplemented in the most fulfilling way possible, by the sounding counterpart, speaking to the professional and the lay listener alike.

In this dissolution of all walls separating practitioner and public, Schnabel attained the zenith available to the educator, whose discourse is limited neither by language nor by metaphor. I may cite as token of honest obligation honorably acknowledged the words of thanks inscribed in a recent book of my own. They were: "directed in homage to a unique breed of interpreters I have encountered during a lifetime of listening. They are the ones who illuminate as they communicate and enlighten as they invigorate. Among them the late Artur Schnabel was the standard bearer . . ."[11]

How Schnabel differed from most of those who have followed the path that he defined may be simply stated: from several who have studied the Beethoven literature and absorbed some essential truths about this work or that (Arrau, Backhaus, Barenboim,

[11] Kolodin, Irving, *The Interior Beethoven* (Alfred A. Knopf, Inc., New York, 1973), Prefatory Note.

Brendel, Kempff, Serkin) you might, if you were fortunate, be confronted with some association or implication that puts a measure, a phrase, a page, in a wholly unexpected relation not only to Beethoven, but to all music. From Schnabel, however, if you don't derive such insights and associations from almost everything by Beethoven that he plays, the fault is yours, not his.

I may cite, vis-à-vis one work of Beethoven that has, for years, been misrepresented by the publisher who gave it the name of "Eroica" Variations (in E flat, opus 35) such an instance. (To be sure, some of its content may also be heard in the finale of the "Eroica" Symphony, but that did not come about until several years later, though more than a few students of my experience assume the orchestral work came *first*.)

For years I shared the prevailing view that the E flat variations were an interesting but digressive stage in the development of a *contredanse* by Beethoven which grew from its first, simple form of 1800, through the *Prometheus* ballet, to that unaccountably great explosion of musical force known as the Symphony No. 3 in E flat (1803). I worked my way through recordings of it by Arrau, Brendel, Curzon, Gould, and Richter, without finding anything to cause a momentary doubt in the attitude of mind that prevailed when I began to write *The Interior Beethoven*.

But a reversion to a Schnabel performance which I had not heard in twenty years commanded a different kind of attention. And when I say "commanded," I mean that quite literally. The voice of the instrument was more than quietly *urgent*, as if the performer had a communication of importance to *himself*, and anyone who would listen, to put into sound. I was arrested by a new creativity in what Beethoven was doing to his all-too-familiar theme, in the player's highlighting and underscoring of emphases, counterstatements, and nuances that had previously escaped not only my attention, but that of all the performers to whom I had been listening.

At the first hearing, it was puzzling but also promising. Why, I asked myself, did the old familiar conformations have something about them that prompted another listening? And why, after responding to that puzzling prompting, was I rewarded with some form of enlightenment I could not define, but was sufficiently aroused to pursue further?

In the course of a dozen or so rehearsals, I began to see in these variations—thanks to my mentor and educator—qualities that defined them as musical crossroads in early-middle Beethoven. From Variation No. VIII, as defined by Schnabel, emerged the ground plan for the rondo-finale of the C major ("Waldstein") sonata (opus 53), thus pointing one direction. From the later variations, and the final fugue in particular, emerged the path that led *through* the finale of the "Eroica" and back to its beginning. Here was an introduction to Beethoven's creative thinking (borne out by the sketchbook to which I later had access) proving beyond doubt that the shape and content of a symphony as a whole, or of a sonata, could flow *backward* from a finale, as well as forward from a motivating theme.

Thus alerted, I listened more intently to Schnabel's re-creation of the subsequent piano works of Beethoven, especially the five last sonatas and the "Diabelli" Variations (opus 120). My conviction was soon total: if there was anything in one of these great works in addition to what made it great Beethoven in that particular work, anything that impelled the composer to weave it into a subsequent work, Schnabel would make it audible. That went, eventually, to his demonstration (merely by quiet, unobtrusive shadings, and purposeful moldings of the sound) that the thirty-fourth of the "Diabelli" Variations (opus 120 is limited to thirty-three) is the great arietta of the C minor (opus 111) sonata, which is based on the same six-note sequence.

The enlivening adjunct is, of course, that Schnabel does not deliver any such allusionary advice to the listener in a didactic, pedantic, or pedagogical way. Like the best of educators—Kenneth Clark, for an example—Schnabel's mind is so full of the subject on which he is discoursing that any particular phase of it gushes forth from the well of knowledge irrigating the whole of it.

As an instance: in the "Eroica" Variations Beethoven throws in (the only way to describe its abrupt appearance and disappearance) a reference to another *contredanse* (the one of which Kreisler made an arrangement for violin). For the average performer, who doesn't know the allusion, the notes are meaningless; for the uncommon performer who might, the point is likely to be punched home, for fear the listener may not take note that he does, indeed, know it. From Schnabel, the reference comes almost as an aside, in a slightly accentuated *dancy* rhythmic beat (the musical equivalent of the wink of an eye), and on he goes. I am also convinced, though I cannot prove it, that Schnabel was acquainted with the sketchbook to which I have previously referred (it is called the "Wielhorsky" after the Russian who acquired it in Vienna in the 1850s and took it back to St. Petersburg-Leningrad, where it is still in a library vault). Here is set forth, in precise detail, the hothouse method of cultivation by which Beethoven bred the seed from the *Prometheus* ballet into the variations, and kept on notating the possibilities of them for an "orchestral work," which became the "Eroica."

IV

In her invaluable collection of reminiscences and observations on Charles Ives, Vivian Perlis allocates an appropriate space to John Kirkpatrick, the pianist whose study and public presentation of the "Concord" Sonata (in 1939) was the first, indispensable breakthrough toward a proper estimate of Ives's accomplishments. In it Kirkpatrick states: "One thing that I tell my piano students in reference to people like Beethoven, for instance, is that you trace the steps of greatness and your own soul grows. I've always felt that way with my own acquaintance with Ives' music."[12] Certainly, "in reference to people like Beethoven," Kirkpatrick's observations could have no greater validity than in the demonstrable, provable instance of Artur Schnabel.

Of all the pianists I have ever heard, the only one who consistently set forth such an interrelating power—on the music of a broader range of composers (insofar as public repertory is concerned)—was Sergei Rachmaninoff. This was an experience that

[12] Perlis, Vivian, *Charles Ives Remembered. An Oral History* (W. W. Norton & Company, New York, 1976), p. 226.

had to be pinned down in flight, so to speak, because Rachmaninoff recorded relatively little by composers other than himself, and not necessarily the works in which his best qualities were most fully represented. Further, the sound of the reproduced *Carnaval* of Robert Schumann and the B flat minor sonata of Frédéric Chopin clangs more than it clings. But, once one had heard Rachmaninoff's dissertation on the dimensions, structure, and true spirit of the Beethoven E minor sonata (opus 90), hearing and rehearing of it were hardly necessary. It remained a presence in the mind, a reminder of a spatial drama to be evoked when the notes were heard again, rarely on such a scale.

The point might be made that Rachmaninoff's musical mind was that of a composer, who looked at a great work of another composer with a creator's eye as well as ear. In a way, so too—some readers may learn from these words—was Schnabel. The impulse that flowed into the music of others also called for a personal realization on its own.

In early Leschetizky days he earned prizes for childish pieces in class competitions. His ambition eventually grew to write symphonies, quartets, sonatas, even a piano concerto, written in the most complex avant-garde idiom he could devise. Those which I have heard (some performed with all art and enthusiasm under the direction of such a Schnabelizer as George Szell) I found to be tedious, dull, and interminable.

I would regard them not as a form of *creation*—which engaged his abilities to their fullest in his collaborations with Mozart, Schubert, Beethoven, Brahms, et al.—but as a kind of rec-reation, or sport. It was a kind of sport which enabled him to "get away from music" as he knew it and felt it, into a form of intellectual exercise—like a writer finding pleasure in particularly difficult crossword puzzles.

I have used the phrase "demonstrable, provable" about Kirkpatrick's contention that tracing the "steps of greatness" can broaden comprehension and engender growth. The same words could be applied to Schnabel's enduring esteem as an educator. Among the first generation of those who profited directly from his physical being (rather than indirectly, as I did, from its by-products) were Sir Clifford Curzon, Beveridge Webster (a great teacher as well as an outstanding performer), Leon Fleisher (brutally penalized though he is by a hand affliction which wrecked his career as a concertizing pianist), Leonard Shure, Webster Aitken, and a scattering of others.

But there is a second generation forming up, which has had the Schnabelesque impulse made a part of their being by deriving it from Schnabel disciples. Prominent among these are André Watts and Misha Dichter. These, of course, are only the known, identifiable ones: those who have made their contact only from recordings and texts must be worldwide. I know of one Israeli pianist studying in New York who wanted only one thing to take back home when his Juilliard studies were finished: the Schnabel cycle of Beethoven sonatas, which still can be purchased in record shops across the country, from bins next to the latest Nashville items. He got what he wanted.

Anniversaries, too, bring about unexpected manifestations and manifesters. The twentieth anniversary of Schnabel's death on August 15, 1951, was commemorated twenty years to the day later with a concert in Lincoln Center (Philharmonic Hall). The program included Bach's C major Concerto for Three Claviers and Orchestra with pianists Eunice Norton, Frank Glazer, and Tung Kwong-Kwong; the Mozart Three Piano Concerto in F (K. 242) with Lili Kraus, Beveridge Webster, and Claude Frank as soloists; and the Mozart Two Piano Concerto in E flat (K. 365) performed by his daughter and son, Helen and Karl Ulrich. All the pianists were identified as "former students of Artur Schnabel." (So was the conductor, Leon Fleisher.) Between the two Mozart works, Schnabel's *Duodecimet* (a four-movement chamber work, with a dozen performers) was heard.

On an earlier occasion (May 19, 1960) a trio by Schnabel was heard at a concert in the Grace Rainey Rogers Auditorium of the Metropolitan Museum of Art. The evening began with a Haydn string quartet and ended with the "Diabelli" Variations of Beethoven, performed by Rudolf Serkin, who has done more to perpetuate the place in the repertory of that transcendental work than anyone since Schnabel.

Was this merely worship from afar by one who has, in his later years, narrowed his own repertory to works he too considers "better than they can be performed"? Not at all. If Serkin's name does not appear among those who studied directly with Schnabel, that great "educator" was nevertheless very much a part of his growth.

When in 1920 (at the age of seventeen) Serkin made his Berlin solo recital debut with a recital in the Singakadamie, he later recalled

> . . . there were only perhaps twenty or twenty-five people in the hall, but among them were Busoni and Schnabel, who came back and introduced himself. How he happened to come, I don't know. But he didn't miss one of my concerts and always came backstage. His comments were not critical, but more like "Why did you play that particular passage such and such a way? Why not this way?"
>
> Sometimes he was there for half an hour or even an hour, talking about a piece I had played, why I played it this way, wouldn't it be better to do it just the opposite. He was the greatest influence on all of us, in every way. By the way he played, by playing all the modern music, by keeping an open house, by knowing everyone. Anything he did was so personal, really wonderful.[13]

Schnabel's concertgoing in Berlin was not likely as random as this modest account suggests. Serkin's name was not wholly unknown prior to his Berlin debut: he had been a composition student of Arnold Schoenberg's in Vienna, and participated in a number of public "readings" of the newest music; and he was, though only seventeen, about to begin his concert career as pianist with violinist Adolf Busch.

But the relaxed nature of the encounter he describes, the thrust of the conversation that ensued, and, above all, the position of esteem that Schnabel (then not quite forty) occupied among the younger musicians of Serkin's time is self-descriptive of the influence of such a man, and such a career. No career of our own

[13] Kolodin, Irving, "The Complete Musician," *Horizon*, Vol. IV, No. 1, September 1961, pp. 83–87.

time can be likened to it, except perhaps that of Serkin himself.

Among the residual likeness that emerges from Schnabel's "educator," and those that he himself educated, is a comment of Leschetizky's about one of his more pretentious pupils: "It is easy enough to act like a great man when you are not obliged to prove it." Schnabel's pronouncements at his 1930 interview in Boston were clearly those of a man speaking greatly: his actions as now known are clear proof of his right so to speak.

In the broader perspective of a century, Schnabel's career looms ever larger as one which has transcended time, and spread its effect ever more widely. In a promotional endeavor to establish the sometimes dubious contention that there is, indeed, immortality to be achieved in the recording of music, the National Academy of Recording Arts and Sciences (sometimes referred to as NARAS) has established a Hall of Fame in Burbank, California, to commemorate outstanding accomplishments.

Though the usual sampling of great recordings currently available for purchase inclines one to the belief that there is more myth than immortality in making a great recording, Schnabel's achievement has been admirably recognized (in a poll of critics, primarily). Among instances of mere "popularity" as a basis for immortality, the recording of the Beethoven sonatas by Schnabel is a tribute to quality eminently in order.

The tribute, in this instance, has more than an honorary value. It contributes to the continuing availability of the material therein contained, and also encourages the present-day duplication of such sturdy stuff by others. The "others" have now climbed close to double figures, the latest of them being the work of Anton Kuerti.

Curiously, however, the pianist I have noted as this time's closest, in influence, to Schnabel has never accomplished his guarded ambition to perform the thirty-two sonatas in public, or to record them all. Here and there, among them, is a scattering which have eluded his complete control, or discouraged him from undertaking a full cycle in public.

If this brings admiration to Rudolf Serkin for sustaining his own standard regardless of the temptation it must be to emulate such an achievement, it brings even more honor to Schnabel for establishing a standard that endures five decades later.

Henry Handel Richardson

I

Too little of the poetic purpose that animates most musicians is contained in the usual biography of a composer or performer, and rather too much of it in the novels that have been written on the subject. An altogether uncommon blend of both makes *Maurice Guest* by Henry Handel Richardson an extraordinary exception to the average. There are things in it to ponder about decades after it was first published.

My interest in it—as in many other things—was aroused by the great English critic, columnist, and biographer of Richard Wagner, Ernest Newman. His volume of essays entitled *A Musical Motley*, encountered in the library of a high school I attended in Newark, New Jersey (the same one in which I heard the recital by Alfred Cortot previously mentioned), made Newman's writings marked for attention wherever they might be found. From older, better-informed people, I learned that they included his weekly column in the Sunday *Times* of London, which was on sale, ten or so days after publication, at a news depot in Times Square that dealt in foreign papers.

The reference to *Maurice Guest* was passed on by Newman in a column in which he described it as one of the best novels ever written about music. This, in itself, was sufficient to start a quest for *Guest*, the quantity of books worthy of such praise from Newman being minuscule. The secondhand copy I finally found (in the Gotham Book Mart, which still exists on New York's West Forty-seventh Street) bears the imprint of Duffield and Company, New York, and the publication date of 1922. It had not been

printed in this country, but imported as sheets from Great
Britain.

To my surprise when I opened the book (it had no slipcover, or
dust jacket, and hence no "blurb" identifying all the contents) it
also contained a preface written by no less a master of (then) contemporary English letters than Hugh Walpole. From it one
learned that "This remarkable novel, first published in 1908, is
one of those few whose influence has been persistently important
and fruitful, almost, as it were, in spite of itself." After detailing
the manner of its reception, the enthusiasm of many reviewers,
and the general admiration it aroused, Walpole wrote: "At the
end of the three months that are supposed to be the average span
of a novel's active life, it apparently vanished and was no more
seen. It was only then, however, that its real history began."

As evidence to this point, Walpole declared: "With the certain
exception of the books of Mr. E. M. Forster . . . there has been
no work by a modern English novelist that has so deeply and persistently influenced the writing of the younger generation . . ."
This generous statement is elaborated upon in the paragraphs that
follow (the preface is somewhat more than three printed pages in
length) to take in the indisputable truth of the author's characters, the ability of the writer to "interfuse environment, character
and incident so closely that the three are not for a moment to be
separated."

That I retained my copy of *Maurice Guest* from then to the
present day suggests that I found it well worth the praise of Newman and Walpole. I wonder now—having just reread all 562 pages
of it—what my initial reaction would have been had I known that
Walpole's references to "Mr. Richardson" were erroneous, that
the author was not Henry Handel but Ethel Florence Lindesay
Richardson.

She had, for publication purposes, appropriated the first two
names of a family forebear, whose "Handel" had been added to
Henry by his Irish mother out of devotion to the great composer
of *Messiah*. She also explained that the male pseudonym was
adapted because there had been much critical talk, at the time
Maurice Guest was completed, about "the ease with which a

woman's work could be distinguished from a man's and I wanted to try out the truth of the assertion."[1]

Ethel Richardson was born in Melbourne, Victoria (Australia), in 1870, and was taken to England (along with her mother and younger sister) three years later by her father. He had been born in Dublin, educated for the medical profession in Edinburgh, and emigrated to Australia in the early 1850s, in the hope of finding a swifter success on the sparsely settled continent than at home. While enjoying his return trip to England he was informed that his investments had gone bad, and that he better come back quickly to see what could be done. For seven years Richardson, his wife, and their children moved from place to place in Victoria in search of a new start. He died insane in 1879.

Out of these circumstances evolved the most ambitious of the Richardson writings, the trilogy called *The Fortunes of Richard Mahony*, created between 1911 and 1929. The three parts (*Australia Felix*, *The Way Home*, and *Ultima Thule*) are obviously derived from her father's faring in the goldfields of Australia's boom period and the misfortunes that overtook him. My knowledge of these circumstances is derived from encountering a paperback set of the trilogy while passing through the Melbourne Airport en route back to the United States after a visit to Australia in 1973. The description on the jacket of Richard Mahony as "the first substantial character in Australian fiction" is a fair reading of the esteem in which Richardson and her works are held in Australia.

Between the first of her novels (*Guest*) and the most ambitious (the trilogy) there would not appear to be much if any connection. There is, however, a deep underlying relationship. When her daughters were grown to adolescence, Mrs. Richardson took them to Europe. To an extent, this was for general educational improvement; more specifically it was to expand the eighteen-year-old Ethel's musical training. Most of the next sixteen years of her life were spent in Germany, acquiring the experiences later related in *Guest*.

[1] Richardson, Ethel, *Australia Felix* (Penguin Modern Classics, Australia Ltd., Ringwood, Victoria, 1971), Preface, p. vi.

In 1895 she married an English scholar of German literature, J. G. Robertson, who became the first professor of that subject at the University of London in 1904. Except for a trip to Australia to refresh her youthful recollections, Richardson-Robertson spent the rest of her life living and writing in England. She died in 1946. Unlike such other memorable musical novels as Romain Rolland's *Jean Christophe* (evoking a composer), Marcia Davenport's *Of Lena Geyer* (published in 1936 and calling on her childhood experiences as the daughter of the celebrated soprano Alma Gluck to create a composite fictional opera singer), Willa Cather's *The Song of the Lark* (an early effort of 1915 which was derived from the background of the famous Olive Fremstad), or Thomas Mann's *Doktor Faustus* of 1947 (for which Arnold Schoenberg denounced him for perpetrating a false likeness of himself as a famous innovative composer), *Maurice Guest* has, for me, even more to do with a place than with a person.

In my judgment, the particular virtue of *Maurice Guest* to us today is not in the depiction of character admired by Walpole, but in the vividness with which the author describes the milieu in which her people functioned: the Leipzig Conservatorium of the 1890s. This was the world that Ethel Richardson knew so well, as a student, from 1888 until she married Robertson. Should you wonder which of the characters in *Maurice Guest* is derived from the part she played in the happenings, look into the artistic failure named Louise Dufrayer. She is also depicted as a native of Australia (not from Melbourne, but Queensland, the Texas of the Antipodes).

Some may disagree with my choice of Louise Dufrayer as Ethel Richardson. I cite it for two reasons: I can hardly believe that the author could have conveyed the stormy, tempestuously schizoid nature of Louise without, for a time, having shared her skin; and the dedication of *Maurice Guest* reads: "To Louise." It is as if Ethel Richardson had put away and left behind in the pages of her novel that other, earlier self.

II

To judge from an entry in Grove's Dictionary of Music and Musicians which reads "it was first and alone in its field,"[2] one would assume that there had never before been such a school as the Leipzig Conservatorium . . . which is not quite true. One doesn't have to know too much musical history to associate Hector Berlioz of the 1820s and on with the Paris Conservatoire (he was both in and out of it for much of his life); or to know that Donizetti was encouraged to become a composer (despite parental opposition) because the director of the Conservatorio at Bergamo, where he was born in 1797, insisted that it was a civic duty for such a talent to be fostered.

One could go back hundreds of years before that to find institutions called "Conservatorio" where music was taught in Italy. This was, however, more a matter of semantics than scholarship, deriving from an institution in Naples—where else?—in the sixteenth century in which "illegitimate, deserted and orphaned children were kept"[3] (*conservati*) until they were old enough to make their own way. In some towns, such waifs were provided with musical indoctrination to prepare them for a useful life in the community.

The word thus became a generic term for such places of training, with results that sometimes defied predictability. A tailor in Parma sent his nine-year-old son to the local conservatory in 1876 partially because he had shown signs of musical talent, but also because the nine-year course of study included board, thus relieving the parent of responsibility for one more mouth at the table. Without the Conservatorio in Parma, Arturo Toscanini might have become some other kind of artisan, rather than the greatest conductor of his time.

Paris acquired its Conservatoire in 1793, under the blessing of the Terror. At first, entrance was free with a view to producing

[2] Op. cit., Fifth Edition, Vol. V, p. 120.
[3] Ibid., Vol. II, p. 411.

musicians for military as well as civilian purposes. The Napoleonic influence amended that program to serve higher artistic purposes. Luigi Cherubini (born in Florence) was installed as one of its three Inspecteurs des Etudes in 1795, and became its director at the age of sixty-two, in 1822. By that time leadership in musical education had shifted from Italy to France. In consequence (under the direction of French regents) the Paris example had spread by 1815 to Milan, Florence, and Naples, and also to Brussels (1813) and Vienna (1817). Under Cherubini's influence, the Conservatoire "formed practically all the important French composers of the first half of the 19th century."[4] But still no Leipzig.

The shift in emphasis that produced a center of music education there in 1843 may be attributed to two things: the liberality of the King of Prussia (Frederick William), who permitted his much-cherished Mendelssohn to apply part of his time elsewhere, and the mercurial mind of that multitalented genius.[5]

The new school embodied the full force of Leipzig's musical associations: with J. S. Bach and the Thomaskirche of which he had been cantor; and with the Gewandhaus made famous by the concerts initiated by Mendelssohn (perpetuated into the twentieth century by such successors as Arthur Nikisch and Wilhelm Furtwängler). Leipzig's earlier fame was augmented, in the mid years of the nineteenth century, by the repute of its native son Richard Wagner, and by the worldwide prominence of its great publishing house, Breitkopf und Härtel.

Joining Mendelssohn in establishing the fame of the "con," as it was known to its students, were Robert Schumann, as a professor of piano and composition; Ferdinand David, the concertmaster of the Gewandhaus orchestra, for whom Mendelssohn had written his E minor violin concerto, as head of the string department; and coordinates of comparable quality in other specialities.

By the latter decades of the nineteenth century, Leipzig, and the great succession of outstanding masters who had succeeded

---

[4] Ibid., p. 200.

[5] Werner, Eric, *Mendelssohn*, translated from the German by Dika Newlin (The Free Press of Glencoe, Collier-Macmillan Limited, 1963), pp. 385–86.

Mendelssohn's self-selected original faculty, had acquired one specific distinction. Italians went to the Conservatorio in their native towns, then to Naples or Milan; the French went to the Paris Conservatoire, as by custom did some Spanish; but the whole world went to Leipzig's Conservatorium.

As the background of Louise Dufrayer attests, this included Australians; the unhappy non-hero Maurice is one of several English on the scene, as is Madeline Wade. Americans, mostly female, are in and out of the action, as are Slavs and Scandinavians. What brought these fictional beings to Leipzig (as it brought the very real Edward Grieg and Arthur Sullivan) was not merely the reputation of the "Con" as a fine school, but its symbolic status as the guardian of the place and background from which the floodwaters of a musical repertory flowed, in all its majesty, from Bach to Brahms.

An arresting by-product of rereading *Maurice Guest* decades after it was written is the new awareness of how well Richardson put into type, and types, students who endure as typical of a conservatory to the present time. Usually, the pianists come with the hope of finding a teacher who will "build technique" without suppressing temperament. Each is alert for privileged information on which one is central to personal aspirations, or the "best" (not necessarily the most famous) at doing the most in the shortest time.

One might be listening in on a conversation at a coffee shop near the Juilliard School in Lincoln Center to hear the advice that the newly arrived Maurice Guest receives from a friendly veteran of the Leipzig scene, Madeline Wade: "You intend to enter the Conservatorium you say. Well, be sure to get under a good man— that's half the battle. Try and play privately to either Schwarz or Bendel. If you go in for the public examination with all the rest, the people in the Bureau [Office of the Registrar] will put you in with anyone they like, and that is disastrous. Choose your own master and beard him in his den before hand." (Page 9.)

Like every conservatory I ever had anything to do with (as student, visitor, or faculty member) the "Con" has its prize pupil. Richardson's name for him is Schilsky: short, slightly exotic, just right for the mix in the student body because he is a Pole. An-other new friend (male this time) gives this word portrait to Guest: He was the school's "finest, very finest violinist." He could "play almost every other instrument with ease." In addition, he was a fabulous composer, with compositions that "were already famous . . ." This recalls to Guest's mind that he had, only the day before, seen someone answering that description: a "genial Pole" who had been "storming up the steps of the Conserva-torium two at a time, with wild affrighted eyes, and a halo of disheveled auburn hair." (Page 24.)

So far, so good for Schilsky. But there are those who know him better than Guest or his new friend, Dove. He soon discovers that others rate him "a talented rascal, the best violinist the Conserva-torium had turned out for years, one to whom all gates would open" but . . . and then come the anecdotes, more to do with "soiled-linen stories" than high-minded artistic dedication. They deal with his "perpetual impecuniosity; this inability to refuse money, no matter whose the hand that offered it; this fine art in the disregard of established canons . . ." (Page 47.)

As time goes on, Guest—who had come to Leipzig really to learn music—becomes aware that the "genial" Schilsky, as he first regarded him, is a man of fatal charm. He all but deserts Louise in pursuit of some momentarily more advantageous involvement, and thus makes her available to the hopelessly infatuated Maurice. But the charm of the unattainable so lingers with Louise that she leaves Leipzig in search of Schilsky, a decision that comes to be fatal for Guest. His only recourse (in Richardson's view) is to blow his brains out.

III

As a conservatory (or conservatorium) can have only one prize pupil at a time, on whom all dote and for whom otherwise non-existent opportunities can be created, or allowances made and rules bent if not broken, the question must be asked: what is its function then for all the others? Is the true purpose of the institution to develop virtuosi? To train teachers? Or is it the basic function of the best schools of today to make musicians?

The average dean or president of an American institution—few of them are now called "conservatories," rather "school" or "institute"—would probably say, if he were honest: "All three, with emphasis on musician." That praiseworthy objective is, on all counts, educationally safe as well as artistically commendable. One may doubt only that it is uniformly pursued.

At the time its enrollees included Ethel Richardson, the Leipzig Conservatorium had a student body of between six hundred and seven hundred, and, as I have suggested, was sought out by the world. The Juilliard School of this time has, curiously, very much the same quantity of students and it, too, is sought out by the world. But the world of today's Juilliard is quite different than that of Richardson's Leipzig.

One might find an Australian or two, a South African (one in a class of mine was actually named Dove), a Slav, or several Israelis. Whether there were as many non-Germans at Leipzig in the 1890s as there are non-Americans in the 1980s at the Juilliard is unlikely. The number of those who annually make their way to the Juilliard from the four corners of the earth is in the range of 20 per cent of the total of music students in the school (there are also flourishing departments of theater and dance). That is the largest number of foreign nationals in the student body of any prominent American educational institution; more, even, than Howard University, whose hospitality to Africans gives it pre-eminence over all other American universities, including Harvard.[6]

Where the profound difference would be is, without question, in the quantity of Orientals. Setting aside the Israelis (some of whom come with Soviet training received prior to migration to Israel) as more European than Asiatic, the dominant quantity of non-American students would be a) Korean, b) Japanese, c) Malaysian or Philippine. The cognizance of Western music in this area of the world is vastly greater than it was in the 1890s (see page 264): the most talented of them tend to a) be more polite, b) attend classes with almost unexceptional regularity, c) take

[6] Information provided by Dean Gideon Waldrop of Juilliard.

notes, as if they had been trained to regard classwork as an opportunity to learn rather than as a chore to be endured.

They have one hereditary difficulty which they yearn to overcome: language. They are sufficiently equipped to understand allusions related to musical examples, to which they can make a collateral association. But interpretation of test material in English—which arouses mental processes in their own languages, which must then be converted into English for written answers—is slow, more often approximate than exact. Of late courses have been introduced to deal with this need, and progress is beginning to be made.

Generally speaking, a talented student of today would find it more difficult to get into the Juilliard than his counterpart would have found it at the Leipzig "Con" in the 1890s. But once in at the German school, he might have found it easier to stay in. As I read *Maurice Guest*, I derive the impression that almost any moderately well-prepared student could get into the Leipzig Conservatorium, provided he or she had reasonably good fingers (for an instrumentalist) and the funds to pay for tuition. Classroom work is rarely mentioned, and regularity of attendance appears to be negotiable between student and individual teacher. Given a satisfactory rate of progress, not too much else was of crucial importance.

The quantity of applicants for admission to the Juilliard is certainly greater; the standard of accomplishment for qualification unquestionably higher; the number of rejects, annually, larger. But there is little question that student assistance—a high-level term for scholarships, fellowships, and grants—exists in a profusion not known to Leipzig in the 1890s. Indeed, at the Curtis Institute in Philadelphia, whose student body is restricted to only 150 (in all categories) a year, those who are accepted receive tuition absolutely free of any charge.

Where a close parallel may be drawn between an American institution of today and the German one of a hundred years ago is in the importance placed by the students on a document, or documents, attesting to attendance and accomplishment. In the Leipzig of the 1890s, it was a certificate awarded after a *Prüfung* (examination), attesting that the student had proven himself worthy of the standards of the Conservatorium. For him, as for the average Juilliard student of the present, time invested in a year's work, without a piece of paper to show for it, might well be considered time lost.

At Leipzig, graduation with a chance at the *Hauptprüfung* (a public concert at which the winners performed with orchestra and critics might be present and which was, in effect, a professional debut) could be accomplished in two years. At today's Juilliard, study for a properly qualified applicant might be extended over more than five years, taking in undergraduate work leading to a bachelor's degree and postgraduate work leading to a master's and —with the writing of a thesis and further work in a major category —a doctorate.

Each of these steps requires a stipulated number of hours spent in classwork, including courses in the history of music and what is called L and M (Literature and Materials of Music). These are necessary to conform to stipulations established by the New York Board of Regents, which controls and allocates the degree-giving function.

All this suggests a procedure far more regulated than what was required of a Maurice Guest or a Louise Dufrayer in Richardson's fanciful Leipzig. Some might describe today's procedures as regimented rather than merely regulated. These might include some students I have encountered who are enrolled primarily to take lessons in their specialities from very good teachers. Almost everything beyond that is irksome, not to say dispensable.

One young lady—now launched on a profitable professional career as a singer—when asked why her mind was consistently on everything else than her classwork, replied: "No reflection on you. I just want to get that piece of paper at the end of the term and get the hell out of here." Whether her inattention at my class, or any other, would have eventually cost her that cherished "piece of paper" I doubt. She still could have gotten it with a C.

IV

Too many American musical institutions, even the best, direct
their efforts primarily to equipping the good talents, the bright
faces, and the eager minds for ways to avoid failure. The course of
study enables them to acquire skills on an instrument (including
the voice), provides them with an indoctrination to take a responsible place in an orchestral or other ensemble performance, and,
above all, when the degree-winning cycle has been fulfilled, sup-
plies them with credentials to qualify for places in other music
schools and universities.

This is an improvement on the other, older procedure in which
the lack of a degree on graduation day sets the student adrift without, so to speak, the ability to row on an education crew. The new
procedure spells s-e-c-u-r-i-t-y, and permits the highest-ranking degree owner with a doctorate. He, or she, will more often than not
assist at the musical birth of others, who will, from a university
school of music, or some other conservatory, go on ad infinitum,
to do what their instructors have done, or are doing.

What the best schools do least—again, speaking collectively—
for the best talents, the brightest faces, and the most gifted minds
is to prepare them for success. By success, I do not refer to the
ability to win competitions, engage in a career, or even attract attention. That is not success in any durable sense: it is merely the
prelude to it.

Where these institutions fail most conspicuously is not providing their students, however gifted, with a broad knowledge of
music, rather than merely a narrow acquaintance with their specialized portion of it. Singers know vocal music; pianists know
enough piano music to get by; violinists and cellists are perhaps
best off, because they play in orchestras and with chamber music
groups. But the student whose musical knowledge crosses *over*
from one categorical boundary to another is more than an oddity,
a novelty, or a rarity. Such diversified knowledge puts him/her in
a bracket far above the rest, for which the words "well informed"
would be the most modest.

After association with graduate students at the Juilliard for more than a decade, taking in approximately 150 in all categories, I can think of perhaps a dozen who would qualify as really knowing something beyond a personal speciality.

There are also shortcuts and procedural detours through which the institution may become an unintentional partner in failing to provide even its best talents with the requirements for what I would call a durable success. The Juilliard, for example, has a procedure by which a talented applicant can qualify for a diploma by concentrating on a speciality, and minimizing classwork. Or, after receiving a diploma—not a *degree*, mind you—may continue such concentrated attention exclusively.

That, to be sure, doesn't qualify such a person to call himself or herself a Juilliard *graduate*. But the record of Juilliard attendance and a diploma to prove it may smudge or even erase the difference in the public mind between diploma and degree. Music rashly performed by a virtuoso whose background includes a period of time spent "at the Juilliard" may cause some people to wonder what the school is coming to.

This gives rise to the question: why? A reasonably acceptable educational answer is that it enables properly qualified young musicians from the Far, Middle, or Near East to derive benefits of high-level training without being forced into classwork in which they are at a disadvantage. I have made previous reference to this reality, and how it can be dealt with (page 51). If they do, indeed, "yearn" to overcome it, there are procedural possibilities.

There remains another order of talent, which is permitted to waive musical work to which, in all charity, he or she should be exposed. That is the he or she who is so special, so promising, so praiseworthy (not to say prizeworthy) that, as in the case of the fictive Schilsky, "rules can be bent if not broken." Between the praiseworthy and the prizeworthy is a whole chasm of educational difference.

The *praiseworthy*, like the poor, are always with us, to be encouraged, complimented, even cultivated. But it is the *prizeworthy* who attract attention to institutions, aggrandize their standing in the academic world, and by association with an outstanding teacher attract others to study with the same "best"

("Schwarz or Bendel," in *Maurice Guest*) who produced a Van Cliburn.

An epochal instance of American capacity, and incapacity, bound up in one tall, universally recognizable body, he is almost certainly the most famous performer of his time to be associated with a Juilliard background (Leontyne Price would be closest in celebrity). At the age of thirteen, having studied primarily with his mother, the teenager known as Harvey Lavan Cliburn, Jr., made his debut with the Houston Symphony Orchestra in 1947.

He came to New York shortly after, and to other young people awaiting Juilliard auditions at the old home uptown (the school took over its new premises in Lincoln Center in 1969), he announced that he was "goin' to study with Madame Lhevinne" because his mother had always "so liked the playing of Mr. Lhevinne" (the famous Josef Lhevinne, a master of the keyboard in its Golden Era of Hofmann, Rosenthal, de Pachmann, Godowsky, et al.), who had died a few years previously. When this was conveyed to Rosina Lhevinne, who had as a widow of seventy-five asserted a teaching ability never associated with her before, she said she had no time for any young man, her teaching schedule was full. Upon hearing him play, and discovering that the hand she shook in greeting was "the biggest since Mr. Lhevinne's," she changed her mind.

In 1954, by winning the Edgar M. Leventritt Competition, Cliburn was given a series of solo performances with prominent American orchestras. Following his appearance with the New York Philharmonic Orchestra in Carnegie Hall, I reported to the readers of the *Saturday Review* (November 27, 1954):

> The most talented newcomer of the young season (and it could be of the whole winter) is young Van Cliburn, still enrolled at the Juilliard, who gave a notable demonstration of pianistic prowess in playing the Tchaikovsky B flat minor concerto on a recent Philharmonic-Symphony broadcast. A striking figure of over six feet two, Cliburn literally commands the piano as he plays and the music too. He is far from a finished performer as yet—an inclination to rush tempi and accelerate accelerandos was evident, also a little lack of technical discipline—

but he has, in abundance, the qualities of fervor, audience appeal, and musicianship which make for distinction.

Withal, and the clear evidences of talent notwithstanding, nothing much happened to Cliburn in the next four years. Such affirmative accounts as mine—no great credit to perception, because everything about Cliburn aurally was as outstanding as what was uncommon about him visually—did not bring many re-engagements with orchestras. His concert bookings flourished for a time, then subsided. He continued to study with Rosina Lhevinne, tended to lose heart as his career waned, and was back home in Shreveport, Louisiana, when she called him early in 1958 with the suggestion that he prepare to participate in the first International Tchaikovsky Piano Competition in Moscow.

He was anything but eager. But her urging was not to be resisted. Some undercurrent of patriotic obligation was doubtless invoked; but Mme. Lhevinne was also persuasive to the point that he was the kind of pianist the Russians would like. Cliburn came to New York, and plunged into hard work with her. Prior to his departure for Moscow he had in prospect one concert engagement at the outdoor summer series in Grant Park, Chicago, Illinois. The fee was $250.

What happened in Moscow in May 1958 to Cliburn was something akin to what happened to Charles Lindbergh in Paris in May 1927: an incredible culmination of an improbable fantasy. That a twenty-four-year-old American pianist should be awarded a prize for demonstrating to Russians how the Tchaikovsky B flat minor should be played was hardly less probable than that a twenty-five-year-old American could show the world how a single-engine Ryan monoplane could be flown across the ocean.

In both instances, the reaction was something more than acclaim for a winner: it was an expression of national pride in achievement, of admiration for doing the undoable, and of affection for typifying the best of which the American society was capable.

Twenty years, two thousand concerts, and several million dollars of income later in his mid-forties (born in 1934) Cliburn is still single (of course), a world celebrity, and something of a gray

ghost to those who see him now and then. The blizzard of dates
with which he was inundated in the months and years after his
first fame has become a scattering. There is some question
whether he has himself recovered from the paralysis of overex-
posure which, at the first, had him playing an afternoon concert
in one state and an evening concert in another. His name recurs
now more often in concerts of outdoor concert series, especially of
openings, galas, benefits, and dedicatory ceremonies, than on winter orchestral programs. He has not, to my knowledge, played a
Carnegie Hall recital in ten years.

My own most recent exposure to Cliburn (one could hardly
phrase it otherwise, because he couldn't have known and wouldn't
have cared whether I was present or not) was in Denver in April
1978. This was at another of the openings of which he has become as much a part as "The Star-Spangled Banner." Cliburn was
physically present, as was the Tchaikovsky concerto.

He took his place, amid a not quite standing ovation, at the
piano on the stage of the new Boettcher Auditorium. There was
little to be noted of a spiritual rapport between him and the conductor Brian Priestman or the audience. More regrettably, least of
all was there a binding, unifying, fructifying relationship between
himself and the notes of Tchaikovsky which he was playing once
again, and one time more too many. I felt, as I watched and listened, that he *must* have wanted to play something else—Brahms,
Rachmaninoff, Beethoven, Liszt—but that he might have been reminded, politely, that the hall could not have been considered officially open without "Van Cliburn and the Tchaikovsky."

That, to be sure, is the nature of the American system, to want
the authentic "ceremonial best" for an Occasion, whether it is the
opening of a supermarket or a new concert hall. Is Cliburn, in
fact, sick and surfeited with that, emotionally drained, psycho-
logically bereft of ambition, direction, aspiration? Or is it, merely,
that the impulse by which he was first propelled through the concerto literature—the composers mentioned above, plus Schumann,
Chopin, MacDowell, Grieg—has been concentrated on one single
objective, and is thus too much of a muchness, for himself as well
as for his audience?

Can anyone imagine Cliburn playing Scarlatti, Haydn, Mozart, Schubert, Mendelssohn, the gossamer or the *galant*, *Le Gibet* of Ravel, the atmospheric *Noches en los jardines de España* of Manuel de Falla, or, for that matter, the concerti of Prokofiev, Ginastera, Samuel Barber?

Even as man cannot live by bread alone, so an artist cannot thrive, spiritually, on the roast beef and the red cabbage of the repertory. He must—privately, at the very least—have the capacity and the composure to step away from the glare of the spotlight now and then, to find a cool, shadowed, reflective corner of the keyboard in which to find mental green pastures.

Is it time to face the question whether Cliburn's education was at fault? Is he one of those so petted and prized that he was overfed on viands such as produce oversized geese for pâté, but deprived of the intellectual exercise to keep the mind supple? Was he the musical equivalent of the overindulged athlete who constantly practices his strengths and reluctantly, if ever, confronts his shortcomings? Was he conditioned for a true success or merely for a gloriously short-lived "triumph"?

There are, to be sure, years ahead for Cliburn. But the road upward is always tougher climbing for those who have known the dizzy exhilaration of standing on a peak all their own than for those still to accomplish such fulfillment. I wonder if Cliburn ever thinks of the indulgence of the 1950s that enabled him to be put in the "diploma" category of a bygone Juilliard administration (the present one is wholly different), and thus to have escaped some of the classwork that might have dulled the razor-sharp edge of his aptitudes, rounded them somewhat by contact with other things, to benefit him more?

I think of the occasion on May 19, 1958, when New York mayor Robert F. Wagner spent some of the city's money to welcome Cliburn home from Moscow (after a ticker-tape parade) with a lunch at the Waldorf. Everything about it, which included a guest list of New York's most officially "artistic" people, was outgoing and enkindling. Nothing was so quietly exhilarating as Cliburn's response to the praise lavished on him with a rapturous playing at the keyboard of a transcription for piano of Schumann's soaring song *Widmung* ("Dedication").

Where has that impulse gone?

V

Above and beyond all the other matters pertaining to Cliburn lurks the Competition—benign, perhaps, in the instance of the Leventritt, which provided him with his first national exposure, lethal when he went to Moscow and won the Tchaikovsky. This is surely an inversion of values: to argue against the mechanism, or means, by which he became rich and famous. But did it make him happy and secure in his career?

Much may be said about competitions, even, specifically, the Tchaikovsky competition in Moscow, depending on who wins, and what he does with the opportunity it presents. Cliburn's victory in 1958 made him the object of a national esteem, not because of *what* he was, but where and when it was recognized. The measure of his talent was so superior to the talents of those against whom he was competing that the Soviet system used it as a weapon to belittle *our* system. Even Dmitri Shostakovich, pushed and badgered into an action about which he must have had profound reservations, was called upon to declaim:

"Until now the musical successes of that country [the United States] resulted not from efforts of Americans, but of famous performers of European countries. We, for our part, are extremely happy that this outstanding young American artist earned his first wide and entirely deserved recognition among us here in Moscow." How wide is "wide"? At the time this article appeared in *Pravda*, Cliburn had already appeared (in addition to the performance with the New York Philharmonic noted on page 56) with orchestras in Cleveland, Pittsburgh, Denver, Buffalo, Cincinnati, Dallas, Detroit, Houston, and Indianapolis . . . *prior* to his success in Moscow.

For the next competition in Moscow devoted to pianists (the solo instrument shifts from year to year) the entrants from the Soviet Union included Vladimir Ashkenazy, then aged twenty-five. He had won first prize at the Brussels International Competition (sponsored by the Queen of Belgium) six years before. Prior to that, he had won second prize in the Chopin International Competition in Warsaw (1955). When he made his American debut with a Carnegie Hall recital in November 1958, he was widely recognized as the most gifted of all young pianists (Russian or otherwise).

The year of Ashkenazy's victory was 1962, when he already had half a dozen recordings on the London label. In my view, and those of some others (possibly including himself), this would have automatically disqualified him from being a "competitor" among other, less established pianists. But the Russian authorities didn't see it that way. The jury, however, salved some wounded spirits by selecting the brilliant English pianist John Ogdon as co-winner. Politics aside, the outcome served both performers well. It was not long after (1963) that Ashkenazy cut himself off from Russian supervision ("defected" was not yet a popular word), acquired a wife of Icelandic citizenship, and made England his home. Ogdon used the prominence conferred on him by his share of the prize to broaden his reputation, make some records, and settle down at home, where he has pursued a solid, serious, non-flamboyant career.

Certainly the political implications of the Moscow competition are always latent in the awards, and who wins them. Invariably, they carry more weight when the winner is a pianist than when other instruments are concerned, doubtless because more people are interested in the piano, and in pianists.

American violinists, such as Eugene Fodor and Elmar Oliveira, have attained high rank in Moscow without being hailed as heroes, or, for that matter, being made much of. In 1978, Nathaniel Rosen, of California birth, who had begun to compete a dozen years before, achieved his objective by winning the gold medal in the competition for cellists. He then returned to America to resume his place as principal cellist in the Pittsburgh Symphony. Now that his contract for such work has expired, he has chosen to pursue the path followed by numerous cellists of similar orchestral background—Gregor Piatigorsky (Berlin Philharmonic), Leonard Rose (New York Philharmonic), Janos Starker (Chicago Symphony), Lynn Harrell (Cleveland Orchestra) among them—on a soloist's career.

As an arena for world attention, Moscow has introduced an element into competitions rarely to be found elsewhere. A counterpart (restricted to pianists) has arisen in this country in the name of Cliburn himself. In the wave of emotionalism that accompanied his return to America in April 1958, a native of Fort Worth, Texas, gratified him extremely by putting up $10,000 for a Van Cliburn Competition to be held quadriennially on the campus of Texas Christian University, in the same Texas city. (Though born in Shreveport, Louisiana, July 12, 1934, Cliburn had lived most of his life in nearby Kilgore, Texas, the home of his father, an oil technician.)

The individual was Dr. Irl Allison, who was also founder and president of the National Guild of Piano Teachers. By the time the first competition was called to order in 1962, the sponsors included, in addition to Dr. Allison as "Founder and President," the president of the Fort Worth Chamber of Commerce, the president of the Fort Worth Piano Teachers Forum, the chancellor of Texas Christian University, and Richard Lee Brown, chairman of the Van Cliburn Piano Competition Foundation. There was also an Advisory Board, with a range of names from Arthur Rubinstein to Madame Rosina Lhevinne, who, in all probability, did not toil, neither did they advise.

In that first year of 1962, there was great enthusiasm, and in addition to the top prize of $10,000, a series of other prizes ($6,000 for second, $2,000 for third, etc.) contributed by other individuals and foundations. Van Cliburn extended to the contestants "The gracious hospitality of Fort Worth . . . in the beautiful state of Texas and, I might add, the United States of America."

When all the notes had been heard, and the jury's votes had been counted, the winner of the first prize was pronounced to be Ralph Votapek, of Milwaukee, Wisconsin, who has seldom been heard from since. Of the other eight who received prizes in some measure or other, the only name recognizably prominent is that of Marilyn Neeley, also American.

In 1966, first prize went to Radu Lupu of Romania, who has utilized the prominence that then accrued to him, to concertize, record, and build a reputation. Barry Snyder, the runner-up, is a member of the faculty of the Eastman School of Music in Rochester, New York, and, as the excellent pianist of its Eastman Trio, esteemed as a specialist in chamber music.

The next competition was held in 1969, rather than 1970. Cristina Ortiz, of Brazil, became the first woman pianist to win. I have heard her of recent years as a soloist with orchestra (also Brazilian): her objectives strike me as more inclined to virtuosity than musicality. Minoru Nojima, who finished second, is a Japanese pianist held by some in high regard. I have no basis for an opinion.

Vladimir Viardo, of the U.S.S.R., and Christian Zacharias finished first and second in 1973. I have heard Viardo give an impressive recital in Carnegie Hall. I have no opinion of Zacharias. The most recent (1977) competition was won by Steven De Groote, a native of South Africa whose forebears are Belgian. Some strong audience sentiment was generated by Alexander Toradze, aged twenty-five, a native of the U.S.S.R. A third pianist —who did not receive a final rating—developed an even greater partisanship with his playing in the early rounds. He is Youri Egorov, also of Russian birth, who chose political asylum in Italy in 1976. He has force and fervor, which are not necessarily the attributes that appeal to competition jurists.

Here, of course, is a key factor to the question: do prize competitions mean anything? Juries vary almost as much as competitors. The first characteristic of competition juries—and I have looked at the makeup of at least half a hundred of them—is that they invariably include as many prominent pianists (or, if not prominent, *pianists*) as the inviting committee can persuade to come. That means that "technique" is a high-priority item.

I put "technique" in quotes to indicate technique in the abstract, as a mechanical, measurable attribute—swift scales, glossy octaves, glittering arpeggios—rather than what suits a particular piece of music. High in the next order of frequency are peda-gogues: people who are imbued with the "right" way of playing a specific piece, and measure such matters as impulse, individuality, sensitivity, and compulsion by what they so often know least of all about. Then there are conductors, who instinctively reduce so much of what there is about music to counts, beats, entrances, etc.

By some lapse of judgment, or, at least, ignorance of desirability, the least common occupation to be found among jurists is: music critic. In the half hundred to which I have referred, the presence among them of a music critic—known, identifiable, assessable in terms of vocation rather than avocation—is all but unknown. I allow the reservation ("all but") because of the breadth of knowledge, awareness of capability, and appreciation of worth shown in the choice of jurists for the first Arthur Rubinstein International Master Competition in Israel in 1974. Or, perhaps, it erred on the side of optimism in extending to me such an invitation, which I accepted.

I cannot claim a wise and effective influence on the deliberations that produced a winner in this competition, because there were none—deliberations, that is. The procedure in this competition—as I believe is the case in some others, including Fort Worth—bypassed lobbying or persuasion among jurists. Votes were cast on the basis of objective, analytical assessment of the contestants, on a numerical scale that prevailed from start to finish.

If I did, by inference, cast a vote that mediated some degree of difference among others, it was because, in functioning as a critic, I was prejudging what would happen when the winner was exposed to the judgment of my colleagues around the world. Emanuel Ax had what it would take for an affirmative response, and so it turned out weeks later, thousands of miles from Israel.

Whether such a straw in the wind would benefit decisions elsewhere, under other circumstances, is almost as difficult a speculation to answer as being a critic in the first place. Take the case of Steven De Groote, winner of the 1977 Van Cliburn Competition.

De Groote (born in 1953) was twenty-four at the time. When I heard about the Fort Worth decision, the outcome struck me as well deserved. He was a finalist in the Leventritt Competition of 1976, in which the jury chaired by Rudolf Serkin (and including a number of prior winners of the award) utilized an option in the conditions of procedure not to award a prize. Sitting a few rows away from where they were in an otherwise empty Carnegie Hall, I thought that De Groote was thoroughly qualified for the jury's endorsement. Whether he was, as the rules specified, of "a quality to embark on a major career" was a fairly speculative assumption. I looked around at some members of the jury after they had voted De Groote down, and wondered whether *they* fulfilled such a qualification after winning a Leventritt endorsement.

The next time I heard De Groote was, again, in Carnegie Hall. What happened on that date (December 12, 1977) is now on the record—De Groote's record—and it isn't etched in gold. Indeed, as winner of that year's Cliburn Competition, it isn't etched at all. Rather it is smudged by the names of the three sonatas he played (Haydn in A, Hoboken XVI 26; Prokofiev in B flat, No. 8; and Beethoven in A, opus 101), none of them really well. The Haydn was dutifully performed, but with little stylistic flair; the Prokofiev smoldered for a while, then burst into a flame of personality, even of temperament, for the summarizing toccata; the Beethoven was, unfortunately, on the other side of an intermission, by which time the energy that De Groote had summoned for the Prokofiev had subsided. To be sure, there was uncommon pianistic power in his Prokofiev: the pianists and pedagogues in the Cliburn jury had noted that well. But the high musical capacity and notable artistic insight I had heard on the earlier occasion were in abeyance.

What does this add up to? Simple: possibilities and probabilities. As any experienced jurist will agree, a competition rarely proves anything, except how well—or how poorly—a competitor may perform at a specific time in his life. The compulsion to proclaim a winner is irresistible (the Cliburn Competition jury has the option to withhold its first prize, but hasn't done so yet). Or, let us say, the pressure from outside sources—the press, the public, the interrelated sponsors—is hard to resist.

So much is common fact, and understandably urgent.

What is far from the fact and hardly urgent is the disposition of awards that concentrate far too much on a first-prize winner, and far too little on the runners-up. As has been demonstrated in all too many instances, competition winners do not necessarily fare as well as those who have been passed over by a jury.

In the present instance, the program of De Groote's Carnegie Hall appearance set forth the following specifications of his rewards from winning the Cliburn Competition: "Cash prizes totaling over $13,000, a Gold Medal, a two-year recital and orchestral tour of the United States (including appearances with such orchestras as those of Philadelphia, Pittsburgh, Chicago, Cleveland, Cincinnati), a special cash award from RCA Records, a London debut, and concert tours of Europe, the Far East, and South America."

By contrast with such *largesse*, the awards to the runners-up in the 1977 Cliburn Competition were of the same cash order as the first, in 1962: $6,000 for Toradze, the second-prize winner; and $3,000 for Jeffrey Swann, the Bronze Medal winner. There were also some consolation engagements for both: a total of seventeen for Toradze, beginning at the Sussex County Music Foundation in Newton, New Jersey, and ending at Bradley University in Peoria, Illinois, of which five were with non-major orchestras (the Spokane [Washington] Symphony, and the Berkshire Symphony in Williamstown, Massachusetts, as instances). Swann was awarded a total of eleven, including the California Youth Orchestra in San Jose, California, and the West Texas State University, Canyon, Texas.

For every contestant in a major competition, there is an element of chance-taking, of success beyond the wildest expectations or an embarrassingly poor showing (such as failing to qualify for the "cut," as competition language has it, which is to say, not qualifying for inclusion among the eight or ten from whom the winner and runners-up will be chosen).

Youri Egorov was exposed to both, if in reverse order. The jury did not include his impulsive, highly personalized interpretations among those from whom they would pick a winner; but a coterie of enthusiasts who had been attracted to his impulsive, highly personalized interpretations raised a total of $10,000 to equal the winner's basic income.

By comparison with Mrs. Richardson's Schilsky and his chances of success in the *Hauptprüfung* at the Leipzig Conservatorium of the 1890s (page 53), or even Cliburn's income from the Leventritt Award of 1954, De Groote's takings qualify as a small fortune. That they are, by implication, a consequence of Cliburn's success in Moscow nearly twenty years before needs no underscoring.

But where is the true line of connection?

In a time when his own career is either sputtering (the orchestral part, which goes uncertainly) or stuttering (the recital part, which goes hardly at all), Cliburn's involvement with a complex, recurrent affair which, these days, may bring him into contact recurrently with a hundred or more pianists from all over the world prompts some curiosity. I have mentioned his part in the opening of Boettcher Hall in Denver in 1978, and the impression it left of him walking on, playing, taking his bows, and disappearing. "That's nothing," commented one with a close view of his recent habits. "The last time I heard him play he did more or less the same thing. Moreover, he was on his way to the airport before the orchestra had finished playing the last piece." And the record company that has been producing his records since the very first wishes that he would pick himself up and finish the incomplete recital they have had on the shelf for a couple of years.

Some might cite the recurrent Cliburn Competition in Fort Worth as part of a public posture, or a pose, perhaps a liking for the limelight, and an easy way of sustaining it. But there are other considerations to be reckoned with.

According to the brochure announcing the Sixth Van Cliburn International Quadriennial Piano Competition, the first prize (now raised to $12,000, on behalf of inflation, come September 1981) is still "Awarded by the National Guild of Piano Teachers in honor of Dr. and Mrs. Irl Allison."

An article of recent years stated that Dr. Allison founded this organization in 1939 and it now has 75,211 members, made up of students as well as teachers. The prize money is derived from the "general fund" of its membership. But there are, of course, other expenses, some of them doubtless accounted for by the Van Cliburn Foundation, Inc., which, according to the same brochure, is "exclusively" responsible for the administration of the Competition.

On May 17, 1977, Van Cliburn and the Fort Worth Symphony collaborated in a concert devoted to three piano concertos:

Beethoven   *Concerto No. 5 in E flat, opus ("Emperor")*

Liszt   *Concerto No. 1 in E flat*

Tchaikovsky   *Concerto No. 1 in B flat minor*

The receipts of $37,000, it was reported in the press, were to be applied "to defray costs" of the Competition. He has put himself out to perform some such fund-raising effort before each Competition since the first.

Is the activity in Fort Worth just "another" competition for Cliburn, or has it taken the place, for him, of "The" competition whose base has always been Moscow?

I have mentioned (page 59) the occasion on which Cliburn phrased his appreciation of New York City's honorary lunch in his honor, in May 1958, in terms of Schumann's *Widmung*. Let us look at Fort Worth and Cliburn's part in the Competition as evidence that the musical heart which prompted that gesture is still there. It needs reawakening.

The Man
Who Rebuked Heifetz

I

Few musicians, including most of his colleagues, would quarrel with the statement that Jascha Heifetz is the greatest violinist of the century. That consensus dates to October 27, 1917, when he made his famous debut (at sixteen) in Carnegie Hall.

As recently as 1971, when he recorded the television program that will, forever, not only convey the peerless sound of his art, but show exactly, and in precise detail, how it was accomplished, he was (at seventy)—as Duke Ellington said lovingly of Ella Fitzgerald—beyond category.

In between, there were some areas of repertory that left me and my speechless admiration for his playing of August Wilhelmj's transcription of Schubert's *Ave Maria*[1] disenchanted.

However, he came very close to liquidating all artistic debts when he acknowledged, with a degree of candor unmatched by any artist of comparable stature known to me, that he had learned something from a critic. The well-known posture, toward critics, of the performing profession being to range from "I never read them" to "What does he know anyway?", the mere expression of such an awareness confers a degree of recognition on their existence. To imply that one of them wrote something worth reading by a Heifetz almost entitles him to honorary membership in their non-existent guild.

[1] The place was a now bygone auditorium in Newark, New Jersey, the year was probably 1920. It was immediately apparent to me that I would never be the "second Heifetz" of which my mother was dreaming.

The full text of this unquestionably true confession may be found in an issue of *Holiday* magazine published in 1963. The "father" to whom this confession was made was the late Samuel Chotzinoff, his onetime accompanist, sometime music critic for the New York *World* (1920s) and New York *Evening Post* (early 1930s), and always brother-in-law. The article may be found reprinted as annotation for RCA album LM/LSC 1903, a reissue of eight violin concerto recordings modestly titled *Heifetz*.

In its verbatim, attested form it reads: "There came a time when my disinclination to practice caught up with me. After a certain New York recital, W. J. Henderson, the music critic of the *Sun*, hinted in his review that I was letting the public (and him) down, and that I had better watch my step. Though it was hard to bear, the warning came in the nick of time. I began to take a good look at myself. I started to practice seriously. I curbed my youthful extravagances. I shall always be grateful to Henderson. He jolted me out of my complacency and put me on the right path. Critics *can* sometimes be very helpful." (Italics in the original.) In another, later version of this testament, Heifetz added a codicil: "He died some years ago, and I will always regret I did not meet him. He did me a great service."[2]

Henderson's long, notable career came to an end on June 5, 1937, when he was eighty-two years old. After several months of debilitating illness, he decided that suicide by pistol shot (a long-forgotten weapon he had found in the bottom of a desk drawer) was preferable to a long, wasting decline. Much as this action appalled his wife and closest friends, and shocked the colleagues and associates by whom he was much admired, it was eminently in keeping with the rational, reasoned mentality to be found in his writings.

My association with Henderson began slightly more than five years before. I had found a place, in the fall of 1931, to risk my private assumption of competence in the public columns of the Brooklyn *Eagle* (for which I was paid by the inch rather than the word). One Sunday night in January 1932 I went, as usual, to the

[2] *Heifetz*, edited by Dr. Herbert R. Axelord (Paganiniana Publications, Inc., Neptune City, N.J., 1976), p. 419.

Western Union office diagonally across Broadway from the old Metropolitan Opera House. Here I would type my comments and deliver them to the *Eagle*'s music critic, Edward Cushing, who had hired me. Then they would be taken, together with his own piece, to the *Eagle* office in Brooklyn.

Shortly after I arrived, Cushing came in from his own assignment, where he had learned that one of Henderson's assistants had quit and New York's senior music critic was urgently in need of a replacement. In a demonstration of selflessness as endearing as it was uncommon, Cushing said to me: "I want to see to it that you get that job on the *Sun*." Precisely how he did it, Cushing never explained in detail. But he let me know the following day that he had spoken to Henderson, who was waiting for a call from me to make an appointment. The call was made, an appointment arranged, and I reported the following afternoon to the hotel in New York's theatrical district where he lived (next to the Belasco Theatre on West Forty-fourth Street). Henderson received me cordially—he was seventy-seven, but widely esteemed as the liveliest, best-informed writer among the city's music critics— questioned me on my background, and thanked me for the examples of my work that he had asked me to bring along.

A really searching interview was hardly necessary. I had been, for the preceding five years, a student at the Institute of Musical Art, where Henderson annually delivered two lecture courses, both of which I had taken. I had also written for the school magazine, and my class grades—not to mention the instructors themselves—were readily available if he wanted further information.

As I left, he told me he was obligated to see several other job applicants, and would I call him later in the week? When I did, he said that he had decided to give me a trial, and I should report the following afternoon to pick up an assignment he would leave at the hotel desk. The "trial" stretched into eighteen years' association with the *Sun*, of which I became music critic before it was merged with the *World-Telegram* in 1950.

Henderson was a luminary, if not the only one, among a high order of critical talent that could be read in the press (weekly as well as daily) of the time. Van Wyck Brooks and Henry Hazlitt were notable among book reviewers; Philip Hale and H. T. Parker (of Boston), Pitts Sanborn, B. H. Haggin, Lawrence Gilman, Carl Van Vechten, Paul Rosenfeld, and Herbert Peyser were prominent writers on music;[3] Brooks Atkinson, Elliot Norton (again Boston), John Mason Brown, and, later, Walter Kerr were young aspirants to the standards of George Jean Nathan, Gilbert Gabriel, Percy Hammond, and Stark Young among astute writers on the theater.

However else some members of this flock might have characterized themselves, Henderson's long-standing description of himself was: "A newspaperman with a speciality." A good, unpompous classification, it hardly did justice to his long-term performance. Unlike some others, writing about music for Henderson was not merely a pleasant way of making a living. It was, rather, a public way of discharging the private pleasure he derived from a lifelong attachment to an art he loved.

A native of Newark, New Jersey, where he was born in 1855, Henderson was educated at Princeton, from which he was graduated in 1876. He later returned to receive an M.A. in 1886. In the years between, he pursued a boyhood infatuation with newspaper work, sometimes assisted his father (a theatrical manager who sponsored the American debut of Gilbert and Sullivan with the country's first production of *H.M.S. Pinafore*), and also served as an assistant to Henry Krehbiel, music editor of the New York *Tribune*. In 1886, he found permanent work with the New York *Times*, and in 1887 became its music critic.

Along the way he played ball at Princeton and also on the Long Branch town team, and did a lot of sailing on the adjacent Shrewsbury waters, while spending youthful summers at the family's vacation home. From this emerged a lifelong affinity for navigation and the nickname of Billy, which clung to him through all his decades. In 1902, aged forty-seven, he became music critic of the *Sun*, a post he filled (despite several wavering affiliations with other papers, from which he rapidly returned to his enduring "home") until his self-willed death, thirty-five years later.

[3] Paul Bekker, the great Berlin-born critic and author of outstanding works on Beethoven, Mahler, and Wagner, left Nazi Germany to become music critic of the New York *Staats-Zeitung* in 1934. He died in 1937.

Musically, Henderson learned his ABCs in childhood, and at Princeton received some piano instruction from Carl Langlotz, a sometime member of the university's faculty whose enduring accomplishment is its alma mater, "Old Nassau." But he was largely self-taught. His writing, of which I have an all but inexhaustible file in more than forty scrapbooks maintained by Henderson with scrupulous care from 1885 to 1937, was characteristically concise, fluently phrased, and clearly articulated. With the broadened scope, breadth of experience, and length of perspective that accrued over time, his work from 1920 was of an authority and insight rarely excelled in the cockpit and crucible of American daily journalism.

I pin the date to 1920 because it was just about then that internal redesign of the *Sun* awarded Henderson an uncommonly prominent budget of space for a weekly column titled (after the manner of Robert Schumann) "Music and Musicians." Eventually it was double-columned from top to bottom, in suitable recognition of the wide-ranging content he filled nearly seven hundred times in his last seventeen years.

II

In this time span, he continued to monitor his many interests— symphonic, operatic, balletic—on the New York scene three, four, or five times a week. Formal "days off" were unknown in a period of journalism when writers pursued their interests, not their convenience. This added thousands of daily articles to the Saturday column. As the factual as well as the nominal dean of the many younger men around him, Henderson was looked upon as a sage. In his case, the honorary title was a measurement of sagacity rather than, as with some others, merely a measurement of age.

Henderson was not averse to sharing his knowledge, but he had his own way of dispensing it. On one occasion, as he was waiting in the lobby of Carnegie Hall for the arrival of the car in which he made his nightly rounds, a critic new to the ways of the craft breached all protocol by sounding him out for an opinion on the evening's soloist. When, to the young critic's amazement, the following day's paper carried Henderson's by-line over a series of opinions exactly opposite to those he had expressed the evening before, he explained to me (a post-performance chat was a nightly ritual): "I just wanted to teach that young man to think for himself."

Similarly, one of the first (of a very few) strictures he laid down when I was taken on for my "trial" period was: "Keep out of the Metropolitan Opera House Press Room. The *Sun* is paying you to give its readers *your* opinions, not what they have already read in the *Times* and the *Tribune.*"

As well and as widely as his day-to-day reports were read—and who could know when he might next take to task some "other" Heifetz for failing his trust to the public?—each Saturday's "Music and Musicians" was an unqualified must. This was not merely for its erudition, for its uncommon sense, for a broadly based summation of some current circumstance that would be better understood in the light of what, somewhat similarly, had happened fifteen years before. All these counted, but so did something more: the smoothly flowing sentences that marched across the double column as if they had been marshaled in ranks, drawn up in battle formation, taught their paces on a parade ground before being displayed in public.

Pervading them, too, was an escalating order of subject matter, based on his own un-indexable predilections. Henderson, the "newspaperman with a speciality," could deal with anything in the range of that speciality. Whether it was a newly discovered motet by Orlando di Lasso, a spurious song attributed to Schubert, or the first symphony by a young Soviet composer named Dimitri Szostakowicz (as the name was then being spelled), he was rational, readable, and reliable . . . three Rs not yet to be found on the curriculum of a school of journalism.

But there is scant question—indeed, no question at all—that the single subject to which he was most attached, and the one on which he had the vastest, widest range of information, discrimination, and illumination, was singing—male or female, sacred or secular, profound or profane, oratorio or operatic. I would state categorically that Henderson's writings on singers and singing are as massively learned on the abilities and disabilities of the people he heard in New York during his fifty years as Henry F. Chorley's are on those of London during the shorter period embodied in the famous volume entitled *Thirty Years' Musical Recollections* (1830–1860). As an instance of the thoroughness by which Henderson was motivated, and his insatiable search for knowledge, references to Chorley's observations may be found in writings by Henderson no less than thirty years (1895) *before* they became known to most other Americans through their reissue (by Alfred A. Knopf, Inc., with an introduction by Ernest Newman) in 1926. Henderson's are crying out, still, to be issued in such depth and variety.

The distinctive quality of Henderson's approach to the subject may be savored by reference to terse summation of attitude uttered on an evening when he was attending the Metropolitan Opera debut of a singer with some European reputation. After the curtain fell on the second act, a colleague seated behind him observed Henderson gathering himself to leave, and inquired: "Aren't you staying for the third-act aria?" "No," said Henderson, "she isn't going to learn how to sing between now and then."

This degree of certainty, which embraced the fairness of mind to reserve judgment where it was merited or to join the issue when it wasn't, had not been derived from random observation. Henderson had actively pursued the study of singing even before venturing into journalism. He acquired, in sustained, year-by-year study of the subject, sufficient practical knowledge to discuss placement, production, emission, breath support, and all the other technicalities beloved of vocal teachers, which added, powerfully, to the value of what he wrote. This qualified him, among other things, for an intimate association with the brothers De Reszke during their days of glory in New York (1891–1905), to probe further to its source the subtle, arcane art of singing.

What this meant to the readers of the *Sun*, after another decade or two of experience, can be read in a comment published in the issue of that paper dated December 21, 1932. It related to the death a few days before (December 19) of Clarence Whitehill, one of the greatest American bass-baritones (Wotan, Sachs, Amfortas, Méphistophélès in *Faust*), who mastered the art that delighted two generations of his countrymen at its sources: Bayreuth and the Paris Opéra.

After extolling his Hans Sachs (one of the best) as "superlative," his Méphistophélès in *Faust* as "noteworthy for its subtlety, its irony and its elegance of vocal delivery," and his Golaud in Debussy's *Pelléas et Mélisande* as a "tragic and memorable portrait of a jealous husband," Henderson addressed himself to an aspect of Whitehill that could have been known to few others:

> Mr. Whitehill had a certain difficulty with his voice throughout his career owing to the supersensitiveness of one vocal cord. When this was slightly congested the singer's tones acquired a little roughness and when the congestion was pronounced he became unmistakably hoarse. The thoroughness of his vocal art enabled him to accomplish much in spite of his trouble, but in later years it became more and more obstinate. He will go down in operatic history as an artist of high rank, whose ideals were lofty and whose devotion to them was unceasing.

Needless to say, little of value can be acquired without paying a price. After Jean De Reszke left the opera in 1902, his brother Édouard stayed on in New York, prospered, and without his brother's watchful eye to keep him trim, grew fat and short of breath for the long phrases of his basso specialities. "It taught me not to become too friendly with artists," Henderson once remarked, "or to be on too familiar a footing with them. When Édouard got fat and short of breath, I told the truth—and lost a friend." Similarly, he once disclosed, a reference in a Henderson column to a "master pianist" brought a complaint from an older performer for whom he had high regard. Why? Because the older performer thought he was *the* master pianist, and there could be no other.

In a perspective of half a century, the vocal talents on which he pronounced equally informed opinions extended from Adelina Patti—of whom he once observed (in 1887), "Everybody knew that Carmen was a cat: but Patti made her into a kitten"—to Helen Traubel, fifty years later.

Following the latter's debut in Walter Damrosch's *The Man Without a Country* (May 12, 1937, less than a month before his death) he commented: "She can be taught to make more of the stature, as well as the voice, for Wagnerian roles." Another critic with a perceptive ear might have noted the suitability of Traubel for the career in which she became internationally acclaimed. Henderson explained *why*: "Mature of voice and figure, she gave clear hints of possibilities in heroic roles, beyond those of fledglings. Her singing had power, her compass was an extended one, her tone solid, steady and true, with the scale well equalized."

So far as I can determine from a far from casual survey of the subject, the only debut of a major singer about which he did not write during his fifty years' work in New York was that of Lauritz Melchior. Henderson was not ill, neglectful, or otherwise guilty of dereliction of duty. Melchior's Metropolitan debut as Tannhäuser in Wagner's opera occurred in a matinee performance on February 17, 1926. This is a date well or ill remembered in the annals of American folklore as the one on which Marion Talley, the Kansas City lark, made her world-reported first appearance as Gilda in the evening's performance of Verdi's *Rigoletto*. In the circumstances, the place of her country's leading music critic and authority on the art she professed to be practicing was where he was—at her debut.

In due course it was Henderson—no one else had the information to venture such a comparison—who ten years later made Melchior the magnificent present, on Christmas Eve, of pronouncing him "the noble Tristan (the best the Metropolitan has known since Jean De Reszke)" in the *Sun* dated December 24, 1936.

III

From this and similar pronouncements *in excelsis* to which he gave expression from time to time, there is not the least doubt

that Henderson was keenly conscious of the difference between
the performer and the artist (whether or not he used the same terminology). In one series of dire circumstances that befell Enrico
Caruso and the musical public of the world in 1920 (and eventually ended with the great tenor's death in August 1921), Henderson wrote (the *Sun,* January 23, 1921):

> For years, the opera which could be given the greatest number of
> times in any [Metropolitan] season has been *Pagliacci.* For years
> the most crowded houses have been those attending a repre-
> sentation of this work with Mr. Caruso as the clown. This fact
> has been a sad commentary on the state of public taste. But,
> worse still, the demand on which it was based caused Mr. Caruso
> to transform himself from a lyric tenor, second to none in the
> history of opera, to a robust tenor relying upon volume of tone
> for its chief effect.
>
> Shouting to split the ears of the groundlings did him no good.
> It reduced his stature as an artist. It diminished the beauty of his
> voice. It robbed him of much of the refinement of his early style.
> It lowered all his standards . . .

Clearly spelled out here is the peril of the *artist* yielding to the
demands of the audience, verging perilously close to the performer
who takes a check for what he can get and thinks of little else.
From the onset of the injury (December 8, 1920, in—as it happened!—a performance of *Pagliacci,* in which he wrenched his
side after "the big aria," as the report in the *Sun* described it)
Henderson reminded his readers of the progressive change in Caruso's style of singing, and the damage it might do to him. As wit-
ness *before* the fact, rather than afterward, Henderson called upon
his own words of ten years before:

"It is a pity that he has, of late, evinced a fondness for extension of the medium range and has striven to carry a big broad
quality too far up. This has done his voice no good and it has
robbed his singing of much of the crystalline transparency which
was one of its greatest charms."

Unhappily, the warning so pronounced, even the example of
Caruso himself, wasn't heeded by later tenors who profess to admire the great Neapolitan above all others. The clown suit and
the big bass drum have taken their toll of more than one tenor's

stamina. The late Richard Tucker and the big bass drum were the last pairing of a vocal life which began at the Metropolitan with Enzo Grimaldi in Ponchielli's *La Gioconda.* He was spared the onstage death of his friend Leonard Warren (it is generally forgotten that the first artist to reach the side of the prostrate Warren in that evening's performance of Verdi's *La Forza del destino* on March 4, 1960, was Tucker), but not the price for wickedly overtaxing his strength.

Nor were excess and overstatement that were dangerous to the well-being of the individual himself the only kinds that Henderson deplored. His admiration for Heifetz was in many ways based on qualities that invited such words as "continence," "restraint," "classic repose," "finesse."

Is it imaginable that Sergei Rachmaninoff ever played the piano music of Claude Debussy in public? When he did, Henderson was there to report his profound admiration for that singular happening (December 11, 1933). He wrote, of one great composer's performance of the other's *Pour le piano:* "Mr. Rachmaninoff's performance was gorgeous in color, splendid in sweep and mastery, and it was one which, contrary to a prevalent practice, kept continually before the hearer that the composer was Monsieur, not Mademoiselle, Debussy."

Schnabel came, eventually, to enjoy Henderson's highest esteem in the repertory of which he was a master; Bruno Walter enjoyed his commendation as a guest conductor with the New York Symphony in the early twenties, years before he became the universally acclaimed master who returned to New York in the thirties. When the two were joined then in a performance of Beethoven's "Emperor" Concerto, Henderson proclaimed that what the audience had heard was "the voice of Beethoven" himself.

His standards remained substantially unaltered through his lifetime; the embodiments of them could be any contemporary, regardless of date, in whom Henderson heard and saw them fulfilled. As each day's comment appeared in a product that bore the day's date and consequently proclaimed it to be the record of the present, so Henderson lived in that endless present, rather than in some forever bygone past.

The unending problem of the mature, conscientious critic confronting the aging favorite with dwindling means of sustaining a memorable reputation was resolved by Henderson in the twenties and thirties with the same weapon he had used to deal with Édouard De Rezke decades before—he told the truth as he saw and heard it. That might not have been the blunt, harsh, *naked* truth as it struck the ear of one totally unfamiliar with the historic accomplishments of the performer's past: it was truth veiled by the esteem hard earned on the performer's part. On the one side there was a coarse non-likeness of an art the younger critic had never experienced; on the other, the interplay of memories and reality, well aware of nuances and subtleties long admired.

When Emma Calvé gave a recital in Carnegie Hall on January 22, 1922, not quite thirty years after her New York debut (as the first of all Metropolitan Opera Santuzzas) on November 29, 1893, Henderson wrote (in part):

> To those who heard Mme. Calve in the bloom of her young womanhood and voice the recital was a faint echo of far off times and an elder art of which almost nothing is known to the contemporaneous opera stage. It was sad and it was wonderful. And it was astonishing.
>
> For with what remains of her natural equipment and in spite of her personal idiosyncrasies, Mme. Calve must have impressed those who never heard her before as a genuinely great singer past her prime. The voice long ago lost its marvelous pliancy, its voluptuous tints, its subtle shades, and acquired a hardness and brittleness which robbed it of much of its pristine eloquence. Long ago, too, the singer abandoned her respect for the written text and violated rhythms, phrases, and even melodic progressions to suit her own whims or vocal convenience. But no matter what she did, there remained the potent spell of a great singer and a commanding personality.
>
> Yesterday, although sometimes the proceedings of the prima donna were almost ludicrous and though she sang off the key not infrequently and shattered phrases at will, the same impression remained. There were voice and art which stood forth the peers of anything known to the contemporary opera stage. The skill in coloring tone which was one of Mme. Calve's most valuable assets, was still present in a sufficient degree to captivate the ear

and the intelligence of the young music lover who is accustomed to incessant monotony and loudness of tone. Mme. Calve still can sing a ravishing pianissimo, a full blooded forte, a brutal chest tone, a fine spun head tone. She can still make her voice as black as night and the next instant emit a thin, cold "voix blanche." She can still declaim text with an almost infinite variety of accent. . . .

Mme. Calve in her later years preserves much of what made her one of the idols of this town twenty-five years ago and is still well worth hearing and study.

Though it was not primarily intended as such, this instruction to the young listener—on the order of "listen and learn but do not imitate"—could be classified as a wise approach to the point often raised by those who hear a greatly honored performer at a late point in a career: "Was there *ever* a voice there?" The answer, almost invariably, is: "Yes, indeed, there was . . . a reputation is seldom created without justification."

The most recent instance that came to my attention was in a class at the Juilliard that brought in a demonstration, via tape, of a Toscanini broadcast (as it happens, Verdi's *La Traviata*). As the beautifully phrased, warmly shaped tenor sound rose to an eloquent peak, I identified it to the listening group as that of Jan Peerce, to which one bright young man responded: "Are you sure that is Jan Peerce?" He couldn't—quite reasonably—relate what he had heard from the tape to the only kind of sound he associated with the living name: the dry, dark, ligneous rasp of a man long past his vocal prime.

This is why I have assembled, from a vastly larger possible pool, a sampling of performers heard by Henderson in such a context as that in which he proclaimed Melchior to be the best embodiment of Tristan he had heard since Jean De Reszke. It is a context in which I would say that Spas Wenkoff, by the measure of a broadcast I heard from Bayreuth in July 1977, is the best, vocally, I have heard since Melchior, thus extending a link to a chain extending over decades. That may be a measurement of quality for those who have heard, or will hear, Wenkoff but did not hear Melchior, just as I heard Melchior but not Jean De Reszke. Arranged alphabetically by the names of the individuals, the circumstances in which they were heard, and the date are a dozen or so instances of comparative excellence, defined with the clarity characteristic of Henderson:

BOHNEN, MICHAEL:
Kezal in Smetana's *Bartered Bride*
(February 8, 1927):

> "one of the most delicious bits of fooling the local stage has known . . ."

BORI, LUCREZIA:
Manon in Massenet's *Manon*
(March 12, 1929):

> "Bori's Manon last evening was undoubtedly the best the Metropolitan has ever known . . ."

Manon Lescaut in Puccini's *Manon Lescaut*
(October 12, 1929):

> "No other singer . . . has been so well able as Miss Bori has been able to lay just the right emphasis on the slender thread of endurance in Manon's love for Des Grieux . . ."

CHALIAPIN, FEODOR:
Boris in Moussorgsky's *Boris Godunoff*
(November 16, 1922):

> "it is no exaggeration to say that the operatic stage has furnished no such portrayal of the agonies of a soul since Tamagno's Otello."

FLAGSTAD, KIRSTEN:
Elsa in Wagner's *Lohengrin*
(March 16, 1935):

> "One of the most moving interpretations of the Princess ever revealed on the local stage . . ."

Senta in Wagner's *Der fliegende Holländer*
(January 8, 1937):

"Her delivery of the ballad was perhaps the most dramatic the Metropolitan stage has known . . ."

GARDEN, MARY:
All-Debussy recital with Walter Gieseking, at Carnegie Hall
(October 27, 1930):

"She sang Debussy with eloquence and with a revelation of the inner spirit of the music. Her interpretations were moving with an indefinable spell. Mr. Gieseking played the *Suite bergamasque*, 'Reflets dans l'eau' and several other numbers with bewitching subtleties of tone, molding of phrase and publication of mood. It was a memorable concert, given by two artists in complete accord with the thought and the method of expression of that solitary genius, Claude Achille Debussy . . ."

GIGLI, BENIAMINO:
Chénier in Giordano's *Andrea Chénier*
(November 15, 1923):

"sings all the music in a manner to command the warmest praise . . ."

JOHNSON, EDWARD:
with Lucrezia Bori in Gounod's *Roméo et Juliette*
(January 21, 1927):

"The balcony scene has not had so much value since the days of Emma Eames and Jean De Reszke . . ."

KIPNIS, ALEXANDER:
Hagen in Wagner's *Götterdämmerung*
(March 3, 1923, with a visiting German opera company):

"There has not been so subtle, sinister and commanding a Hagen . . . since Édouard De Reszke . . ."

PINZA, EZIO:
Don Basilio in Rossini's *Il Barbiere di Siviglia*
(January 3, 1928):

"One of the best impersonations of the village organist since the days of Édouard De Reszke . . ."

[This pair of opinions on widely diverse characterizations confirms that, whatever else had affected his personal friendship with Édouard De Reszke, nothing could reduce Henderson's impersonal esteem for him as an artist.]

Pons, Lily:
Lucia in Donizetti's *Lucia di Lammermoor*
(January 5, 1931):
> No illusion of madness, nevertheless— "We do not get florid singing like hers more than once in a decade . . ."

Ponselle, Rosa:
Leonora in Verdi's *La Forza del destino*
(November 16, 1918):
> "She is the possessor of one of the most voluptuous dramatic soprano voices that present-day operagoers have heard. Some day doubtless Miss Ponselle will learn how to sing, and then she will be an artist."

The same singer, seven years closer to Henderson's confidence in what she was capable of becoming:

Giulia in Spontini's *La Vestale* (with Tullio Serafin conducting, November 13, 1925):
> "She has ceased to content herself with splitting the ears . . . and gone in for real singing . . . Hers is one of the most beautiful organs of tone the Metropolitan has ever known . . ."

Schipa, Tito:
Don Ottavio in Mozart's *Don Giovanni*
(December 19, 1932):
> "Mr. Schipa has not a remarkable voice, but he is a very fine artist . . ."

Steschenko, Ivan:
Doctor in Berg's *Wozzeck* (with Leopold Stokowski conducting the Philadelphia Orchestra in the Metropolitan Opera House) (November 25, 1931):

"all the sinister power and sardonic glee demanded by the role . . . Berg has written with a glow of imagination in many places and always with aptness, vigor and orchestral virtuosity of a high order . . . The story is drab throughout. There is no moment of fine feeling or high contemplation. It is a squalid tragedy of low life . . . Worst of all it exudes fatalistic symbolism from which we protect the reader . . ."

TAUBER, RICHARD:
Debut in Town Hall
(October 29, 1931):

"a spontaneous emission of tone, with a firm attack, good phrasing and delightful diction . . . The latter part of the program was devoted to four airs of Franz Lehar. Mr. Tauber is famous in Europe for his singing of such music and the reason was easy to discover . . . Instead of singing these light airs lightly, he sang them with remarkable finesse in phrase and color and with a depth of sentiment which is rarely bestowed on such melodies . . . He raised them to the level of high art and furnished ground for speculation as to whether we of New York have ever become truly acquainted with the best music of this popular composer."

IV

Here, by inference if not by intention, are included some of the recurrent phenomena of the singer's art, associated (for the most part) with the great names of a particular generation: the one endowed with great material which she eventually learned how to use (Rosa Ponselle); the one of limited endowment but great artistry (Tito Schipa); the one who went on singing far into her fallow days, leaving some doubt that she ever had had a notable voice (Lily Pons); the one of high operatic attainments lastingly remembered (by the largest public to whom he was known) for his non-operatic activities (Ezio Pinza); the surprising embodiment of a vocal aptitude little known to the general American public (Richard Tauber).

Here, too, the challenge, to a master critic of an art form called "opera," by the appearance of a new, vigorous work little related to the vast literature with which he had grown up, matured, and, perhaps, mellowed: Alban Berg's *Wozzeck*. The adaptability and recognition of quality come where some might least expect it: vis-à-vis Berg's writing for the orchestra, and the "glow of imagination" that might have impressed the ears of other critics of seventy-seven as more searing than stimulating. Against this aural receptivity is to be reckoned the total hostility to the "drab" story and the "squalid" tragedy, despite the literature of Gorky, Dostoevski, Zola, O'Neill, Hauptmann, and many, many others which had, by 1930, accumulated in the *century* since the play of Georg Büchner's on which *Wozzeck* is based came into being.

The contradiction is by no means an inconsistency. Henderson's musical mind, which had encountered all the shocks and dislocations to which the nineteenth-century framework of values had been subjected in the first quarter of the twentieth—Stravinsky, Schoenberg, Berg, Scriabin, Bartók, Ornstein, Varèse, Prokofiev—was resilient enough, analytic enough, to separate the artistic from the merely eccentric. He didn't always revel in what among the new music he found artistic, but he found a place among the artistic for the best of Berg to which he had been exposed.

But his aesthetic sense—with which he was, perhaps, born before he found its counterpart in music—was formed in another, less flexible mold. By 1886, when Henderson had completed his university training, it was fixed forever within nineteenth-century perimeters, in which the moralistic and the religious stood staunchly at the boundaries. Art should, somehow, be demonstrably uplifting, contributory to a catharsis of mind and body that cleanses and purifies. He was one among a half-dozen other prominent music critics (Henry Krehbiel, especially, Philip Hale and Richard Aldrich among them, but *never* James Huneker) who were in agreement on this if on little else. They had their counterparts in such literary critics as Stuart Sherman and William Lyon Phelps.

Early in life, Henderson wrote a biography of Wagner, guarded in its raptures of such unseemly goings-on as the "strange love" (as he termed it) of Siegmund and his sister Sieglinde in *Die Walküre*, or even the illicit passion of Tristan and Isolde. What washed out moral doubt was an irresistible flood of music that established, beyond quibble, the presence of Love—pure, wholesome, compelling, compulsive Love, against which everything else was not merely meaningless but powerless.

If this was a rationalization that could be invoked on behalf of brother and sister of a noble (Wälsung) race, and of prince and princess, why was it not equally appropriate to a seamstress and poet in Paris, or a painter and actor in Rome, or a poet and dressmaker, again in Paris? The answer defies definition: but it is nevertheless a fact that *La Bohème*, *Tosca*, and *Louise* (and many, many others) were roundly denounced as obscene, cheap, and immoral by several of New York's leading critics (Henderson and Krehbiel among them) until the enticing music had made them so popular that nobody cared, really, very much what the characters did in the spare time when they were not singing.

As for the crude and vulgar Richard Strauss, he was undeniably overpowering as an orchestrator and musical sorcerer, but such subject matter! The necrophiliac Salome ("kinky" had not yet been added to the vocabulary), the maniacal Elektra, the lustful Marschallin and her infidelities with Octavian (they were not allowed to *lie* on the same bed at the Metropolitan until the fifties), each was scrutinized and rejected as no more suitable for extended discussion in a proper newspaper than the "fatalistic symbolism" of *Wozzeck* from which Henderson sought to "protect" the sensitivities of his readers.

Where he stood and by what motives he was animated were spelled out and defined in a letter by Henderson written in 1936 and published after his death.[4] It was addressed to his longtime friend Richard Aldrich (for many years, music critic of the New York *Times*). Henderson had been suffering from midwinter malaise, and Aldrich had written him a note of inquiry and sympathy. Here is Henderson's answer:

[4] In *Musical America*, June 1937.

New York, Jan. 30, 1936

Dear Richard: I thank you most sincerely for your letter . . . I'll confide to you that I feel it my sacred duty in these, my closing years, to stand up for the spiritual quality of music, its soul, its imagination, its poignant emotion. That means I am bound to oppose all this formation of methods first and writing according to them afterward. Even Wagner discovered his new paths before he tried to sell maps of them to the world. Chopin and Mozart just wrote as their spirits compelled them to. I'm fighting materialism and its close associate, sensationalism.

That's enough. I hope to be out next week, and to see you before long.

W. J. Henderson

Aldrich had been retired for a dozen years (he was succeeded as music critic of the *Times* in 1924 by Olin Downes) when he died in Rome on June 2, 1937, at the age of seventy-two. Henderson's suicide a few days later was attributed in part (by some of those who knew him best) to desolation at the death of one of his oldest friends, and the last of his surviving close colleagues.

v

That Henderson had some share of moral bias—call it puritanical or otherwise—against the trend of subject matter with which he was confronted as his career moved forward in its long course is unquestionable. That it foreshortened his vision of the merits of some things he could have been more objective about is clearly on the record. *Der Rosenkavalier*, for example, he found "not a great creation" when it was new, though he had great admiration for the Marschallin's monologue at the end of the first act. Later he took to calling it "charming," but took exception to the "crass and shameless realism" with which the music delineated "matters which are customarily, among decent people at any rate, discussed in private and in subdued voices" (November 18, 1922).

If *this* was Henderson's critical shortcoming, it merely affiliated him, to some extent or other, with every critic who ever lived. The difference would be in degree or in kind, rather than in the presence or absence of it. The critic who believes himself to be lacking in shortcomings is one of two things—a liar or a fool (and sometimes both).

But the man who believed it to be a "sacred duty" to pursue a particular path fulfilled his credo in more than the merely abstract matters with which he dealt. When Arturo Toscanini left the New York Philharmonic in the spring of 1936, the directors of that organization decided that the man best qualified to succeed him was Wilhelm Furtwängler. Musically, this choice had merit, for Furtwängler was among the greatest conductors of his time. Morally, it was abysmally inappropriate, as Henderson specified in his column for March 7, 1936:

> It is with considerable reluctance that the musical editor of *The Sun* approaches this theme, but, unfortunately, it cannot be avoided. The discussion of European politics, international relations, troubles arising from conflicts of race or creed, does not belong to the department of music; but in this case reference to these topics is forced upon it. Mr. Furtwängler is a prominent and active Nazi: at least one half of the patrons of the Philharmonic-Symphony concerts are of the race which the Nazi government of Germany has singled out for severity of treatment unhesitatingly defined by the press of several lands as persecution.
>
> What will be the inevitable attitude of the Jewish music lovers of this city? Let it be conceded that in the world of art personal or racial antagonism should be unknown. That indeed would be an ideal state. But what should be and what unquestionably will be are different matters. It is manifestly impossible that the sons and daughters of Israel can disassociate their feelings from their artistic judgement at a concert directed by a man they regard as an enemy of their race. To avoid painful experience they will take the simple and logical course of staying away from these concerts. And if they abandon the Philharmonic-Symphony Society it will perish. There is no musical enterprise of any kind whatever that can prosper in this great Jewish city without the support of the Jews.
>
> The most casual observer at musical performances cannot fail to see that full half of every audience consists of people of the

Jewish race. They are ardent, devoted and for the most part intelligent music lovers. To give up the Philharmonic would be a serious deprivation to them; but what else can they do? It would be interesting to know why the directors of the Philharmonic-Symphony Society did not ponder this matter before taking their action. No convincing reason for such action presents itself to the mind of the disinterested observer. To him it must look like an incomprehensible blunder.

The resolution of the "blunder" was accomplished in an all but minimal number of days. The editorial page of the *Sun* for March 16, 1936, carried the following paragraphs:

EXIT MR. FURTWAENGLER.

The Philharmonic-Symphony Society is to be congratulated on the outcome of the Furtwaengler affair. Without raising the baton, the distinguished German conductor has resigned the post for which he was engaged, offering as his reason a profound objection to the mingling of art and politics. It apparently has not occurred either to Mr. FURTWAENGLER or the directors of the Philharmonic that the mingling did not follow the engagement, but was inherent in it. In the discussion of the matter made public in various letters to this newspaper the point at issue has frequently been obscured or missed entirely.

When the directors gave a contract to Mr. FURTWAENGLER to conduct the local orchestra, they disregarded the constitution of their body of subscribers. Mr. FURTWAENGLER was generally believed to be a Nazi; and he unquestionably enjoyed the favor of the Nazi government. His differences with some of the officials were lately smoothed out and he returned to all his musical honors. At least 60 per cent of the supporters of the concerts of the Philharmonic-Symphony Society and of every other musical enterprise in this city are Jews. Mr. FURTWAENGLER's engagement could not possibly be anything but an offense to them. Hundreds of them would have no hesitation about withdrawing their names from the subscription list. Without their contributions the Philharmonic could not continue to exist.

That is the one and only point which was raised. Publicity was given to it in THE SUN of March 7. The relation of art to politics was not approached; the point of view was established wholly by the box office. It was purely and exclusively a matter of business and it was handled with amazing clumsiness by the astute business men of the directorate. They are now happily out of the quagmire into which they so casually walked. Mr. FURTWAENGLER has been enlightened. He gracefully retires, proclaiming himself no politician, but solely an exponent of German music. The proper field for the exercise of such an exclusive talent is Germany.

By custom an editorial bears no signature or other evidence of authorship: it is the statement not of an individual, but of the newspaper in which it appears. The original from which this reproduction was made is to be found almost entirely alone in a page of Volume XXXX of the Henderson scrapbooks dated April 15, 1935–March 16, 1936. The man was proud of what he and his paper had done, and for good reason.

Were there a comparable situation today and a present-day writer with Henderson's sense of justice, the question is not whether he would have equivalent power of expression but—given the poverty of newspapers in New York—where would he publish it?

In total commitment to his craft, W. J. Henderson may be described as a critic of performers and artists who became, eventually, an artist on the level of the best of them.

Fischer-Dieskau
at the Summit

I

If there is a deficiency in the preceding sampling of Henderson's opinions on singers, it is not that it is lacking in fulfillment of its promise: that could be accomplished in a book entirely devoted to the subject. Unfortunately, that would still leave us bereft of his views on singers who came to prominence after June 1937. So I can only speculate on his response to a pair of singers whose likes, I believe, would have prompted him to the kind of comparisons he once composed on Kirsten Flagstad and her place among the great Wagner sopranos of the past.

They are Birgit Nilsson and Dietrich Fischer-Dieskau.

Nilsson would have given him ample provocation, and no problem (though she excelled all prior category-combiners in having in her repertory *at the same time* Sieglinde and all the Brünnhildes, Isolde, Salome, and Elektra in German, plus Turandot, Tosca, and Aïda in Italian). Fischer-Dieskau would have provided him not only with equal provocation, I believe, but also considerably more problem (if only to find an equivalent among singers of the past).

He is, for one thing, a specifically second-half-of-the-twentieth-century apparition . . . the most recorded vocal artist in the first hundred years of Edisonian epoch. His life, thus, is artistically an open book. This applies not only to what he thought of himself as a Mahler singer in the early 1950s as well as what he thinks of himself as a Mahler singer in the 1980s: but also as a conductor.

His eminence as a performer of a wide range of operatic roles I will have to set aside because these performances occurred in a part of the world where I was not able to be present (with the highly revealing exception of his Hans Sachs in Wagner's *Die Meistersinger von Nürnberg*) and recordings are but a shadowy indication of competence in this branch of vocal art. He differs from all other species—animal, vegetable, mineral, or musical—in being not only an artist rather than a performer, but one whose favorite form of food is white paper covered with black notes, which he digests with ease and gives out as communication. He has been known even to go on an all-Schubert diet extending over weeks and months, and showing no sign of non-digestion at the end of it.

How could Henderson or any other critic of the generations in which he lived have possibly been able to relate himself to a man who studied, learned, and recorded 450 of Schubert's 600 songs? He couldn't, really: because there has never been a predecessor, and may never be a successor (who would, in any case, be open to the charge of being a Pseudo-Dieskau).

To absorb the magnitude of his accomplishment one would have to have started more or less concurrently with the Fischer-Dieskau career, and pursued it month by month, year by year, box by box of recordings, through wear and through tear, through weal and through woe, from Bach to Berg. To be sure, there might be extended chronological stops along the way at such seldom (by singers) visited inns as Hospices Peter Cornelius (1824–74) and Othmar Schoeck (1886–1957) as well as at the more familiar Schloss Mendelssohn (1809–47) and Parkhotel Hugo Wolf (1860–1903). But if one could indict any categorical complaint vis-à-vis Dieskau (as he is sometimes referred to) it would be that, to vary an old German witticism, he is lacking in artistic *Sitzfleisch* ("to be always on the go" is one dictionary's definition of that anatomical deficiency).

It is hardly necessary to say, but I will say it anyway: I am not implying that any of the great critics of the past such as Henderson (who said, of one lamentable Siegfried in *Götterdämmerung*, "nothing so much became his life as the leaving of it") or Philip

Hale (who reported of the accomplished but somewhat aloof Emma Eames's singing of Schubert's "Who Is Sylvia," "She sang it as if she were not quite sure Sylvia should be included on her guest list") could not handle the Fischer-Dieskau phenomenon brilliantly. But they would have had to devote themselves to a good deal more record listening than was customary prior to the 1940s.

Music and mountaineering are by no means unknown to have affinities. I have seen photos of the young Leopold Stokowski (what a spectacle he was!) dressed, stick in hand, for a day's climbing; Dimitri Mitropoulos looked to the sky beyond many a mountain top; Gustav Mahler put his love for the hills into more than a few pages of his Sixth Symphony; Richard Strauss expressed his appreciation of the Zugspitze near his Bavarian home in his "Alpine" Symphony; and Anton Webern had an almost pathological need for an occasional "mountain break" (see page 20).

But it is particularly akin to the vocal art. All singers of whatever gender or category start from ground level, as do mountain climbers. The higher you go, the greater the temptation to look back, which invites dizziness and possible disaster. Each time you reach a plateau, it is only to be reminded anew of the distance to the peak. And the higher you are, the more elusive it becomes. Most dangerously, a single slip can mean the end of a singer's security, as well as a mountaineer's. How many singers have implied, if not said so in as many words (some have), after an interruption in performance due to an illness, or a bad night onstage: "If I could only get my confidence back!"

Soon after Fischer-Dieskau began his climb in 1951 (the first real appearance of prominence, after lesser engagements elsewhere) at the Salzburg Festival with the late Wilhelm Furtwängler as conductor and a much prized recording of Mahler's *Lieder eines fahrenden Gesellen* in consequence, the basic question was: "Could the newcomer become good enough to equal the best of his contemporaries?" Within a decade it had to be rephrased: "Was he on a level with the best of his immediate predecessors?" Now, having left age fifty behind (he was born in 1925), Fischer-Dieskau has attained a personal plateau for a final assault at the top, and has qualified to ask himself, in a paraphrase of "Mirror, mirror on the wall": "Can I be the greatest of them all?"

In several ways, he already is. Few male singers since John McCormack have been so popular in the concert halls of America, so readily assured of a capacity audience anytime an appearance is announced. As one who observed both men under similar circumstances (indeed, in the same place: Carnegie Hall), I can attest the truth of the contention that McCormack offered his audiences half a program of what he wanted to sing before giving them half a program of what they had really come to hear. In effect, an excerpt from Méhul's *Joseph* was a down payment for "Danny Boy," a Schubert group a promissory note for ballads by del Riego, Ethelbert Nevin, and Mary H. Brahe. It was a compromise in which both parties to the bargain profited, or—perhaps if GBS were writing this commentary—suffered.

There were also male singers—such as the great *Lieder* master Heinrich Schlusnus—who sang programs exclusively of music *they* wanted the audience to hear. They did not, however, have the popular appeal to fill so large an auditorium as Carnegie Hall. One could measure their reappearance, comet-like, in years rather than months. The one male singer who could be described as a Germanic McCormack was Richard Tauber, whose art in Brahms and Wolf touched the ears and minds of the listeners who packed Carnegie Hall to hear him sing. But what went to their hearts was his irresistible delivery of the Lehár literature praised by Henderson (see page 85). As for the female recitalists whose repertory paralleled Fischer-Dieskau's, their New York address was, for the most part, 113 West Forty-third Street, which is to say, the same Town Hall in which he made his New York debut in 1955, and has rarely visited since. Now they too must perform in Carnegie Hall or the almost equally large Avery Fisher Hall in Lincoln Center, or suffer professional loss of face.

Beyond the numerical quantity and the categorical range of the records Fischer-Dieskau has made and their unquestionable effect on the creation of a public which craves to hear him in person, are such vital statistics as: the greatest variety of material ever recorded by a single artist; the longest, broadest chronological survey of musical matter ever undertaken in live and recorded form; the embracing response to the most difficult challenges—in song cycles, concert hall literature for singer and orchestra, *and* operatic incentives—ever identified with a vocalist, male or female.

It would be an absurdity to say that Fischer-Dieskau made *Lieder* singing respectable or even beloved, for there have been those of the past with equally devoted audiences—at well-spaced intervals. But it has been his achievement to make it thoroughly *enjoyable,* not only for people who had approached it timidly and suspiciously, but for the vastly larger number who had never approached it at all. In consequence, they become, in many instances, converts who look forward to their next opportunity to wait in line for tickets to buy their way in.

The graphic evidence to all of these contentions was summarized in a cartoon in *The New Yorker* (January 1975) by William Hamilton, in which the female fraction of a married couple bent on separation is captioned as saying: "Just a minute—you don't get three years of my life *and* the Dietrich Fischer-Dieskau recordings."

II

There are vogues for which there are reasons and there are vogues for which the reasons are vague. The vogue of Fischer-Dieskau is eminently of the first order. Ask a dozen musicians familiar with his work what specific, central factor they would single out to explain his pre-eminence, and the probability is that you would get a dozen different reasons. Among them could be intelligence, seriousness of purpose, personality, versatility, rhythmic vitality, stage magnetism, dramatic resource, emotional gamut, imagination, enunciation, poetic impulse. Each touches on an unquestionable attribute: the number of them, added together, measure the size of the towering figure he is.

To those I would add the finalizing dozenth: an overriding, indeed indispensable adjunct to all the others. Central to them and the spinal cord supporting all the artistic vertebrae is the ever present strength that he is, above and beyond everything else, a superb vocalist.

The immediate impression, I suppose, is that I am saying that he has a superb voice. That is another, and different, thing. I much prefer the voice of Karl Schmitt-Walter in Strauss's *Ständchen,* or of Heinrich Schlusnus in Brahms's *Wo bist du, meine Königin,* or of Gerhard Hüsch in Schubert's *Erlkönig,* or of Herbert Janssen in Schumann's *Widmung,* to restrict a line of comparison to singers in Fischer-Dieskau's own baritonal category. That would mean, in my view, that each had a God-given, verdant kind of vocal bouquet inimitably right for some particular song, or even of the category of song of which it was representative.

But it takes a great vocalist to mold a less than great voice—and I don't think that Fischer-Dieskau's vocal endowment was, per se, great—into the instrument for a superior performance of *all* the songs listed above. Here the accomplishment relates not so much to what was God-given as to what was man-made. This enabled him to sing dozens and dozens of other songs that the best of the artists enumerated above were well advised to avoid.

In most discussions of a singer's attributes, such a statement would have to be taken on faith—faith in the person making it. But so attentive has the microphone been to Fischer-Dieskau's sound—beginning with a tape of Schubert's *Die Winterreise* on Berlin's RIAS (Radio in the American Sector) station in 1948 which earned him an operatic debut as Posa in Verdi's *Don Carlo* —that there is scarcely a turning point in his career that cannot be documented.

The 1952 version of *Lieder eines fahrenden Gesellen* with Furtwängler conducting (to which I have previously alluded) is still available (on Odeon SME 91 387, and Seraphim 60272). It is unquestionably a pleasant sound, intelligently applied to the problems of the Mahler songs. But it is also a "short" baritone sound, strained at the top and rather foggy at the bottom. The quality is concentrated in the middle, which does well enough by these Mahler songs, whose range is not extreme.

By 1955 there were enough Fischer-Dieskau recordings in circulation, enough word of mouth about this tall young man with the exceptional aptitude, to bring a capacity audience to his New York debut in Town Hall. The work was Schubert's *Die Winterreise*, nothing more, nothing less, with Gerald Moore (who has demonstrated a capability to bring a capacity audience to that hall on his own) at the piano. There was much to commend in it; but I wondered then, as I wonder now: how many of those acquainted with Fischer-Dieskau's recordings had heard the best of those by other *Lieder* singers, or, more precisely, the singers themselves?

Some reviewers commended the performance by implying that improvement was impossible. I thought the larger songs taxed his top notes to the point of fraying, and that a few of the faster ones were breathy and without color. If he could not equal in moments of dramatic and dynamic pressure what he did at Schubert's quietest and his best, the high promise and exciting possibilities might never be realized.

My guess is that Fischer-Dieskau thought likewise. To venture so ill armed into the trackless wilderness of repertory for which he was, by disposition and temperament, destined would be to wind up breathless and eventually voiceless. He continued to work with his great pedagogue, Hermann Weissenborn, until his death in 1959 at eighty plus. Then the issue was joined. If there has been any outside guidance—other than that derived from Moore in their work together—it hasn't been publicized.

All the evidence suggests that it wasn't needed. If the microphone has been listening to Fischer-Dieskau since 1948, all the indications are that Fischer-Dieskau has been listening to what it has to convey, as carefully as any other student of the subject. And beyond what it has to say about his own work, listening to what it has to say about the singing of others, past and present, in the repertory in which he is interested. Gerald Moore has written: "His library of books on the subject and of gramophone records is vast. Do you wish to compare a Schlusnus with a Slezak performance of a Wolf song? The records are found in a moment—for they are all carefully indexed, and each has its particular niche on his capacious shelves."[1]

[1] Moore, Gerald, *Am I Too Loud?* (The Macmillan Company, New York, (1962), p. 173.

Fischer-Dieskau's musical equipment includes the ability to accompany himself at the piano. As is well known, he memorizes repertory by tape-recording his self-accompanied performances and studying the playbacks. It may be assumed that a man diligent enough to study as many examples as he can find of work by his predecessors would have a similar degree of objectivity about his own output. One may also assume that an artist of such capacities would be equally mindful of the condition of his own vocal capital. In self-interest, he would be combining the shrewdness of a banker and the objectivity of a surgeon to make it yield maximum returns on withdrawals, investment in time and energy, and, of course, prevailing interest, personal and public.

Some may have forgotten that when Edison, all but accidentally, discovered that a track inscribed on a waxed surface could give back the sound that had created the track, his first thought was of its utility to speech. It would take dictation, permit the blind to "hear" a book, and teach elocution. The reproduction of music was relatively far along in the sequence: Edison himself was hard of hearing and pathologically uninterested in music.

When GBS came to write *Pygmalion* in 1912 (and, indirectly, lead to the creation of *My Fair Lady*) he brought about not only a marvelously observant study of speech and its innumerable mutations, but also, in his preface,[2] a diagnostician's account of the efforts by such men as Alexander J. Ellis and Henry Sweet to lead the world in the direction he applied to Liza Doolittle.

However, the techniques Shaw devised for Liza and her dedicated instructor 'Enry 'Iggins were decidedly more of a "modern" manner. Liza not only spoke her Lisson Grove "lingo" into a horn, to be recorded on a blank from which it could be played back for Higgins and his friend, Colonel Pickering, to analyze. She could herself be exposed to the results, from which to learn and change.

Valuable as this was for speech purposes, it was not yet equally acute for correcting flaws in singing. Some enterprising teachers of the *Pygmalion* (and later) periods utilized it for whatever benefits might be derived—a makeshift crutch is better than no

[2] Shaw, Bernard, *Androcles and the Lion. Overruled. Pygmalion* (Brentano's, New York, 1916), pp. 109–14.

crutch at all. But it was not until the development of the microphone, and more particularly, magnetic tape—which, unlike the
blanks that Higgins used, could be erased and reused—that a singer
with Fischer-Dieskau's mentality had a tool worthy of it.

With the development of home tape recorders (which required
no second-person participation) an artist with the inclination and
application of Fischer-Dieskau now has a closed circle of useful
input and output by which he may scrutinize, *ad infinitum*, the results of his own effort. Add to it the convenience of the cassette
and its portability, and self-study can be not merely unending, but
worldwide.

Nor need it be confined to rehearsing at home, in the studio-
workroom. Given a comradely collaborator-connoisseur—and
every artist of Fischer-Dieskau's quality has them, around the
world—a very decent likeness of any concert hall performance can
be picked up from a seat down front, reheard, evaluated, reconsidered, even before the next day's press comes in with its possibly
deflating aftermath.

III

What serves so well the intelligent artist of today can serve
equally well the critic, intelligent or otherwise. What Henderson
was required to do in words, in order to evoke, decades ago, the
early sound of Caruso, can now be done by reference to a sounding counterpart of the thing itself. To be sure, there were early
recordings of Caruso's voice, but it was a dim, distant, noise-rid-
den whisper compared to the vibrant whisper with which Fischer-
Dieskau recorded Strauss's *Ständchen* with Moore (on Angel
356000) in 1956.

That Fischer-Dieskau sound is, of course, not the sound of the
voice a decade later, or a decade after that. As Henderson's description of the Calvé voice of the twenties reminds us, every
voice used for public, professional purposes changes over the decades. Anyone who argues to the contrary is engaged in self-deception, or in praise of a paragon not known to many others.

The truly pertinent question is: does change invariably mean deterioration, or, in some instances, growth? Does it promote access to a wider range of roles (Birgit Nilsson) or a decrease, perhaps a termination of reliability (Maria Callas)?

To my way of hearing it, the changes in Fischer-Dieskau's voice, both in character and responsiveness, have all been on the side of artistic advantage. Arguments may be entertained vis-à-vis the altered beauty of the sound, but hardly to question the expanded command of range, color, dynamics, articulation of the text which enable him to do vastly more with it in the seventies than in the fifties.

A random demonstration could be derived from his two versions of Brahms's *Magelone-lieder*. This is a demanding, and a rewarding, series of songs based on poems by Ludwig Tieck. His first version appeared in the late 1950s with so responsive a pianist as Jörg Demus and earned the accolade of the "best ever." This was not irrational praise, no recording of comparable quality having been previously offered.

But the critical "best ever" spoke for the one who heard and wrote, not for the one who did and evaluated. His second version of 1971-72 clearly aims, through the participation of Sviatoslav Richter as pianist (Angel S 36753), for higher ground. To be sure, the mere presence of so commanding a pianistic personality engenders chemical reactions, spiritual heat not previously present. But more of the change in Fischer-Dieskau's effort derives from his increased ability to keep the vocal sound *consistent*, whatever the range, and a newfound ability to match the longest Brahms phrases with the breath support to hold them securely in place.

To deal for a moment in specifics: in the first song (*Keinem hat es noch gereut*—"He who rides the steed of youth") the sound of the tone in Version II is much better focused, distinctly more secure in the "break of the voice" (between E and F in Fischer-Dieskau's). In the phrase *und einsame Wälder* the surging rhyme of *Stunden* and *Wunden* (the English equivalent would be "story" and "glory") is pronounced with much greater confidence, the ending consonants bitten off (the "n" sound) to give the words sharper impact on the ear.

Such a command of vocal mechanics serves a resourceful singer as much as a mastery of other muscular mechanics served Edmund Hillary on his way to conquer Mount Everest. Does it, however, serve Fischer-Dieskau equally well in his effort to conquer an audience in the concert hall? Is there sufficient awareness of such subtleties among a majority of those in the average concertgoing audience to make a difference? Will they recognize the niceties of nuance which spring to the ear of you—the connoisseur —and me?

On the whole, possibly not. But that is not to say that they do not have a part in the effect of the notes and words on the listeners, any more than it is necessary to know whether Mstislav Rostropovich bows with a loose wrist or a tight one to rhapsodize about his playing of the solo part in Strauss's *Don Quixote*. One of the most remarkable vocal demonstrations I ever heard was delivered from the stage of London's Old Vic by Sir Laurence Olivier as the Captain (Edgar) in August Strindberg's *The Dance of Death*. In it he is required to simulate an incident which leaves the Captain truly purple with rage. He said no word: but the breath control that enabled him to do what he wanted to do was truly spectacular.

In every instance, the solid foundation of skill provides the firm ground on which the great performer stands taller, reaches further, attains a higher elevation from which to cast the artistic net that captures the attention of the least learned.

In his engaging exposition of working with, and sometimes learning from, a man who was unborn when he was already a practicing professional, Moore describes Fischer-Dieskau as "Big in every way: physically, intellectually, and musically," with the surprising addition "the commanding presence of a Chaliapin."[3] An interesting analogy, that one: especially to come from a musician whose sources were in neither case passive observation, but active participation in the most revealing of all relationships—on the firing line of public appearances, touring, and personal relations.

For if ever two men of the same profession were polar, both in

[3] Moore, op. cit., p. 168.

personality and performance, they were Chaliapin and Fischer-Dieskau. They had in common the ability to surround an audience with a magnetic field of artistic attraction, and to hold them, almost immobile, for the length of whatever they were performing. They even had a "big song" in common: Schumann's setting of Heine's great poem *Die beiden Grenadiere*.

There is a famous recording by Chaliapin (now readily available in a collection on HMV—His Master's Voice—by way of Japan, if not otherwise), from which I first became aware (c. 1920) that there was such a man as Schumann. It was a great, stirring experience to encounter, as Schumann's climax to the narrative of the two grenadiers and their devotion to the Emperor, the quotation of *La Marseillaise!* At that moment I also became aware there were things that could be done only *in* music, and *with* music. There is also a very well-known recording by Fischer-Dieskau and Jörg Demus (DG 139 110). It, too, has a triumphant proclamation of that transcendant conversion of one aesthetic experience (the verbal) into another (the musical). Yet the nature of that transformation could hardly be more different.

With Chaliapin, who sings in Russian, the effect on the listener is predominantly derived from the effect of the song on Chaliapin himself. Some of the notes are growled; some of the rhythmic values are his own rather than Schumann's; it is, in every way, a great roaring soliloquy (or would have been, had Chaliapin been singing into a microphone rather than a horn) of a man transformed from a square-shouldered husky product of the Stanislavsky school of acting into a ragged, bedraggled straggler on the road from Moscow.

In the Fischer-Dieskau conversion, the emphasis is less on what the song does to the performer than what the total delivery of it does to the *listener*. Every word of Heine's text is cleanly, crisply articulated, audible to the ear; every nuance and tonal value magically molded into the syllable as Schumann imagined it; and when *La Marseillaise* dies away in the dark, tragic postlude, nothing has been left to the listener's imagination. Everything the page contains has been given to him, colored and enhanced by Fischer-Dieskau's perception of meaning.

In other words, Chaliapin's *Die beiden Grenadiere* is a great example of a song acted out, in which we respond to a consummate dramatic recitation. Fischer-Dieskau's, however, is less an enactment of how the song affects him. Rather, it is an insight into how he conveys a composition in all its complex detail to make the full conception of Schumann directly available to the listener.

In a conversation with James Goodfriend, music editor of *Stereo Review*, he called to my attention another way in which Fischer-Dieskau's perception of a composer's purpose—also Schumann—heightens the listener's understanding. The song is *Waldesgespräch* (in the *Liederkreis*, opus 39), which may be described as Schumann's response to Joseph Eichendorff's response to Johann Wolfgang von Goethe's *Erlkönig*. Here, however, the horse galloping through the woods is ridden not by a father with an ailing child in his arm, but by a beautiful young woman. The young man who sees and stops her is aroused by a chivalrous motive—can he assist her in finding her destination? Too late, alas! In one of Schumann's great melodic surges, he recognizes her as a fateful charmer who will lead him to *his* destination—death.

Too often, singers deprive the key phrase of the great melodic surge Schumann meant it to have: the upward momentum is blunted when the singer emphasizes *bist* ("you are") rather than the climaxing words *Hexe Loreley* ("Sorceress Loreley"). The common mistake (adherents are legion) is an understandable one: *bist* comes on the *downbeat* of the measure, and that, normally, is where the accent falls. But it is greater musicality, as Fischer-Dieskau demonstrates, to follow common sense rather than a common mistake.

As an instance of the kind of creative imagination which can rouse an audience to understanding of a song it has not heard previously, one could hardly surpass directing attention to his singing, with Leonard Bernstein at the piano, of *Nicht wiedersehen* by Gustav Mahler (Columbia KM 30942). The text (from *Des Knaben Wunderhorn*) tells us of a schoolboy who has been parted from his summer sweetheart until another year and another visit will bring them together again. When he returns, it is to discover that the "farewell" (*Ade*, pronounced "Ah-DAY") they had exchanged the previous summer is forever: he will find her, he is sadly informed, in the village churchyard where she is buried.

I have heard several good, honest, touching restatements of what this song appears to contain. Simple in construction, *Nicht wiedersehen* (one of the early *Wunderhorn* songs) is without elaboration, vocally or pianistically. But there are instances in which the difference is not in the song, but in the singer. On coming upon the Fischer-Dieskau/Bernstein collaboration, I discovered that it is a litany of remorse for anyone who ever lost a beloved, a lament of bereavement on a Schubertian scale.

IV

Or, to vary the image, the by-product of a light and shade in vocal brushwork that Fischer-Dieskau did not possess ten years previously. If one wants a diagnosis of palette-ability there is a whole canon of artistic shading Fischer-Dieskau, or any other singer of his caliber, can employ. What the eye discerns in thickness or thinness of line, the ear can pick up in weight, timbre, and roughness (or evenness) of sound.

But as a chef may become addicted to the use of salts (rock, white, sea?) or peppers (cayenne, red, white, black?) so a singer, even one as good as Fischer-Dieskau, may not appreciate the virtue there is in leaving well enough alone.

Still another *Winterreise?* One more *Schöne Müllerin?* DG 27 20 059 is the *Winterreise* of the seventies as Angel 3640 B is the *Winterreise* of the sixties. Perhaps, one muses, if the appearance of another in the eighties carries with it, as in the automotive world, the possibility of a trade-in, the updating, if not upgrading, would have more appeal. I shun the possibility of a Fischer-Dieskau/ Alfred Brendel *Winterreise* because I know all too well the nature of their collaboration from a Carnegie Hall performance of October 21, 1975. Unlike those equally shared, single-minded re-creations (live as well as recorded) by Fischer-Dieskau and Moore, this was less a re-creation than an autopsy. Brendel was searching measure by measure for some trace of life in the deceased —and not finding it—while Fischer-Dieskau was pronouncing a eulogy that did not quite ring true.

The spirit of the long-gone Schubert was much more in the air at the series of recitals with Demus in which Fischer-Dieskau commemorated the hundred and fiftieth anniversary of the composer's death during the last week of March 1978 in Carnegie Hall. Taken together, the three recitals were both more, and less, than might have been anticipated. At the first recital, the reunion of Fischer-Dieskau with his audience was fervent, on both sides. The audience gave him a greeting, even before the program began, that would have rewarded an evening of singing on the highest conceivable level.

Fischer-Dieskau responded with a selection of songs that he might have set aside for all those privileged connoisseurs I previously alluded to (page 101), had they been gathered from around the world in his own home. He had chosen a sequence of eighteen songs, of the highest quality and the least familiarity. The audience realized from the very first few—*Versunken, Des Sängers Habe,* and *Wehmut*—what he was about, and the unwinding sequence magnetized attention on two levels: "What a great song this is!" and "Why haven't I heard it before?" In both respects the program's content was a compliment to the performer and a reflection on the lesser enterprise of his contemporaries (he has no competitors).

The *Winterreise* followed several days later, a little "down" in spirit, something that can occasionally happen to the greatest of artists.

The third program (a week later, an interval during which Fischer-Dieskau had sung elsewhere in the country) showed him at his most effortful and least compelling. Unlike the first evening, on which he had invited the audience into an intimate communication with his closest-treasured, least-favored songs of Schubert, this program found him parading his capacity to deal with the most difficult, highly challenging ones. Their only relationship was the infrequency with which any good, or even fine, interpreter of Schubert would arrange them like targets on a rifle range and proceed to demonstrate his marksmanship, one after the other.

The sequence began with *Prometheus,* followed by *Meerestille, An die Leier,* and *Memnon,* on the way to *Der Tod und das Mädchen, Gruppe aus dem Tartarus,* and *An Schwäger Kronos.* The second portion was relatively modest, beginning with *Der Wanderer an den Mond* and ending with *Der Musensohn.*

Looked at with maximum kindness, this could be regarded as a sacrificial offering by a communicant at the altar of his idol. Regarded with several degrees more objectivity, it has to be viewed as a form of aesthetic weight lifting, starting with a two-hundred-pound press (*Prometheus*) and going on from there.

Or, reducing it a few pegs to reality and practicality, what the program and its performance said to me was: "You know that Hans Hotter's *Memnon* was fine, *Der Wanderer an den Mond* by Schlusnus was something, or that Elena Gerhardt's *Musensohn* was marvelous and Marian Anderson's *Tod und das Mädchen* was bone-chilling. Here is the way they should really sound." As for Demus at the piano, he was required to equal or excel not only Gerald Moore and Alfred Brendel, but here and there, Franz Rupp, Coenraad V. Bos, Michael Raucheisen, Hanns Udo Müller, and practically every other great accompanist who ever lived.[4]

Bad show.

Curiously, an equally disjointed succession of great Schubert songs has a degree of unity which such a parade of blockbusters does not. I am referring to the *Schwanengesang* ("Swan Song," a title of finality obviously not attached to them by Schubert, but by a sales-hungry publisher).

Given the prior circumstances, it is idle to invoke such a ques-

---

[4] In his last appearances in New York before these words were printed (May 1980) there was something of an echo of this kind of exhibitionism in a program devoted to songs of Schumann, also with Demus. It began, promisingly enough, with *Widmung* ("Dedication"), followed by a dozen and a half of the least-known Schumann songs. In several, such as *Soldat,* a voice formerly utilized with great discrimination was being pushed to produce more than it could. It left the impression that after many years of high regard as a singer celebrated for choice of material suitable to his voice, Fischer-Dieskau was acting the part of a star sure that his audience would listen to anything he chose to sing.

tion as "What interpreter, acting on his own, would program *Der Atlas* and *Der Doppelgänger* within minutes of each other?" That supreme sacrifice could be induced, by the addition of *Aufenthalt* and the superb if slender *Ständchen*, to show how Schubert was feeling in March and April, May and September, in the last year of his life (1828).

Fischer-Dieskau has himself paid tribute to the much sung "Serenade" by describing it in his fine book as a song "framed in mandolin music" which was nevertheless "written in a vale of tears."[5] Even the words, with all their felicity, cannot compare with Fischer-Dieskau's lightly veiled (but not tearish) vocal quality, and the superbly tinkling, super-mandolinish background by Moore, the most imaginative I have ever heard.

V

There is a fine restaurant in Milan's spacious Galleria answering to the name of Savini's which daily offers a dozen different kinds of soups. Is it reasonable for an American to complain because one of them is *not* clam chowder (Manhattan or New England)? I find myself similarly beset by the unbelievable abundance of Fischer-Dieskau recordings which does not, nevertheless, include Fischer-Dieskau on Grieg, Fischer-Dieskau on Yriö Kilpinen, Nikolai Medtner, Modest Moussorgsky, or even Peter Tchaikovsky, Berlioz, Chausson.

In an interview in the Paris *Figaro* in the later sixties he acknowledged that he still had not developed sufficient skill to sing French songs in France. An apt instance of self-evaluation, this explains why the name of Fauré is absent from those above. Early in his career, he ventured Fauré's *La Bonne Chanson* (Electrola E 70 370) and other matter by Debussy and Ravel (DG 138 115). All possible care had been applied to the linguistic necessities, with Moore at the piano, but the outcome is persuasive to the point

[5] Fischer-Dieskau, Dietrich, *Schubert's Songs, A Biographical Study* (Alfred A. Knopf, Inc., New York, 1977), p. 278.

that a French pot in German hands is a German pot still (see page 321).

Rather recently (the jacket is dated 1977) HNH Records Incorporated of Evanston, Illinois, has reissued a collection of French material by Maurice Ravel (*Chansons madécasses*), Francis Poulenc (*Le Bal masqué*), and Fauré (*La Bonne Chanson*), again, in which Fischer-Dieskau participates with Wolfgang Sawallisch as pianist, and director of a small instrumental ensemble from the Berlin Philharmonic (HNH 4045). FonoTeam is named as the licensing agency, thus identifying a German source. It is in almost every way superior in sound to what Fischer-Dieskau has done previously in French, fastidious in vocal detail and textual enunciation.

However, the baritone has this time chosen to perform *La Bonne Chanson* in a version in which a string quartet is joined by double bass and piano. Martial Singher, who has recorded it previously on Columbia (MS 6244), vouches for its authenticity because it was advertised on the back of the sheets bearing the original voice and piano edition. It is, alas, lacking in the intimacy of the version to which we are long accustomed; and the conspicuous piano part, in the hands of Sawallisch, sounds like another instrument than the one played with such finesse by Moore. However, Poulenc's *Le Bal masqué* (with oboe, clarinet, bassoon, trumpet, piano, violin, and percussion) is a lively romp through Max Jacob's text, which would make a smashing conclusion to an "evening at home" with Fischer-Dieskau (HNH 4045). Such falsetto at the end!

I would also welcome some such evidence of humor in Fischer-Dieskau's additional examples of his skill as a conductor. The sequence began well (Schubert "Unfinished" on Angel S 36965 and Schumann No. 3 on BASF DC 22 705-7) but hasn't progressed much since. As a conductor Fischer-Dieskau is hampered by shortcomings that a conservatory student of the art would have well in hand (rushed tempi, not quite disciplined entrances), but he is also impelled by the same musical qualifications which have made him the foremost *Lieder* singer of which there is record.

All this is to imply that Fischer-Dieskau could be as plausible a music maker with his back turned to the public as he is when facing it, given adequate indoctrination. Doubtless as he grows older, he will be finding it increasingly attractive to transfer some of his impulse to make music from himself and an accompanist to the members of an ensemble (should he say, à la Toscanini, "*Canto*," they would have to agree that he knows what he is talking about). Unhappily, one reality does intrude: the kind of self-improvement possible for a singer and a tape recorder cannot be duplicated by a conductor. What Herbert von Karajan refers to as the "inertia" of the orchestra, and the challenge it presents anew to the conductor each day—no matter his abilities—cannot be circumvented. Without the resistance to combat and conquer, the beginning conductor can accomplish little.

I have set aside his career as an opera singer, for obvious reasons of incapacity. But I will, nevertheless, speculate on the answer to a speculative question: with which of his illustrious predecessors does Fischer-Dieskau have the most affinity? I would say that the possibilities narrow down to just a pair: Julius Stockhausen (1826–1906) and Georg Henschel (1850–1934).

Both were friends of Brahms (in different age relations to the composer [1833–97], as the dates suggest), both were baritones and *Lieder* singers. Henschel, who became Sir George, in 1914, for all that he was born in Breslau, performed a group of Schubert *Lieder* at the age of seventy-eight in a London concert in 1928 commemorating the hundredth anniversary of the composer's death; and both became conductors of note. Indeed the unquestionable annals of the Boston Symphony Orchestra show that Henschel was the first of all its conductors when its history began in 1881. Stockhausen, who was a choral specialist as well as a participant in a number of Brahms premieres as a vocalist (the *Magelone-lieder* is dedicated to him), never came to America. With such a pair between him and the highest peak to which he might aspire, Fischer-Dieskau might find the way to the top rather cluttered. But what company on a chilly night!

There is, also, an objective which, with good health, proper care, and a sense of purpose, Fischer-Dieskau might reasonably bear in mind. The two hundredth anniversary of Schubert's birth will arrive on January 31, 1997. That would find Fischer-Dieskau a robust seventy-two (he was born May 28, 1925). And, I should think, still in voice.

If that remote date implies the unattainable, there is still one attainment no other singer in history can claim. He was able to convert so peerless a pianist as Vladimir Horowitz into an accompanist in Schumann's *Dichterliebe* at a benefit concert in Carnegie Hall.

Other participants included Isaac Stern, Mstislav Rostropovich, Yehudi Menuhin, Leonard Bernstein, and the New York Philharmonic. Could it have been called "The Concert of the Century" minus Fischer-Dieskau and Horowitz?

Better Fruits
and Fairer Flowers

I

Among musical flora and fauna which have flourished not merely for decades but for centuries, Dietrich Fischer-Dieskau is clearly a late-blooming hybrid. A Lutheran by birth, he was, by evolution and conditioning, another sort of Lutheran. My thought is of Luther Burbank, one of the greatest of horticulturists, who was inspired by the reading, at an early age, of Charles Darwin's *Variation of Animals and Plants Under Domestication* to spend his life (1849–1926) pursuing its implications.

Burbank's life began, not in Santa Rosa, California, where he became famous, but on a farm in Massachusetts. One could say that his future was determined even before birth, when he was endowed with the curiosity and the persistence that underlie his accomplishments. The chance observation of a seed ball on a garden-variety potato vine, where it had no biological right to be, led to his experiments in selectivity and cultivation. From the sale of the marketing rights to what soon became known as the "Burbank potato," the young man migrated to his Nirvana, where the sun always shone and plants grew almost without the help of man. To be sure, California wasn't always that, but it gave him the surroundings in which to dedicate his life to what he modestly called the production of "better fruits and fairer flowers."

Fischer-Dieskau may be likened, aesthetically, to a garden variety of vocalist who, with the help of a few devoted advisers and the resources of twentieth-century technology, made himself into a species of musical interpreter not previously known. But it

would take more than advisers and technology to restore to one
strain of human beings what Burbank had done with a broad
range of plant life. In other words, to regenerate a species of musical creator long known and cherished, but now all but extinct.

The appearance today of a composer with the ability, the interest, and the impulse to take a principal's part in the performance
of his own music would be regarded as a "throwback" or "sport,"
biologically speaking, to a practice that was present on every side
in previous centuries. I speak of a time, to begin with, when music
was performed *only*, or largely, by the person who wrote it: Bach
at the organ, Mozart at the piano, Haydn in front of an orchestra.
The publication of music achieved a breakthrough when young
Ludwig van Beethoven played (1795) the solo part of the D
minor concerto for piano and orchestra by his idol, Mozart. This
was a mere roughening of the surface that widened into a crack
when Franz Liszt gave the first of his "recitals of piano music" in
the 1830s. In one demonstration the long-established line of identity linking composer-performer began to deteriorate, and a gap to
take the place of the hyphen.

Even so, the biological determinism of the connection was so
true, so right, so staunch, and foreordained that it endured for decades, into the twentieth century and halfway through it. Strauss
and Stravinsky, Prokofiev and Poulenc, Bartók and Britten were as
much a part of the performance of their music as their music was
a part of them. Gradually, however, what had once been a common expectation in a winter's round of concerts in a metropolis
became a rarity verging on extinction. Toward the end, two of the
long-established custom's most vital, prominent survivors were
men of less than the first magnitude as composers, but still of
such distinctions as interpreters to convey not only their music,
but that of others, with distinction.

Fritz Kreisler's qualities as an artist were no less present in his
playing of the violin concertos of Beethoven and Brahms than in
the re-creation of the endearing vignettes of his own. Sergei Rachmaninoff's re-creation of Schumann, Chopin, Beethoven, and
Debussy, among others (see page 37), reflected the capacities, in-

sight, and musical imagination of the mind which created the *Rhapsody on a Theme by Paganini.*

Both were well placed to be familiar with a whole literature of music described as *Kapellmeistermusik* ("conductor's music"), implying that anyone capable of being a conductor was capable of writing some kind of music. With the exception of Leonard Bernstein, most conductors of today are satisfied to be the specialists most of them claim to be (and some of them are).

Doubtless the classic example of the composer-conductor-pianist-etc. reached its zenith in Georges Enesco (1881–1955). In his eventful seventy-four years, Enesco became a master of the violin, an excellent pianist, a competent cellist, a truly great conductor (of Beethoven and Brahms among others), and one of the most productive composers of his time.

And, as a teacher, he also shared his life with two of the most remarkable performing talents of the twentieth century: Yehudi Menuhin, who came to him as a protégé of ten, and Dinu Lipatti, the lamentably short-lived (1917–50) Romanian pianist-composer, for whom Enesco was godfather. That of all the work Enesco produced in almost every imaginable form, from songs to opera, and suites to symphonies, history has decreed that he be remembered for the Second Romanian Rhapsody should be construed as a sign of favor rather than disfavor. Dozens of others, equally industrious and no less learned, have labored a lifetime and achieved nothing comparably communicative.

Indeed, the residue of Enesco's lifetime speaks directly to the point of music as communication, and where it stands in the last quarter of the twentieth century. From a time (in the eighteenth century, as well as earlier) when it was a direct communication from composer as performer, to an intermediate status in which the performer was sometimes the composer, it has dwindled to a condition in which the performer is seldom the composer, and the composer is practically never the performer. All this concentrates more of sound's purpose on the impersonality of the superficial shell, and less of it on the personalized content of its interior being.

It will doubtless surprise many, who wonder why the music of

Béla Bartók (in such works as the *Concerto for Orchestra*, or *Music for Strings, Percussion, and Celesta*) speaks to them with such personalized power, to be told that he had capacities as a composer-performer which are all but forgotten today. I am speaking of Bartók as a performer not merely of his own music, including the piano concertos and the works which he wrote for self-performance with his wife, Ditta Pasztory, but of music by so distant a predecessor as Beethoven.

In some centuries, such a statement pertaining to the activities of a man who died thirty-five years before it was made (1945), pertaining to a happening even earlier, could be passed off with an indulgent smile and a tap on the forehead, with well-known implications. But fortune prevailed on an occasion which proves the truth of this statement.

The place was the Library of Congress in Washington, D.C., the date was April 3, 1940, and the participants in the evening's music making were violinist Joseph Szigeti and Bartók. A foresighted person in a position to do so arranged for the music to be perpetuated on acetate discs, and it was eventually issued on a Vanguard tape bearing the designation VTP 1701.

Half the program was devoted to music by the eminent composer-pianist: the Rhapsody No. 1 and the Sonata No. 2. What is even more remarkable, for present purposes, is that the program also contained the Debussy sonata for violin and piano and the A major opus 47 ("Kreutzer") sonata of Beethoven.

Obviously Bartók was a man who viewed a musician as part of a trinity consisting of creator, re-creator, and listener, or, if the circumstances were especially favorable, of a dialogue between creator-re-creator and listener. Unfortunately, the Library of Congress program did not include a work by Bach. If it had, it would have rounded out Bartók's reply when he was asked, a year before, to identify the three composers from whom he had learned the most. He replied: Bach, Beethoven, Debussy.

From this century-spanning selection, I would, personally, have adduced such thoughts as: Bach, of the eighteenth, for structure; Beethoven, of the nineteenth, for substance; and Debussy, of the twentieth, for color.

Fortunately for the world of music, that was *my* answer, and as stereotyped as his was unexpected. In his view, he told Serge Moreux in 1939: "Debussy's great service to music . . . was to reawaken among all musicians an awareness of harmony and its possibilities . . . Beethoven . . . revealed to us the meaning of progressive form . . . Bach . . . showed us the transcendental significance of counterpoint . . ."[1] The question that Bartók then posed to himself, as "overheard" by the interviewer, was: "Is it possible to make a synthesis of these three great masters, a living synthesis that will be valid for our own time?" Let us reconsider the date, and the speaker: he had already answered, or was about to answer, that self-raised question in the most persuasive, well-defined way: in the *Music for Strings, Percussion, and Celesta* (1936), the *Divertimento for String Orchestra* (1939), the *Concerto for Orchestra* (1943), and the Concerto No. 3 for Piano and Orchestra (1945).

In a vivid account of the rebuilding of the war-damaged cathedral at Coventry, England, its eminent architect, Sir Basil Spence, chose as his guideline and philosophic framework, not the words of a fellow builder in stone, but those of a builder in tone, Bartók: "Only a fool will build in defiance of the past. What is new and significant must always be grafted to old roots, the truly vital roots that are chosen with care from the ones that merely survive. And what a slow and delicate process it is to distinguish radical vitality from the wastes of mere survival, but that is the way to achieve progress instead of disaster."[2]

II

Certainly that sentiment would have earned the approval of Burbank, who said the same thing in somewhat different words: "I have been imbued from the outset with the idea that, inasmuch as existing plants have evolved from inferior types, it should

---

[1] Moreux, Serge, *Bartók* (Harvill Press, London, 1953), p. 92.
[2] Spence, Sir Basil, *Phoenix at Coventry* (Harper & Row, New York and Evanston, 1962), Prefatory Note.

be possible to develop any or all of them further still."[3] Burbank
proved his point in the garden and the greenhouse; Bartók vin-
dicated his own faith in a trinity of forebears whose seminal force
had, in his judgment, not been exhausted. And the works that
crowned his career—shortened though it was by leukemia—have
steadily affected the minds of two generations of composers.

Though Stravinsky outlived him by nearly a quarter of a century—they were born only months apart, Bartók in 1881, Stravinsky in 1882—Bartók did not outlive his own richest period, as
Stravinsky did. The most sophisticated music of which Bartók was
capable came in the context of his own self-imposed question:
whether it was possible to derive a "living synthesis" from the examples of those who meant the most to him musically. The outcome was embodied in music of such freshness and vitality that
many of those who were growing up in the fifties and sixties have
found in it their own "truly vital roots."

The results, at a distance of an appropriate time span (twenty-
five years), are to be found in what I call "first-generation
Bartók," the by-products of his *Concerto for Orchestra* (1943).
The idea of the players in such an orchestra as the Boston Symphony (for which it was written) being capable of filling a solo
role in an extended work was not original with Bartók, neither
was the title. What he did was to extricate their abilities from a
storytelling function in Rimsky's *Scheherazade* or Ravel's *La
Valse* and, by the brilliance of his own purpose, evolve a new kind
of abstraction.

There are currently in existence post-Bartók concertos for orchestra by Elliott Carter, by the English composer of Spanish
birth, Roberto Gerhard, by such other Americans as Ezra Lader-
man and Benjamin Lees, by the Polish Witold Lutoslawski, the
Japanese Akira Miyoshi, and the English-born Michael Tippett.
These are the ones that have been recorded; how many more
there are in print, only ASCAP and BMI know. However much
these works and their composers may differ from each other, they

[3] Burbank, Luther, *His Methods and Discoveries and Their Practical Application* (Luther Burbank Press, New York and London, 1914), Vol. VII,
pp. 272–3.

have in common Bartók's conception of a work in which the orchestra rather than an extraneous instrument is the soloist.

Now a trickle-down appears to be accumulating from another of Bartók's works: the *Music for Strings, Percussion, and Celesta* (1936). In this masterful interplay of sonorities and vibrations, pulsations and silences, to which an alert listener responds not merely by ear, but also by an almost skin-sensation of nerve-end perceptions, Bartók demands the playing skill of the best orchestral specialists with the intimacy of a chamber music ensemble. This work recasts the conventional conception of "families" of instruments nestling close together into communal brothers and sisters, nephews, nieces, and cousins teaming up (one almost said bedding down) with total strangers.

Thea Musgrave, of Scottish birth, may be said to have forged a link between first- and second-generation Bartók. She has added to the list of concertos for orchestra, and, more recently, devised a concerto for orchestra and what might be called Strolling Clarinet. When it was introduced to New York by the Philharmonic under the direction of Sarah Caldwell in 1975, the soloist was the orchestra's peerless master of that instrument, Stanley Drucker.

He began the performance in a normal position to the conductor's left. After a bit he walked away to confer, musically speaking, with a smaller ensemble of brass instruments. That colloquy completed, he joined a group of reed instruments, and added the voice of his instrument to theirs. And so it went, with Drucker playing as he strolled.

What it amounted to, formally, was Drucker playing *with* the orchestra and its components, rather than for the audience. We all heard, or perhaps more accurately, *overheard*, what he was doing, but the creative purpose was, for the most part, focused inward rather than outward.

A variation on this decentralization of the symphony orchestra was introduced by Ned Rorem in a work of 1976 called *Air Music* (a title derived from a statement by Wilhelm Heinse [1746–1803]: "Music represents the inner feeling in the exterior air"). There are, within its twenty-five minutes, ten sections, of which only the first and last utilize the full orchestra.

The variations performed in this work are not so much on a theme as on sound itself: patterns of reeds and percussion, followed by violas plus bassoons, with a quartet of horns and a harp. Do you like opposites? Rorem provides you with tuba and violin, surrounded by flutes and oboes, violins and string bass. It is, in a way, a pastime for the ear, distantly related to the soloistic kind of orchestral writing derived by Schoenberg from Mahler.

The implication of it all—and "all" includes works by Jacob Druckman, Charles Wuorinen, Toru Takemitsu, and Pierre Boulez—is that composers who are comfortable with the symphony orchestra may very well be uncomfortable with the thing it was created to perform: symphonies.

Does all this convey a hang-up with a name, a notion, a convention? Perhaps there is some semantic, pseudo-romantic factor at work: but surely these well-educated, widely read composers of today are well aware that decades ago Gustav Mahler (who died in 1911) said that what he really meant by a symphony was: "to build a world, with all the means at my disposal" (including words, when appropriate).

The evidence is clear that even when Elliott Carter calls a work *Symphony of Three Orchestras* or Toru Takemitsu prefers *Arc*, the men and women who file onstage to perform could very well be those for the Mahler Ninth. It is *where* they sit that creates a new consequence.

To this I have no objection whatsoever. Break down the orchestra as you will, but don't break it up. There is still a lot of work it can do better than anything else.

III

Is there conceivably a common ground on which a contemporary composer might combine Mahler's cosmology with Bartók's selectivity? Such ground not only exists but has been explored with a rare kind of productivity by Luciano Berio. Not a man to mince words, Berio does not hesitate to confront the phobia of some of his colleagues by using the word *Sinfonia* to characterize what he has done, even if it is in no common respect a symphony. Berio, who conducted the work's first performance (by the New York Philharmonic Orchestra on October 10, 1968), uses the term in its older Italian sense of "a work for instruments."

Berio himself is a variant, a hybrid in the best tradition of both Darwin and Burbank. Darwin would have recognized in Berio's family heritage of church musicians a predisposition to some form of tonal expression. Burbank would have appreciated the manner in which these aptitudes were influenced, by cross-pollinization, to produce a variant quite unlike the original.

For a time, Berio did everything possible to foil nature, heredity, and predisposition. Born near Genoa, he could not escape musical indoctrination as a child. He was barely into his teens when the war began: he graduated from the equivalent of high school when the Allies invaded Italy in 1943. He was then of draft age, and taken into the Italian Army. He deserted not long after, and finished the war as a partisan. When peace came, he followed an older sister (now a professor of Italian and Italian literature) into the University of Milan as a law student.

The postwar revival of musical life in Italy had two powerful effects on Berio. The introduction of long-existing but previously unheard works by Bartók, Stravinsky, and Webern revived his dormant family heritage. It also made him a convinced, permanent enemy of the Establishment (any Establishment, anywhere) which had the power to exercise such "thought control."

Berio gave up both the university and the study of law, and enrolled at the Giuseppe Verdi Conservatorio in Milan. It was a fortunate choice, for here Berio encountered Giorgio Ghedini, a stimulating teacher of composition whose mind helped to form the talents of such musicians as Victor de Sabata and Guido Cantelli. Berio also found a conducting mentor in the young Carlo Maria Giulini.

He then settled down to discover Luciano Berio.

To help meet day-to-day living expenses, he accompanied classes in opera repertory directed by such celebrated singers of the past as soprano Carmen Melis and tenor Aureliano Pertile. He also conducted performances by small opera groups in the vicinity of Milan. He was thus well indoctrinated in the practicalities of performance before he was swamped by the impracticalities of composition.

The quest for identity took a new direction in 1952. Aided by a postwar flood of philanthropy, Berio was able to visit the United States, to spend a summer at the Berkshire Music Center (Tanglewood), and there to follow his countryman Luigi Dallapiccola, as teacher, into the maze of twelve-tone discipline. He also heard his first electronic music in a concert at the Museum of Modern Art in New York. This he liked. Twelve-tone discipline he didn't.

By 1954 he was back in Milan, married to the now well-known mezzo Cathy Berberian, and working at the Italian Radio. In pursuit of his electronic interests, he set the first forty lines of James Joyce's *Ulysses* to such a background, and called it *Omaggio* ("Homage"). He also established a publication on new music titled *Incontri musicali* ("Musical Encounters"). One of its first contributors was a Frenchman exactly of Berio's age (both were born in 1925). Pierre Boulez appears to have remembered the title when he became music director of the New York Philharmonic Orchestra fifteen or so years later, and called one of his innovative programs "Prospective Encounters."

Berio was part of a unit in the Italian Radio which stimulated his interest in words. It was the Studio di Fonologia (Studio of Phonology). Among a series of compositions which have shown a gift for inventive titles, the first was *Allez-hop*, performed in Venice in 1959. By this time his interest in twelve-tone composition had dwindled, after he found it "formalist and escapist . . . ignoring what sound really is . . ."

In 1960 he returned to Tanglewood, now as a member of the faculty and a composer-in-residence. He spent 1962 and 1963 on the Oakland side of San Francisco Bay at Mills College. *Passaggio* (which bears the subtitle *messa in scena,* or "staged mass") had a success that attracted international attention at its first performance at La Scala in 1963. The central performer is Everywoman ("Her"), who is hunted down by "forces of conformism." In the end, she drives them from the theater. Berio became a member of the Juilliard's compositional faculty in 1965. The arrangement also permitted him to teach at Harvard.

The climax to this phase of his career occurred when he was commissioned to compose a work for performance by the New York Philharmonic Orchestra during its one hundred and twenty-fifth season (1966–67). Having by now spent the better part of a decade in America, it was rational—if you were Luciano Berio—to combine a trinity of interests in which he had long been interested: the symphony orchestra, a verbal text, and a decided strain of non-conformism. As the verbal text laid heavy emphasis on syllabic values, and offbeat rhythmic contrasts, he added to the orchestra the vocal group called the Swingle Singers. Contrary to some supposition, the name does not derive from a sometimes swing-y sound (which indeed it has) but from the name of its American founder, Ward Swingle.

More by chance than by purpose, Berio found the stimulus for his scherzo, the most considerable movement in the work, at a concert of the Philharmonic Orchestra. A vivid performance of the Mahler Second Symphony directed by Leonard Bernstein left its wordless scherzo, based on the *Knaben Wunderhorn* song *St. Antonius von Padua fischpredigt*, lodged in Berio's mind. The treatment by Mahler as an orchestral scherzo minus words has a certain insistence of rhythm and a highly ingenious scheme of orchestral detail which can leave it running on and on. Gradually, other values began to form in his mind around the slithering ostinato, and Berio jotted them down.

Unlike countless predecessors who have taken a theme, or a thought, from an existing work and made it over into something of their own, Berio utilizes the total texture of Mahler's scherzo as the backdrop, or screen, on which to impose, and superimpose, innumerable other things: textual references to student riots in Paris, outcries by Harvard undergraduates against the war in Vietnam, other matter reflecting the heat and clamor of a time of unrest.

In the first movement are to be found quotations from *Le Cru et le cuit* (Claude Lévi-Strauss); the second is made up of dirge-like iterations of the syllables Mar/tin/Lu/ther/King to a mournful marchlike background suggesting one of Mahler's *Kondukts* (funeral processions) to commemorate the Atlantan's assassination. Both are preparatory to the "journey to Cythera," the composer calls it, "aboard the scherzo of Mahler's second symphony."

The words[4] come and go in such patterns as "I am in the air, the walls, everything yields open, ebbs, flows, like the play of waves . . ." against the repetitious command in other voices. "Going, going, going." This eventually becomes the *Leitmotiv* of the whole experience as an exhortation "going, going, going" and then as an invocation "keep going, page after page, keep going, going on, call that going, call that on . . ." and, all the while, so, too, do references and allusions to works by composers from Bach to Berg, Beethoven to Strauss, Ravel, Ives, and, the composer adds, myself. Some are immediately recognizable in an eruptive phrase from *La Valse* or *Der Rosenkavalier*, others are swallowed up in a whirl of inner voices which challenge identification.

In a letter to me dated February 12, 1975—prompted by a comment of mine on other contemporary music, in which *Sinfonia* was mentioned—Berio describes the musical references as "only incidental, like signals, like flags, to the structure of the harmonic developments" in Mahler. That, of course, is one of the ongoing elements in Berio's transformation which symbolizes its craft—the upper and lower levels of communication which coexist simultaneously. What may be objective in the mind of the composer can become very subjective in the mind of the listener. Given a certain amount of recall and association, the references make a fascinating warp to the woof of Mahler's texture, a veritable *here and now* to a musical *there and then*, in the best traditions of visual flashbacks and superimpositions.

Against a general temptation to refer to this procedure as some form of montage, I would, rather, describe it as the first occurrence of a "*sontage*" (*son* for sound) in which the ear is invited,

[4] Berio refers to them (in his comment on the self-conducted recording, Columbia MS 7268) as "excerpts from Samuel Beckett's *The Unnamable* which in turn prompts a selection from many other sources, including Joyce . . ."

nay prompted, to make the same allusive associations as the eye does with visual images.

On another, post-Bartókian level, the aural scheme includes division of the twenty-four strings not into equal groups of twelves (firsts and seconds) but into three groups of eight, percussion players are urged to be "as far apart as possible," and there is, of course, provision for a mixing panel to monitor and control the output of the vocal group through speakers in the hall.

These are, in various ways, by-products of Berio's interest in electronics. But, it should be stressed, he uses these adjuncts creatively, to make the sound of the voices *closer* to the ear than would otherwise be the case. That *Sinfonia* is even more absorbing and rewarding in its recorded form than it is in the concert hall doesn't disturb me in the least . . . any more than Strauss's use of a wind machine in the "Alpine" Symphony is to be held against it. If the assets and opportunities of the recording process prompt a composer to create a work which is more directly experienced that way, why not?

Sinfonia has been widely performed in this country, in Canada, and in Mexico, not only as a concert work but also by dance groups. Audiences have, in all instances, gotten a message *because* there is a message to be gotten. My own perception of the work's durability has been strengthened not only by the 1970 performance by the New York Philharmonic but also by rehearings of the recording. Now that Berio has added a fifth movement which collects and reorders elements from earlier movements (as heard in the 1970 performance directed by Bernstein) the impression comes clear that Berio was not aiming to capture the ear of posterity, but the mood of the moment; and, as may happen when the artist is completely immersed in his work, he did it enduringly.

In the aftermath of *Sinfonia*, which is a non-symphony, Berio brought to attention (at Santa Fe in 1970) not only a non-opera, for all that it is titled *Opera* (work), but also a non-attraction, *This Means That* at Carnegie Hall. Both were served before the cooking process had been finished, with not only an unappetizing but non-aesthetic result. A concerto for two pianos (Berio-like, each was placed at opposite sides of the stage, rather than nestling

—Siamese-twins-like—in each other's curves) has come to my hearing in both New York and London (1976). I was partial to what I heard but what I heard was, because of the work's complexity, only a fraction of what was going on.

Recently, Berio has joined his "old," new, young friend Pierre Boulez at the research center in Paris known as IRCAM (Institut de Recherche et Coordination Acoustique/Musique). Here, I have heard it said, Berio has returned to his longtime interest in *électroniques* (a summary of last year's activities describes him as *Responsable* in the Département Électroacoustique).

My comment to that is: "Stop that tonal doodling, Luciano! Back to portraiture!"

IV

This is not to suggest that Berio should write more *Sinfonias*. Ravel had an apt commentary on the place of risk and success in a career when, on a visit to Monaco, a friend suggested a visit to the casino. "No," said Ravel, referring to *Boléro*, "I have won my gamble." The same highly discriminating musician had a profound insight to another work of great distinction (which might refer to the work with which Berio won his gamble).

In the time when musicians were vying with each other to produce a terse summation of the evolutionary element in *Le Sacre du printemps*—rhythmic force, harmonic sparseness, orchestral might—Ravel told the composer that its greatest innovation was "in the musical entity." That pleased Stravinsky very much. The same could be said of Berio's *Sinfonia*.

While Berio is pondering his next move—and I wouldn't be surprised to discover, one day, that it has been happening *while* he has been "researching" in Paris—his example of what Bartók calls "the living synthesis" invites some retrospect of the circumstances that brought it about. Had Berio remained in Milan, never visited America, taught at the Juilliard, Harvard, and Mills, been present in Paris during the student insurrections, or even had not polished his English to the point of Mar/tin/Lu/ther/King, would there have been a *Sinfonia?* Perhaps Stravinsky would have produced *Le Sacre du printemps* had he remained in St. Petersburg rather than relocating in Paris with the Diaghilev ballet, producing *L'Oiseau de feu,* and starting *Petrouchka.* But the odds on both happening are longer than a prudent bettor would consider inviting.

Luther Burbank considered one of the prime successes of his career was in producing—to order—a pea of a certain size which a canner wanted to process in quantity. In addition to size, flavor, and uniformity of quality, it should be produced on vines where it would mature at the *same* time through the whole crop, in order to simplify harvesting and canning.

In commenting on the successful outcome, Burbank candidly acknowledged the good fortune that "the extraordinary experiments through which the Austrian monk, Mendel, made the discoveries that have created such commotion in the biological world," were made with the common garden pea.[5] Recessives and dominants are worn coins of the clinical vocabulary that Gregor Mendel (1822–84) created, but the pass-on of information gave not only Burbank, but innumerable researchers since him basic doctrine by which to abide.

Attention to botany, and the impulse that produced "better fruits and fairer flowers," have some elements that Berio found, in common, for Mahler and Bartók,[6] recycling a creative conception and regrouping the orchestra. Certainly it would be costly to ignore a precedent that could be informative and even illuminating.

Burbank acknowledges that it was not until he had been through many years of hybridization and cross breeding that he learned an important basic principle: "the all-important lesson that the second-generation hybrid, rather than that of the first generation, is the one that must be looked to, in a large number of cases, for important development." By that token, the generations of Bachs (beginning in 1561) were bursting at the seams for the arrival of Johann Sebastian in 1685.

Berio's *Sinfonia* is an innovation of genuine significance. Whether in terms of Berio's forebears or the "generations" of

[5] Op. cit., Vol. VIII, p. 86.
[6] Ibid., Vol. VII, p. 112.

Bartók, it contains considerations not to be ignored. What entered into it and how it came about is worthy of close study, especially on the educational level, where a Burbank-minded musician is sorely wanted.

Mildred

I

I have made no secret of my belief that every critic has short-comings (page 88) and the one who believes otherwise is either a fool or a liar. Being perhaps a fool but not a liar, I readily confess that my personal deficiency—or at least the one I am prepared to acknowledge—is a nodding rather than a speaking acquaintance with foreign languages. At a time when in addition to musical and academic studies, I should have been busying myself with learning the three basic European languages—German, French, and Italian —I was engaged in learning a then new North American language, the language of jazz, in all its dialects, variations, and subdivisions.

"Then" was the 1920s—the Roaring Twenties, they have been called. But not often at the time. By common consent, it was a hectic, exciting, fairly undisciplined time. Probably every time in which an alert, responsive individual grows up is hectic and exciting. Even with the "unbearable" miseries of adolescence, it is that oyster, the world, at its most inviting.

Perhaps the fifties were the last time period roughly comparable to the twenties. Both were postwar decades in which hopes of a new start could, at least, be contemplated. But before the hope could escape from the cradle into childhood, Korea intruded as a new place of battle, deaths, and family disruption—all of which the twenties had left behind—and the new infant's name was apprehension, not hope.

Furthermore, the fifties brought a new awareness of the United States as something it had never before been—a superpower, and one of only two.

In the twenties one could, at least in a figurative sense, think of isolation, about fleshing out a continent not wholly inhabited, and discovering, amid Prohibition and the social eruption it engendered, the new worlds of radio and film and an upstart, unbridled, raucous form of music. To some it was an irritant, to some a stimulant: but it was un-ignorable, an unceasing source of interest and some joy, to all for whom being ear-minded is a special privilege among all the countless others who are only eye-minded.

The upstart—and it was to some as maddening a deviation from prior forms of music as rock has been and disco now is, to those unprepared for it—was hard-driven, uncouth, outrageously unconcerned whether cultivated people put it down or took it up. As the expression proliferated and more and more minds became involved in it, so too did the varieties of personalities it could accommodate. What Ansermet learned from Bechet (page 7) in minutes took Americans of comparable learning years to become aware of, often to their own deprivation. Time was fleeting, and so too was the rich, racy, live experience of what was going on all about them.

Within the twenties, there was already a place in America's popular music for the small voice of a large person (female) born (February 27, 1907) to an Irish father and an Indian mother (Coeur d'Alene tribe) on an Indian reservation at Tekoa, Washington. She was educated in Spokane, including the high school attended also by the late Harry (Bing) Crosby; and began, at an early age, to sing at family functions and small social affairs. Her father played the violin, and her mother, the piano, so music was in her blood. But the music to which she was attracted was neither Irish nor Indian. It was what all the other kids around her were hearing, the American popular song.

By the time she was seventeen (1924) she was engaged in a then familiar, now forgotten form of employment: demonstrating, by voice, new songs of which sheet music was for sale in the five-and-dime (Woolworth's or the equivalent), perhaps the record shop, by which she was employed. Obviously she was bent for a professional career, and could have become known by her family name, Mildred Rinker. Or perhaps as Mildred Norvo, the name of the celebrated xylophone performer to whom she was later married. In between, she married a man named Bailey, and it was as Mildred Bailey that she imprinted the sound of the small, warm voice on American musical history.

The nature of her employment at seventeen in Spokane, Washington, had two profound effects on her future: she was forever after dedicated to the American popular song, in all its limitless variety, and she perpetuated, enduringly, the person-to-person directness of manner that demonstration-singing calls for. She could no more overwhelm a listener with punch, sex appeal, or brute force than Beatrice Lillie could, for a coarse effect, intersperse a monologue with a vulgarism. In all the forms in which the Bailey voice became unforgettable—in a Spokane music shop, a San Francisco restaurant, on radio, or from records—it was inescapably personalized and infinitely endearing.

Unlike other specialists of the thirties and forties, Mildred rarely embellished what she sang with notes not written, scatted (used nonsense syllables), or deviated widely from a melody. After all, if you cared enough for such a melody as "Heather on the Hill" (from Alan Jay Lerner's and Frederick Loewe's *Brigadoon*) to sing it time and again, why change it into something else? At her best, the Bailey singing was anything but repetitious; but the variants came in subtle shifts of emphasis from word to word, in the bend of a note's intonation (slightly above or below pitch), in the colorations from bland to fervent with which she infused her sound, in the memorably *affectionate* caress she imparted to the key *word* in a phrase ("All this I know").

And, of course, *time, time, time*: that crucial jazz musician's term, which has nothing to do with the clock on the wall, but everything to do with the beat, the pulse, the throb of life in the music, especially in singing with a small band against soloists equally aware of *time*. As Franz Schubert is known to have asked, on being introduced to a new acquaintance, *"Kann er was?"* ("What is he good at?"), the first thing a seasoned jazz musician wants to know about a newcomer is: "Has he got time?"

The subject came up once in a conversation with Ruby Braff, that rare cornet player. He was alluding to his New England background and mentioned an occasion when Leonard Bernstein sat in on piano with a band of which Braff was a member, to play some tunes of his own (*Wonderful Town, West Side Story*, etc.). Asked what he thought of the world-famous conductor-composer's participation, Braff replied: "He's okay—but he ain't got good time."

Mildred Bailey died in 1951 (at the age of only forty-four) before Braff (born in 1927) probably had the opportunity to play with her, but I doubt that he would have found fault with her time. The hidden ingredient in all music worth the listening, whether grindingly insistent in the finale of Beethoven's Seventh Symphony, the lightly regular pulsation in the *pizzicato ostinato* of Tchaikovsky's Fourth Symphony, the slight *lean* on the second beat of a waltz by Johann Strauss or Franz Lehár, or the ritard which gives a tremor of life to a mazurka by Chopin, *time* is as essential to music as breath is to life.

In jazz, time is more than a hidden ingredient: it is the internal, ongoing value that relates player to player and listeners to players, the moving entity in any truly great performance because it engages the motor impulse flowing from the group to the individual. In the song performance to which I have alluded, a choice Bailey instance of time comes in foiling the listener's expectation by *delaying* the input slightly between "the" and "heather" in "the '/heather on the hill." All manner of other refinements and reactions are built into jazz, whose best phraseologies are inexplicable, and whose great impacts may come from a well-chosen silence.

There is, of course, an infinity of other instances in Bailey's other work, on more conventional jazz tunes, in which delaying or anticipating the beat is exploited. I draw particular attention to "Heather on the Hill" because the perceptible detail may be described in terms of a *verbal* usage rather than being wholly related to notes, or notations of them. All, however, have much to do with the expected and the unexpected as the embodiment of a refinement, a subtlety, a *caring* about what she is doing not often to be found in music making of any kind.

I don't know whether Bailey ever had a formal lesson in singing. Who could *teach* her to do what came forth in such a natural, untaught way? Doubtless she *learned*, as almost all fine singers (of any kind) do, from listening to those whom she admired, and those whose results she envied: with Bailey, it was Ethel Waters and Bessie Smith who are most often mentioned. She also must have learned from listening to the instrumentalists with whom she worked, such as the legendary Bix Beiderbecke; and, most important of all, from listening with an unremitting critical sense to herself.

All singers, after all, have the same basic equipment to work with: starting from the bottom, it is the lungs which draw in the air, the diaphragm below with which to support it, and the pelvic area with muscles that are utilized to anchor the diaphragm; above, in ascending order, are the larynx, throat muscles, and resonating chamber (facial cavity, palate, nasal structure, and the like) with which to form the sound. Differing degrees of lung capacity and the mass of the vocal cords account for variations in volume and range.

To liken Mildred Bailey to Fischer-Dieskau is to invite ridicule and disbelief. But a quest for perfection may be as inbred in an Al Hirschfeld, say, as in a Pablo Picasso. It is an attitude of mind, a determination of will, an expression of spirit and resolution that makes no more demanding a mountain than a molehill. In her work, the microphone was an inseparable part of the result she achieved; for Fischer-Dieskau it is merely an intermediary for converting what he can do without it into a result he cannot achieve otherwise. For her it became a tool with which to shape breath control, placement of tone, and articulation of text into a stream of sound that came together, finally, into a result as difficult to achieve as that of any fine *Lieder* singer.

Helen Traubel, great artist though she was, had the poor judgment to pretend that jazz singing was an easy mark for someone who had sung Isolde and the three Brünnhildes. She made those whose standards were as high in one world of singing as in the other shudder at the ineptitude of her efforts on television, in supper clubs, and on the stage (particularly in the Rodgers-Hammerstein *Pipe Dream*) to find *time*, literally, for what she was doing.

Mildred Bailey, on the contrary, had the good sense to regard perfection as an end in itself, and thus left an incomparable image and a wide range of recordings, as a stylist beyond compare. Embodied within the image and the records are an intimate sound (curiously at variance with an ample body that was rarely less than two hundred pounds, tableside), the loverly confiding passion from the motherly frame, and a cordial, good-natured ridicule of her own awkwardness.

II

To relate Mildred Bailey to jazz is to invite, from another quarter, no less ridicule than to relate her to Fischer-Dieskau. All right for ballads and pop tunes, they might concede: but jazz? Could she ever really sing the blues? In a traditional sense, no. She readily recognized her special order of ability on an occasion in the early thirties when she attended a night club at which Bessie Smith (one of her idols, and billed as "the Empress of the Blues") performed. The MC then suggested that perhaps Miss Bailey would like to perform.

"What?" said Miss Bailey. "After Bessie? No, sir."

But then—how would Leadbelly do with "Summertime"? Poorly, I venture. Miss Bailey paid her respect to the blues in a variety of ways of her own. As an instance, the traditional chords of the blues are present, the kind of folk philosophizing often heard in them, and, of course, a strong beat, in the adaptation she sings called "Don't Worry 'bout Strangers" ("keep an eye on your best friend"). And Miss Bailey was keenly aware that to equate the ability to sing or play the blues with being a jazz musician was as much a form of discrimination as color itself, condemning the outsiders to what might be called a whited sepulcher. Or, to pretend that what others believed in and performed was poor stuff, would be to outdo the hypocrisy that Matthew was decrying in his biblical analogy.

I am referring to a whole generation of ethnomusicologists who have deigned to tell others what the "real jazz" is, though they were not here when it was happening, and were rarely exposed to it as a reality rather than a recording. I refer to Messrs. Hugues Panassié, Charles Delaunay, Joachim Behrendt, Benny Green, et al., who were either elsewhere or not born in the twenties.

The insistence that jazz is Afro-American or nothing leaves out a whole side of it related to the Creoles of New Orleans, the strains of Indian blood in Bailey and her great contemporary singer and master of the jazz trombone Jack Teagarden (who was highly regarded by no less a Titan than Louis Armstrong), the Scotch-Irish Dorsey brothers, the Italian-Americans such as violinist Joe Venuti and guitarist Eddie Lang, the Russian-Jewish Irving Berlin (admired by Ansermet), his younger colleague George Gershwin, the German-Americans of sundry identity. Which is more truly jazz: Gershwin's "I Got Rhythm" or Louis Armstrong's playing of it? In my lexicon of jazz, it is all as American as the men and women who participated in its birth pangs and growing pains, from which emerged a pantheon big enough to accommodate all who made their individual contributions: blacks and whites, gentiles and Jews, poor and rich, plus all the gradations between.

In that pantheon, a special wing belongs to the Baileys of jazz, those of the quieter but no less insinuating persuasion, whose art is in the chamber music category. Curator and head man would, of course, be Teddy Wilson. A pianist whose instrument, like the man himself, never raises its voice in anger, he has, over nearly fifty years, been a joy and a pleasure to hear. Some typical instances of what he can do are contained in a prizable collection devoted to Bailey (Columbia CRL 22), ranging from 1929 to 1946.

The contents (most of the best derived from sessions directed by, or, as the more current word has it, "produced," by John Hammond) include nearly ten (of forty-plus) in which Wilson is the pianist. More than once Bailey's voice can be heard not merely resting comfortably on the piano background provided by Wilson, but, when he has executed a particularly subtle example of his beautifully inflected embellishments, crying out in pure pleasure.

Such public expressions of satisfaction are not encouraged in a singer-pianist relationship of the Fischer-Dieskau/Demus variety, but the endorsement comes easily among performers in jazz of the chamber variety. I say "among" rather than "between," because it is part of the rapport that should, but does not always, prevail. Moreover, it is something *shared* by *all* the participants, not merely those directly involved.

As for those "directly involved" in other respects, the alphabetical listing begins with trumpeter Bunny Berigan and ends with Wilson, articulating a choice collection of musical names whose company hardly could be kept by a singer other than Bailey: such saxophonists as Chu Berry, Coleman Hawkins, and Johnny Hodges; the Dorsey brothers; clarinetists Benny Goodman, Artie Shaw, and Hank D'Amico; pianists Billy Kyle, Ellis Larkins, and Mary Lou Williams, as well as Wilson; drummers Gene Krupa, Dave Tough, Eddie Dougherty, and George Wettling; and, of course, the innovator of the xylophone as a jazz instrument, Red Norvo (previously identified as Bailey's husband).

Possibly some would say that identification should be provided of which were blacks and which were whites, beyond those whose names are of sufficient fame to be self-identifying. Inasmuch as the choices were made on a basis of musicianship, not color, the equality of ability was something more than skin-deep, its pigmentation inconsequential.

As a footnote to the history of this particular subject it might be of interest to mention that the whole subject of what I call "chamber jazz," which eventually brought into being that notable group the Modern Jazz Quartet, actually had its beginnings in 1935, through Bailey. It was at a gathering in her New York home that Goodman and Wilson first found their musical affinity. Not many weeks later, the first Goodman Trio recordings were made (with Krupa, of course). Not much more than a year later, Lionel

Hampton, greatest of vibraphonists, and also an excellent drummer, was added, thus creating the first jazz quartet.

It was, as those who are old enough to have enjoyed it live will remember, a very colorful organization.

III

Hugues Panassié did an enormous public service in creating the publication HOT JAZZ in the thirties (the Ansermet essay on Sidney Bechet may have long ago faded into obscurity had it not been reprinted, as noted on page 5, in that publication). The book of the same name earned Panassié universal praise, and thanks (including mine) for organizing and codifying the jazz scene from its recorded beginnings to the mid-thirties, as it had never been organized and codified before. But it also patronized some aspects of a situation that, as a Frenchman with only a limited on-site observation, he comprehended only incompletely.

At the outset Panassié gave a degree of reasoned perception of the part that white musicians—a term as general and unspecific as Negro musicians—had in that development. In a later book, called *The Real Jazz*,[1] almost all were, in a sense, drummed out (despite Gene Krupa, Dave Tough, Buddy Rich, and other innovational drummers) because they had the misfortune to be born white.

The apotheosis of the rejection came in the fifties and sixties with the appearance of what was called the Tom Uncle movement. This was an inversion of the "Uncle Tom" phrase (after Harriet Beecher Stowe's character) applied to Negroes who accommodated themselves to the white man by being subservient to discrimination, segregation, emasculation, and other catchwords of the day. Now it was the whites, especially jazz musicians, who were being excluded, in a reverse racification.

Eventually it reached flood tide when the text of the Oscar Hammerstein-Jerome Kern classic "Ol' Man River" had to be changed from "Darkies all work on the Mississippi" to "Colored

[1] Panassié, Hugues, *The Real Jazz* (Smith & Durrell, Inc., New York, 1942).

folks work on the Mississippi" because "darkies" was considered a racial slur. A date of reference might be cited as 1955, when *The Jerome Kern Song Book*[2] appeared with the amended text. This is akin to the protests of some Jews to the identification of Shylock in *The Merchant of Venice* as "a Rich Jew." The premise is that the association of the usurous Shylock with a racial identification was a slur on all members of that race. Fortunately, there are enough Jews like myself who have been victimized by other Rich Jews to recognize Shakespeare's characterization as a reflection on the Rich, not on the Jews.

I had a long, affectionate, and mutually rewarding association with the composer of *Black, Brown, and Beige* (which was first performed at a Carnegie Hall concert in 1943 with program notes I had written), and know that he schemed it to celebrate the diversity of his people, not on their solidarity as a bloc of blacks. As Duke Ellington was himself something between brown and beige, to identify him as a black composer is less than even coloristically correct.

As for the music to which he made such a profound, inimitable contribution, it can no more be reduced to black and white than the ability to reproduce it can be prescribed by formula. In each decade since Ansermet was celebrating it as "ragtime," the American way of playing popular music has changed, sometimes quickly, sometimes slowly. What it was in the thirties was different from what it had been in the twenties, and what it became by the seventies was vastly different from that of the fifties or sixties.

Each decade washed up something to pass on to the next. The twenties were singularly rich in the kind of music that almost all Americans heard, enjoyed, and cherished. There were as many talented composers of popular music as there were highly endowed performers of it—a rarity in any decade. The interchange was much as Ansermet described vis-à-vis Berlin: "Having absorbed the negro style perfectly it is to this style that he applies his gifts

---

[2] *The Jerome Kern Song Book*. Edited with an introduction and text by Oscar Hammerstein II. Arrangements by Dr. Albert Sirmay (Simon & Schuster and T. B. Harms Company, New York, 1955), p. 78.

of musical invention, which is indeed remarkable . . ." (page 4).

As I have noted previously, I would question "perfectly." But there is little question that Berlin responded to an impulse, and had his own contribution to make to it. By the twenties, another transformation was in the making. "Ragtime," for which Ansermet had such an acute ear, was out; another way of breaking up a tune into individualized, rhythmically and melodically varied figurations was in. But the challenge, if long-lasting, was not permanent. By the seventies, the vitality of ragtime reasserted itself in the insinuating, melodically bright art of Scott Joplin (1868–1917), knocking at the door of the pantheon to which I have previously referred (page 135) and reclaiming in it a hall of its own.

What picked up the tempo and quickened the pulse of American popular music—as much in the theatrical works of Eubie Blake ("Shuffle Along") and Fats Waller ("Hot Chocolates") as in the cabarets and night clubs—was a powerful wind from the South. Negro jazz was gutty, as in gut bucket (a place for discharging vomit, when necessary, in a bar, or barrelhouse). It was out of the brothels and the cribs (cheaper form of rendering the same important service), the whorehouse and other places of pleasure. Often enough, the prices differed according to the furnishings and social-climbing aspirations, provided by the madams.

But white jazz of the same period wasn't exactly polite either. The impulse had more to do with high school dances and back porch romances than it did with barrelhouse and the blues. But in the intermingling previously mentioned, and the vigor that accrued from it, the strain developed a hardiness all its own.

The difference of the jazz played by the whites of the twenties from that of the blacks varied less in kind than in degree. Those who did it best, on either side of the color line, had something special to say without which American popular music would not be the singular, highly distinctive variant it became.

To be sure, it started as far apart as the two races themselves were. For the whites, the source is to be found in the crude, nearly parodistic performances of New Orleans jazz purveyed by the Original Dixieland Jazz Band. Its acceptance did not derive from quality, but from availability: their recordings, cheap as well as available, were the first likenesses—however distorted—of the real thing to be heard by young Americans of a certain, highly impressionable age. The impact and the aftermath have a classical representative in a male, instrumental counterpart in white jazz of the part represented by Mildred Bailey among female vocalists.

IV

Precision in place and date is provided by one who miraculously survived such occupational hazards as night work, bad hours, dissipation, intoxication, and exploitation to attain the biblical quota of threescore and ten, in 1976.

He was, properly enough, born in Chicago, Illinois, in 1906, as Lawrence Freeman. He attained fame as Bud Freeman, master of the tenor saxophone, and is one of the few still-living members of the Austin High gang who made white jazz that endures (others included Eddie Condon, on banjo-guitar, Frank Teschemacher, clarinet, Jimmy McPartland, cornet-trumpet, etc.).

Speaking several years ago of the forces that played around the music of the twenties, as he knew them and it, Freeman said: "My good friend, Frank Teschemacher [killed in an automobile accident in 1932, at the age of twenty-eight, and hence known more by reputation than proof as a great clarinetist], called me one day and said: 'Bud, our idol's in town.' That could mean only one person: Bix Beiderbecke, the greatest on horn we had ever heard. So we made it to the club where he was playing, and during a break he went to the piano and began to play something we had never heard before. 'My God,' I said, 'that's a fabulous thing you've written. Let's hear more.' 'It's not mine,' he said. 'It's a thing called "Boneyard Shuffle" by a friend in college named Hoagy Carmichael . . .' " (1923).

The "idol" named Bix Beiderbecke, born in Davenport, Iowa, became part of literary lore (after his death in 1931 at the age of twenty-eight, primarily of alcoholism) because of Dorothy Baker's *Young Man with a Horn*, published in 1936. How he became a catalyst, reagent, motivating force, and creator of some of the most beautiful musical phrases ever put into reproducible grooves by anyone—white, blue, green, yellow, tan, brown, beige, or black —is better-known today than for many years past, because of a work of loving documentation published more than forty years after his death.[3] As a way of revisiting an era long since vanished, the painstaking assemblage of data is comparable, in its own way, with the exhaustive work of restoration on Gustav Mahler accomplished by Henry-Louis De La Grange.[4]

Why Davenport, Iowa? That is a question that could only be asked by one, like myself, to whom the whole of Iowa is a vast farmland and Davenport is somewhere in the middle of it. I know now, of course, that Davenport has, timelessly, occupied ground where the Rock and the Mississippi rivers meet, and thus is a part of a traffic network reaching from Minnesota to the Gulf of Mexico. Davenport, almost as timelessly, had been a "German" town (as Cincinnati once was) with a fair amount of musical interest, a vaudeville theater on the Orpheum circuit, and close enough to Chicago (sixty-five miles to the east) to afford a stopover for talent moving from east to west, or north to south.

One biographical detail should be mentioned before any other. The quick, easy name by which Beiderbecke became famous derived from his Germanic father's first name, Bismark. Untrue, however, is the legend that alleges his son's name to have become Bix because his childish lips could not form the word Bismark. The birth certificate exhibited by Messrs. Sudhalter and Evans shows that Beiderbecke Sr. had incorporated his *own* nickname into the given ones of his second son: Leon Bix Beiderbecke.

A piano in the home was an early source of fascination for the boy born in 1903 (which would make him four years older than Mildred Bailey). He played with it, rather than on it. Some lessons along the way were helpful, allowing the largely self-taught Bix to get around the keyboard well enough for simple jazz pur-

[3] Sudhalter, Richard M., and Evans, Philip R., with Dean-Myatt, William, *Bix Man and Legend* (Schirmer Books, published by arrangement with Arlington House Publishers, New York, 1974).

[4] De La Grange, Henry-Louis, *Mahler* (Doubleday & Company, Inc., Garden City, N.Y., 1973).

poses, and to make a pass at some pieces of Debussy. However, as his professional career was perpetually penalized by an inability to read music at sight, he cannot be said to have been provided with the most elementary of all musical skills. (The references to Debussy could mean that if he heard something that attracted his ear, he could reproduce it on the piano, even if the notes on the staff were a blur to him.)

A vocation came to Bix when an older brother, just home from the 1914–18 war, celebrated by buying a hand-wound phonograph and an assortment of records. Among them was the sensation of the moment, "Tiger Rag" played by the Original Dixieland Jazz Band. Why Beiderbecke, aged fifteen, chose the cornet line of D. J. ("Nick") La Rocca to call his own, nobody knows. By turning the knob that reduced the turntable's revolutions by half, the boy could identify each individual note as it came out in a baritonal rumble, and follow it on the piano. A few weeks later he turned up at home with a cornet he had borrowed from a neighbor. Despite urging that he learn proper fingering from a teacher, Beiderbecke set about learning how to play it on his own. The result was a fingering system unknown to anyone else in the profession. From 1918, aged fifteen and a high school freshman, Beiderbecke did little else for the remaining thirteen years of his life but play, and listen to, music.

The world has long been taught, and accepted, the historical fact that jazz was born in New Orleans, and came up the river. But beyond the lore that it had something to do with the riverboats, the factual details have been mostly obscured. Presumably the young Bix, like the young Abe Lincoln, could have made a trip south on a boat and had a life-forming experience. But that wasn't necessary. Beiderbecke didn't have to go to New Orleans. New Orleans came to him.

Summer 1919 found Beiderbecke sufficiently qualified on his "pickup" piano jazz to join some school friends in a band that performed for their fellow students. They also had an occasional opportunity to play aboard a local boat that made brief river trips out of Davenport. According to the custom of the time, it carried musicians to entertain the travelers on their way and to play for dancing, the predominant social pastime of the period.

As a result, the young performers were well versed in what was happening on the big boats from the South whose run from New Orleans to St. Louis and the North occasionally had a trip that terminated in Davenport or passed through on the way to St. Paul, Minnesota. When the opportunity beckoned, the young music-struck kids visited the docks, as a young Viennese music lover might frequent the fourth ring at the opera house, in quest of what was more necessary than bread and butter.

One day in summer 1919, it was the imposing *Capitol* of the Streckfus line which docked in Davenport, complete with a band from New Orleans. Aboard, and in charge, was the famous Fate Marable (born in Paducah, Kentucky), who literally conducted a jazz conservatory from the keyboard of his riverboat piano. Included in the "class of 1919" were Warren (Baby) Dodds on drums, Johnny St. Cyr, and, on cornet, Louis Armstrong.[5]

The instant interaction of the two young brass players I leave to the imagination. The formidable numerology comes out to nineteen all the way. The century was nineteen years old, and so too was Louis (having been born on July 4, 1900).

Armstrong, who died in 1974, had a lifelong memory of the meeting, and of many subsequent ones with Beiderbecke. A man of great generosity as well as of innate musical genius, Armstrong was especially impressed with the serious, single-minded way in which his younger friend pursued his objective. Sudhalter and Evans quote Armstrong as saying: "He'd come down to hear the bands, and then go home and practice what he heard . . . No matter how good the solo was that he played, he wasn't very satisfied with it. He never seemed satisfied with his effort, this was true in later years, too, even while he was driving all the cats wild."[6]

Louis, at nineteen, out of an orphan's home, had something that Beiderbecke could never match—an instinctive attachment to the blues, the mother's milk of all Negro musicians of the time. Beiderbecke, at sixteen, had something as distinctively his own—a middle-class white background, and all the attachments it suggests. Both put their youth into their music, and what came out

[5] Sudhalter and Evans, op. cit., p. 39.
[6] Ibid.

was as distinctively their own as the backgrounds from which they emerged.

The white man's jazz of the twenties was, curiously, both a lower- and an upper-class phenomenon. In the first instance, it was produced by small combos and the pickup groups that sprang up in many communities of the Midwest. Driving was just coming in, and with it came roadhouses and the so-called "clubs," which needed music to satisfy customers in search of dancing as well as drinking. (Prohibition also made this more a sub-rosa public pastime than a readily accessible private one.)

Those who had the money to spend danced and drank. Those who didn't, played—and also drank. When the young players thought their skills were good enough, they were drawn, mothlike, to the cheaper spots in the larger cities (Chicago in particular) which gathered around the bigger, more expensive places where the top Negro bands from the South flourished. When the teenagers (mostly white) weren't jamming together, or scuffling for money on the river (or lake) boats, they were haunting the bandstands at the big cafes or ballrooms (the Lincoln or the Royal Gardens in Chicago) listening to their idols.

Well above such involvements, as the twenties progressed, were the emerging, better-organized, better-paying, and larger bands typified by the one led by Paul Whiteman. A native of Denver, where his father (Wilberforce Whiteman) was superintendent of school music, Whiteman was well versed in the "classics," and played the viola in the Denver Symphony Orchestra. A stretch of service in the Navy during World War I gave him a taste of bandleading, and it became a lifelong infection. He was also attuned to the popular music of the time. Together, they led him to a career that achieved a milestone (if not a climax) in the famous Aeolian Hall concert of February 12, 1924, at which George Gershwin played his *Rhapsody in Blue* for the first time.

Whiteman has been glorified by some, vilified by others (especially jazz connoisseurs), but rarely identified for what he was: a man with a high instinct for talent which lent itself to his purposes. By the end of the twenties, the musicians he sought out, and paid well, to appear with him at the best hotels from coast to coast, on recordings, and eventually on radio and in films, were a Who's Who of obscure players who became famous as band-leaders in the thirties. The ominous word "commercial" has been leveled ad infinitum at the music he produced, and the im-pure means (money) with which he seduced all the great talents he discovered (Crosby, Jack Teagarden, the Dorseys, Red Norvo, eventually Bailey and Beiderbecke). Nobody was required to ac-cept a Whiteman offer, and more than a few didn't. The ones who did acquired some insights and a lot of on-site training that later served them well. If his "conservatory" wasn't as rough as the one Marable conducted on the riverboats, it had its notable graduates of a different breed. In the nature of his gifts, Beiderbecke was an outstanding example of one who never graduated. Bailey, who did, found Bix there when she arrived in 1927.

V

There had, of course, been agonizing stations along the way, from dockside to topside. Beiderbecke Sr. had no sympathy for his son's jazz ambitions. He took him out of Davenport High in 1921, aged eighteen and getting no closer to graduation. The family de-cision was that he needed stricter supervision than the kind he was getting in public school, and a private school was the answer. After suitable investigation, the choice finally settled on Lake For-est Academy, which had been recommended for its success in other difficult cases. Beiderbecke Sr. visited the school in Illinois, approved of its facilities, and was assured by the headmaster of productive results.

Only one, unimaginable flaw corrupted the reasoning. Lake For-est was not, like Davenport, sixty-five miles from Chicago, but only thirty-five. The moth was that much closer to the flame. Beiderbecke soon found a way of slipping away from the dormi-tory after lights-out, catching a train on one of the suburban lines that surround Chicago, turning up just as things were beginning to heat up, sitting in with other young musicians in one of the cheaper spots, or hanging around the bandstands of the high and mighty. Before a school year was out, Beiderbecke's disappearances were uncovered. He was suspended from school and sent back to Davenport. His father ordered him into the family coal business, but that didn't last. By the summer of 1923, he was back to playing in Chicago, as noted above by Freeman.

In their separate ways, and a century apart, the paths of Bix Beiderbecke and Franz Schubert were curiously similar. Schubert's schoolmaster father wanted his son to follow the same profession, and not waste his time on music and loose living. When he didn't take the advice, he was ordered out of the house. Beiderbecke's case was substantially similar. Schubert contracted a venereal disease, and, the pathology of the time being what it was, died five years later. Beiderbecke's ailment was alcoholism, and the quality of liquor being what it was in the twenties, he succumbed—after interludes of sobriety—in 1931, at the age of twenty-eight.

The suggested likeness of Beiderbecke, cornet player known primarily for some remarkable records, to Schubert, composer of quartets, symphonies, sonatas, and more than six hundred songs, will strike some readers as even more farfetched than a comparison of Mildred Bailey and Fischer-Dieskau. Social circumstances and cultural exposures aside, the two young men shared many of the same impulses, and each was denied a full opportunity to pursue them with parental blessing.[7]

As an indication of the rapidity with which his career took fire, once he applied himself to nothing else, Beiderbecke cut his first record in February 1924, at the Richmond, Indiana, plant of the Gennett label, a famous cheap product of the time which was highly responsive to young talent. Before the end of the year, he was offered a chair in the famous band of Jean Goldkette, whose headquarters were in Detroit, and who was sometimes described as "the Paul Whiteman of the West." Beiderbecke's lack of facility in reading music cost him the job. Under family pressure, he enrolled in Iowa University as an "unclassified" (non-matriculated) student.

[7] When Beiderbecke left Davenport, finally, his high school sweetheart, Vera, married a man named Ferdie Korn (Sudhalter and Evans, op. cit., p. 293). When Schubert could not persuade the father of Therese Grob to allow him to marry her, she married a man named Johann Bergmann. Bergmann and Korn had the same profession. They were bakers.

He left Iowa City and the university in February of 1925, and went back to "jobbing," playing here and there as the spirit moved him. Some of the happiest months of his life began in the fall of 1925, when he joined a band in St. Louis led by saxophonist Frank Trumbauer (the clarinetist was the later famous Charles Pee Wee Russell). This eventually led back to Goldkette in Detroit, and, in the fall of 1927, to Whiteman, in both instances with Trumbauer.

Unquestionably Trumbauer was a man who read Beiderbecke's talents at their maximum and his weaknesses at their lowering worst, and did what he could to find a productive way between them. Another was the "friend in college," of whom Bud Freeman made mental note when Beiderbecke said he had not composed the piano piece he admired (page 140).

A focal point in the relationship of Biederbecke and Hoagy Carmichael can be located in May 1924, when the piece, now known as "Riverboat Shuffle," was recorded by the Wolverines, of which Beiderbecke was a member. Like the slightly younger Beiderbecke, Carmichael was also music-struck. Bloomington, Indiana, was his home, and he too left high school to play a bit as a pianist, become acquainted with the Negro musicians he encountered in the Midwest, and learn their lore. He returned to high school in 1919 (at *twenty*), entered Indiana University, and eventually qualified as a lawyer. But his fame has, of course, been related to his songs, and to a particular, single song.

The conversation with Freeman, to which I have made mention, was prompted by the appearance a decade or so ago of a disc devoted entirely to Carmichael's songs. They were performed by a band in which the headmaster of the old school of tenor saxophone players was joined by such other elder statesmen as Bobby Haggart (bass) and Ralph Sutton (piano), together with a younger link in the long chain, Bob Wilber, today's master of Bechet's instrument of old, the soprano saxophone.

In response to a question pertaining to the ways in which Carmichael's songs of the late twenties differed from others being written at the time, Freeman replied: "Hoagy's writing, in contrast with most other writing that was going on at that time, was a composition of true jazz . . . his songs seem to improvise themselves in that they are based on true jazz phrases . . . A very important point is that Hoagy and Bix were very close in those days, spending a lot of time together, and I don't think it would offend Hoagy to say that his writing was very much affected as a result . . ." "As a matter of fact," I added, "in his book[8] he extols Bix in unrestricted terms and pays him every conceivable tribute . . ."

Freeman nodded as he went on: "Now I'll try to give you an example of what I mean. A Hoagy tune differs from almost all others of that time in its structure . . . like the beginning of 'Stardust':

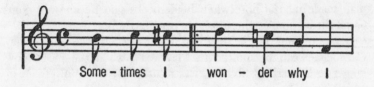

Some – times I won – der why I

spend the lone – ly night

"Dat dat dat, dee dee dee dee dee dee dee dee dee.

"That would be the end of a phrase in an ordinary song, and a very good phrase too . . . But it improvises *itself* with the following

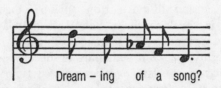

Dream – ing of a song?

[8] Carmichael, Hoagy (in collaboration with Stephen Longstreet), *Sometimes I Wonder* (Farrar, Straus & Giroux, New York).

"La da da da dum . . . Now that was either taken directly from the way the great Frank Trumbauer phrased, or was reproduced from Hoagy's absorption of his style . . . In effect, he put into *permanent* written form a way of playing that had been originated around that time by a handful of great musicians . . ."

A curious linkage, of the kind that constantly crops up in folk art, draws the line of connection even closer. In their researches for *Bix Man and Legend* Sudhalter and Evans interviewed hundreds of musicians who lived long enough to put their recollections at the authors' disposal. One was the man who had been the idol of Freeman's idol—Nick La Rocca, whose playing with the Original Dixieland Jazz Band made a cornetist out of a teenager in Davenport, Iowa.

In 1923, Beiderbecke came briefly to New York, haunted the bandstand where La Rocca was playing, and persisted to the point where La Rocca agreed to hear him play. One of the tunes that came into the audition was by the band's pianist, J. Russell Robinson: "Singin' the Blues" (of which the later version by Beiderbecke and Trumbauer is now in the Phonograph Hall of Fame in Burbank, California): "While I played the melody of 'Singin' the Blues,'" said La Rocca, "he used this countermelody which had parts in it which Mr. Hoagy Carmichael later incorporated into his song 'Stardust.' Now when I say this countermelody was similar I mean this man derived his idea or drew on Bix's ideas as I heard this boy play . . ."[9]

Too bad that Ernest Ansermet was not in the room as Freeman and I were talking. He very possibly might have raised the question: what about the products of Irving Berlin, George Gershwin, and the many others whose songs reflect the Negro influence? Freeman would have had the answer from him as he had the answer for me: "It's simple. Gershwin wrote lovely melodies like 'Summertime' . . . but when a jazz musician plays 'Summertime' he feels a need to *improvise* around it, in order to express something he feels. But a Hoagy tune has the improvisation already in it, and there is no need to add to it . . ."

When Freeman heard his "idol" play something on the piano

[9] Sudhalter and Evans, op. cit., p. 82.

and concluded that it was something *he* had composed, the suggestion is clear that he thought of Beiderbecke as a composer as well as an instrumentalist. That, of course, is a familiar fact: but the results are to be found in those Debussyish piano pieces called "Flashes," "In a Mist," etc., which Beiderbecke had a colossal problem in working out and putting onto paper (finally with the assistance of such a skilled musician as Bill Challis, a Whiteman retainer who made some of that bandmaster's best arrangements).

How much of Beiderbecke there is in "Stardust" may never be resolved. But there certainly is something of him in a song known to as many people as Schubert's "Serenade," and in its own idiom, no less perfect. And, I think, there is also in it something of Mildred Bailey, who mothered Beiderbecke through his last difficult days with Whiteman, in 1930–31, cursed him when he got drunk, and agonized—as did many musicians—when the end, however expected, finally came.

As to the whiteness or the blackness of this kind of jazz, both colors are subordinate to the redness of the blood in them.

As to Trumbauer, Frank, and an instance of penetration surpassing pigmentation, a standard reference work reads: "Frankie Trumbauer was [his] original idol; he attributed his original sound on tenor sax in later years to an attempt to duplicate the quality of Trumbauer's C melody saxophone . . ."[10] The words are written of Lester (Prez) Young, the great tenor man of Count Basie's band, close friend of Billie Holiday, and as Negroid (black?) as a jazz artist can be. Regardless of who plays what, the immemorial test—is it good or bad? are the colors fast when the shrinkage test is applied?—must prevail.

The achievements of Beiderbecke and Bailey, and all of those who were part of what they did, haven't shrunk in the vat of time, nor has the substance of what they had to say shriveled in the wringer of usage. Durable, strongly woven out of talent, conviction, and a true emotional impulse, they carry within themselves the wearability of the best goods.

If, as I have said, the meaning of artist, to me, is someone who

[10] Feather, Leonard, The Encyclopedia of Jazz (Horizon Press, New York, 1960), p. 471.

puts back into music more than he takes out of it, Mildred Bailey and Bix Beiderbecke were stunning examples of artistry in a performer's world.

One could liken them to the great exponents of another treasured folk art, the flamenco dancers of Spain. They, too, perform for money, but not because of money.

Nadia

I

The kind of "expressive substance" that Ansermet discerned in jazz was a fundamental factor in the reshaping of America's popular music in the twenties that enabled Mildred Bailey, Bix Beiderbecke, and a legion of others to discover an identity of their own. And it was Ansermet's enthusiasm for his discovery that prompted his friend Igor Stravinsky to write a piece called *Ragtime* in 1918. This certified such syncopation as proper for use by others who, in the fashion of the time, considered Stravinsky their "leader."

But the breakthrough for American serious music, which was also then the *non*-popular American music, needed more than a single device, or the use of folk tunes, even of Negro spirituals (both of which had been tried), to liberate it from its pedantic past. American serious music found what it needed in Nadia Boulanger, a French woman of high academic qualifications who was, also, non-pedantic.

She was, in effect, an outsider who became an insider, the one who was responsible for enfranchising American music, or, perhaps more accurately, for en-Frenchising American music.

"To enfranchise" means "to set free":[1] "to en-Frenchise" is to suggest how it was done.

The possibility of such a development had there not been a World War I is unlikely; the probability of such a development had the war resulted in a stalemate or a German victory is on the order of impossible. It took a complete dislocation of American

[1] Oxford Concise Dictionary, p. 401.

attachment to European musical priorities (in which German was first, and others followed at a distance) to achieve not only a spiritual but a physical relocation.

The palace at Fontainebleau has become so familiar a part of America's educational apparatus that few of those now there, from year to year, in search of summer training have any idea of how it came about, or when. It was a result, in all illogicality, of a need for the training of American bandsmen in the war. A school, supervised by Walter Damrosch, was established at Chaumont (somewhat north of Paris, and headquarters of what was called the AEF, or American Expeditionary Forces). Its function was so well performed, and the liaison with the French educational system so harmonious, that Damrosch (and a group of American Francophiles) arranged for its postwar perpetuation.

Why the choice of Fontainebleau rather than Chaumont, or some other locality? In all probability, because space was available in its palace, it was reasonably close to Paris, and it had an identity with the arts which was appealing (in a tradition associated with the forest of Fontainebleau, young American painters were later welcomed to the school). And so it exists to the present time.

As the twenties began, Nadia Boulanger was little known to the non-French musical world, least of all to the American musical world. She was, in French musical circles, respected as an organist and a teacher; she was also known as the older sister of Lili Boulanger, a brilliant musician and a composer of high promise, who was the first woman to receive the Prix de Rome, in 1913. The sickness and death of Lili Boulanger in 1918 at the age of twenty-five was a sad loss to French music, and a lifelong sorrow to Nadia and her mother. In the decades that followed, Nadia Boulanger's non-professional life was devoted to filling the place of both children to her widowed mother.

Also, as the twenties began elsewhere, Aaron Copland was known to his classmates at Brooklyn Boys' High School (from which he graduated in June 1918) as a talented pianist and an aspiring composer. He had already pursued the latter ambition, post-high school, to study with Rubin Goldmark, then esteemed as New York's "best" teacher of composition.

Rubin Goldmark was a nephew of the celebrated Karl Goldmark, Austrian-born composer of the attractive "Rustic Wedding" Symphony, of an opera, *Die Königin von Saba*, which had been widely performed in Europe in the 1890s and also at the Metropolitan in New York. Doubtless Rubin Goldmark profited from his kinship to a famous uncle. His pieces (especially one called A *Negro Rhapsody*, utilizing spirituals) were performed from time to time by orchestras in search of "American" repertory, and his reputation as a teacher was considerable even before he became head of the composition faculty at the Juilliard School when it was opened in 1924.

Among those who studied with Goldmark, pre-Juilliard, was George Gershwin. Whether Gershwin and Copland ever compared notes on their studies with Goldmark, I cannot say. But Copland found his teacher's conservatism repressive. After a conflict about a bit of compositional latitude he had ventured in a mildly adventurous piano piece (*The Cat and the Mouse*), he continued to "take lessons from Goldmark" but kept the creative consequences to himself. In maturity, Copland has paid tribute to Goldmark's "excellent grasp of fundamentals."[2] But in immaturity, he had by the summer of 1921 (when he reached twenty-one) begun to look for guidance elsewhere.

"Elsewhere," in 1921, was by common consent and political elimination France. Germany and Austria were off limits, the wounds of war not yet healed. Perhaps Copland knew, in 1920, that such a thing as the American Academy in Rome was in the making. But he hardly had the qualifications to enter a work in a competition whose first winner, in 1921, was the older, more experienced Howard Hanson.

The new venture in Fontainebleau found one prospective student so anxious to be included that his name headed the list of applicants: Aaron Copland. His particular objective was to work

[2] Berger, Arthur, *Aaron Copland* (Oxford University Press, New York, 1953), p. 5.

with Paul Vidal, a prizewinner in various categories at the Paris Conservatoire in the early 1880s, and a recipient of the Prix de Rome in 1883. Upon arrival in Fontainebleau, Copland was disappointed to discover that Vidal was as much an academician as Goldmark: different language, different training, but much the same point of view. The prospect of spending a whole year in Paris under such auspices was hardly inviting. Even the suggestion of a fellow student that he look into a session or two with a teacher of his (a lady) was anything but tempting.

Nadia Boulanger's subject that summer was harmony, of which Copland was quite sure he had had quite enough. Too, she was a woman, and who had ever heard of a woman qualified to teach composition? No woman had ever attained distinction as a composer by 1921 (the record is hardly changed fifty years later), and how could a woman who was not a composer help a man learn how to compose?

Fortunately, the friend's urging prevailed. The subject of the session on which Copland sat in was Moussorgsky's *Boris Godunoff*. The off chance could hardly have been more on target. The lady teacher's insights were astonishing, the discourse so absorbing—no doubt with Moussorgsky's cross-connections to Debussy, on which she lectured admirably elsewhere[3]—that Copland's doubts melted away. He came away with the belief that maybe he had "found his teacher."[4]

When the summer session was finished, Copland arranged to continue his studies with her, privately, in the fall, at her home and studio, 36 rue Ballu.

The first of many Americans to follow Copland came by his association with Boulanger more directly. At Harvard, Virgil Thomson had attended classes with two rare exceptions to the general rule of German-trained professors of music at American universities. One was Archibald Davison, the other was Edward Burlingame Hill. Thomson had an interest, collateral to composing, that catered to a French affinity—he was planning to pursue a career as an organist. This qualified him for the special consideration of

[3] Boulanger, Nadia, *Lectures on Modern Music* (Rice Institute, 1928).
[4] Berger, op. cit., p. 7.

Professor Hill, who was—as one source has said—"born into the Harvard tradition, being the son of a professor and a grandson of a president."[5] He was also a pupil of organist Charles-Marie Widor, who had succeeded César Franck as professor of organ at the Paris Conservatoire.

Even though short of graduation, Thomson had risen to academic prominence as conductor of the Harvard Glee Club, with which he made a tour of France and down into Italy at the end of the spring term of 1921. The tour terminated in Genoa, but not Thomson's determination to stay on. A traveling scholarship in the name of John Knowles Paine (first professor of music at Harvard) was available.

Though granting such a traveling scholarship to an undergraduate was, in Thomson's words, "not customary," fortune favored him: his "good friend Hill was chairman that year, and Davison was [also] warmly disposed."[6] On the proviso that he pledge to return to Harvard in fall 1922, and qualify for his degree, the grant was made. This gave Thomson access to Paris on rather better terms than Copland, who had in large part earned his own way by part-time work in New York, while studying with Goldmark.

Thomson's on-site adviser in Paris was Melville Smith (a Harvard graduate whom he succeeded as holder of the John Knowles Paine scholarship). Smith had found his way to Boulanger and commended her warmly to Thomson. Thus the way, for him, to 36 rue Ballu was open and waiting. On Thomson's side, the academic attractions of Boulanger were twofold—she taught organ at the Ecole Normale de Musique, a course in which Thomson enrolled, and he also became a private pupil of hers in strict counterpoint.

The fortunes of war—French and German—that brought Copland and Thomson to Paris only months apart to study with the same teacher are the kinds of which history is made. They were, to be sure, men of talent: but the diversity of their talents and the

[5] Grove's Dictionary of Music and Musicians, Fourth Edition, American Supplement, 1939.
[6] Thomson, Virgil, *Virgil Thomson* (Alfred A. Knopf, Inc., New York, 1966), p. 51.

versatility of the efforts Boulanger brought to bear upon them greatly widened the range of other Americans who responded to her influence. Moreover, what Copland possessed in one respect, and Thomson in another, enabled them to absorb something more than music in Paris.

Both were acute observers, and alert to the ways in which the arts prosper in a society in which artists make them prosper. This was an indoctrination, for life, in the skills for organization and proselytization which attract as much attention to artists of quality as art does.

The full effect of such observation was not to come all at once. But from the outset, the talents of one were marvelously complementary to the gifts of the other.

When, after a while, Copland was settled in New York, securing his reputation as a composer, Thomson's career revolved more and more around Paris. Here he acquired, from close study of the system in action, the techniques and procedures of self-promotion that were, eventually, to serve him, and his friends, so well at home. Would they have fared as well, in either respect, in Germany?

II

At this distance, the coincidence that brought together two young men of talent—from backgrounds as diverse as Kansas City, Missouri, and Brooklyn, New York—in the Paris studio of a teacher to become lifelong colleagues has the echo of bygone fiction. But like the collateral meeting of Armstrong and Beiderbecke on a dock in Davenport, Iowa, it was the history that followed which gave birth to the fiction derived from it.

The history of American music represented by Copland and Thomson may be given a sounding counterpoint in the part of it related to the career of Howard Hanson (page 155). He, too, was in Europe, enjoying the advantages of the American Academy of Rome, as the first winner of the Prix de Rome. What he took with him for the three-year period of foreign residence it provided was derived from birth in Wahoo, Nebraska (1896), and education at the Institute of Musical Art in New York City, from which he graduated in 1916.

At the Institute, he studied with Percy Goetschius, a gentleman well known to me. I never studied directly with Goetschius, but it may be said that I studied indirectly *under* him, learning harmony from his much-used treatises (in print from 1912 to 1942). Though born in Paterson, New Jersey (1853), Goetschius entered the Stuttgart Conservatory at the age of twenty, and applied himself so well that, only three years later, he became an instructor there in the inclusive subject called "theory." Such was the subject on which he became a lifelong expert. Indeed, his gifts were so well appreciated in Stuttgart that he became a Royal Professor at the Conservatory in 1885. After five years, he returned to America, to pursue a teaching career through nearly half the century that followed.

The precepts that Goetschius organized into canons of faith—the science of harmony is, essentially, derived from what Bach, Beethoven, Mendelssohn, Brahms, etc. made the essence of their *practice*—served as guidelines for others so long as the mainstream of music stayed within well-charted channels. When the reckless French and the improper Germans (Strauss, Mahler, etc.) let themselves follow wherever their fancy led, Goetschius had recourse to such classifications as "wandering harmonies" and "irregular neighboring notes" to explain what was, in his system, inexplicable. Such composers as Stravinsky and Schoenberg were scarcely recognized.

As might be derived from the statistics, Goetschius was a brilliant young man. So, too, was Hanson. When he returned to America, in 1923, he brought with him a "symbolic poem" titled *North and West* for chorus and orchestra, which Walter Damrosch encouraged him to conduct with his New York Symphony. The totality of achievement and promise the young man had to his credit prompted George Eastman, at the urging of the much admired Albert Coates (then serving as conductor of the Rochester Philharmonic Orchestra in its first flush of youth), to offer the directorship of the new school bearing his name to Hanson. The latter accepted, and from 1924 until he retired forty years later, he was the man who ran the power plant in one of the three generating forces of musical education in America. The others, in sequence of appearance, were the Curtis Institute of Music in Philadelphia (1924) and the Juilliard School in New York (1925).

As a composer-conductor-educator, Hanson rendered particularly useful service to the compositional community by offering Americans much prized opportunities to hear their works performed in Rochester. Nor was this an empty, costly honor. The invitations were accompanied by payment of expenses. "From the beginning," it is said in an authoritative source, "he has insisted on the right of the serious and responsible composer to hear his music—at least once."[7] Those favored by repeated invitations tended to be in the vein of Hanson's own compositional preferences, described as relating "to both American and Scandinavian traditions, the American influences being those of MacDowell and his contemporaries."[8] This puts the status of Hanson neatly into perspective, affiliating him with the composers acceptable to the academic procedures of the past (while Charles Ives was selling insurance and writing "unperformable" music).

Of them all, Edward MacDowell (1861–1908) made the grandest of gestures to write music that would be widely esteemed on its merits, not merely because it was "American." A greatly gifted pianist as well as composer, the New York-born MacDowell went abroad at the age of fifteen (1876) and really did not return home to live and work until he was approaching thirty. He spent two years in Paris, at the Conservatoire, before settling into German musical thought and German ways of making music at the Conservatory of Frankfurt (1879).

Here MacDowell became something of a living wonder, a composer from America whose work earned the encouragement of Franz Liszt! This occurred in 1882, at the intercession of Joachim

[7] Riker, Charles, *The Eastman School of Music. Its First Quarter Century 1921–1946* (The University of Rochester, Rochester, New York, 1948), p. 40.

[8] Grove's Dictionary of Music and Musicians, Fifth Edition, Vol. IV, p. 67.

Raff, who was director of the Frankfurt Conservatory, MacDowell's teacher of composition, *and* a friend of Liszt. Such recognition naturally endeared MacDowell to his surroundings, and when his work with Raff ended, he settled in Wiesbaden.

Save for a brief visit to America in 1884, during which he married Marian Nevins, who became the famous "Mrs. MacDowell" of the artists' colony established in her husband's name in Peterborough, New Hampshire (in 1910), MacDowell lived in Germany from 1878 to 1888. When he closed out a long absence from America, he chose Boston for a home. He came back to the city of his birth in 1896, when Columbia University established a music department and invited MacDowell to be its head. However, academic constrictions were not to his liking, and he resigned in 1904. A state of depression and mental debility affected MacDowell until he died in 1908.

Two incidents of importance should be added to this brief summary of the life of a man of unquestionable musical greatness. It has been mentioned that he wanted to be considered a composer, unqualified by place of birth. In February of 1904, he forbade the inclusion of any work of his on a program announced for performance in the Metropolitan Opera House as "all American." He protested such exclusivity as not being in the interest of the American composer: "Unless we are worthy of being put on programs with other composers to stand or fall, leave us alone."[9] The program, conducted by Felix Mottl, proceeded without any work by MacDowell.

In a retrospective look at his career rarely to be found in summaries of his ideas and attitudes, MacDowell once commented on the long period of time he had spent away from the United States. During a composition class at Columbia around the turn of the century, a student later reported, MacDowell remarked to his young class that what they "whistled, sang, or played in moments of relaxation more often than not was ragtime. Well, if syncopated rhythms were natural to us, why not try to make of

---

[9] Shanet, Howard, *Philharmonic. A History of New York's Orchestra* (Doubleday & Company, Inc., Garden City, N.Y., 1975), p. 443.

them something important? 'I would do it myself,' MacDowell is quoted as saying, 'if I had not lived so long in Europe.' "[10] The student, whose commitment to literature took precedence over his interest in music, was John Erskine, who achieved positions of prominence in both worlds. He was professor of English at Columbia from 1909 until (after winning a reputation as a novelist with his *The Private Life of Helen of Troy*) he accepted the presidency of the Juilliard School in 1928.

III

Provocative as the idea of MacDowell's comment on the period of time he spent away from the United States may be, it also contains one other revealing attitude: it was altogether natural for him, as a musician, to equate Germany with "Europe." Of the many others of American birth who might be described as his contemporaries if not his peers, almost all would very likely have said as much, in similar terms. Among the few exceptions were such Harvardians as Hill and Davison, already mentioned, and in a direct line of descent, Daniel Gregory Mason, a native of Brookline, Massachusetts, where he was born in 1873.

To be a Mason in nineteenth-century New England was to be a musician, and so to make a common name part of an uncommon profession. Lowell Mason, his grandfather, was one of the first musicians of American birth to make a name for himself in Europe; William Mason, an accomplished pianist and sponsor of Brahms in America, was a member of the same family; and the father of Daniel Gregory was the Mason of Mason & Hamlin. Their pianos, manufactured in Boston in small quantities and with great care, were the elite of all American-made instruments. Their fame persisted until they became a part of a conglomerate known as Ampico, for American Piano Corporation. (Others included Chickering and Knabe, of which only the latter endures prominently to the present.)

[10] Erskine, John, *The Memory of Certain Persons* (J. B. Lippincott Company, Philadelphia, New York, 1947), p. 77.

Daniel Gregory Mason was a Harvardian whose studies, in and out of schools, were with Goetschius and George Chadwick, director of the New England Conservatory of Music. Having sampled the best that America could provide, Mason went to Paris in 1900. Here he sought out Vincent d'Indy, composer of *Symphony on a French Mountain Air* and author of a well-known commentary on the music of Beethoven. The verdict today would be that the input Mason received was more distinguished than the creative output that resulted. Mason composed busily during his thirty years as a prominent member of the musical faculty at Columbia University (1910–40). His works were frequently performed and politely praised, but with no lasting consequences. He is better remembered today as a lecturer-educator on the music of the nineteenth-century giants to whose music he was attached (Beethoven, Schubert, Schumann, Mendelssohn, Brahms) than as a composer.

In something of an in-between category was John Alden Carpenter, born in 1876, also a Harvardian (where he studied with Paine), who divided music with participation in his father's prosperous Chicago business. Intermittently he took time out for studies with Elgar (in Rome, 1906) or with Bernhard Ziehn in Chicago (1908–12). His talent was engaging rather than arresting: he deviated from the pomposity or pretentiousness of some other American composers of the early years of the century to deal with such subjects as childhood in *Adventures in a Perambulator* (1915), the comic strip in *Krazy Kat* (1921), and urbanology in *Skyscrapers* (1926). Though there was nothing overtly French in his education, the lines of thought, rather than the outcomes they produced, have a Gallic *esprit*. He became a Knight of the French Légion d'honneur (1921).

These instances aside, the list (illustrative rather than inclusive) that follows defines a period when Europe and Germany, as equated by MacDowell, were musicologically synonymous. Choice varied as to locale, but a consensus prevailed. The George Chadwick mentioned above as director of the New England Conservatory of Music and teacher of Daniel Gregory Mason might have discoursed eloquently on the Leipzig Conservatory of Music just before it was discovered by Maurice Guest (see pages 46 ff.). He studied there between 1877 and 1878, and then spent a year in Munich before returning to Boston. His compositions were frequently favored by the conductors of the Boston Symphony Orchestra, and he achieved many educational good deeds as director of the New England Conservatory from 1897 to 1930.

The highly regarded, if infrequently performed Roger Sessions had what might be called a maternal predisposition toward a musical education elsewhere than with Boulanger in Paris. His mother, born Ruth Huntington, studied piano at the Leipzig "Con" of the 1880s. When he left Harvard, where he worked under Davison, with a B.A. at nineteen (1915), he spent some time with Parker at New Haven, Connecticut, and then with Ernest Bloch in Cleveland, Ohio. Between 1926 and 1933 Sessions lived primarily in Europe, enjoying the hospitality of Bernard Berenson's villa in Florence (on Guggenheim scholarships) and also the vista of Rome from the American Academy during his Prix de Rome years (1928–31). Concurrently he joined in the sponsorship of the New York series (1928–31) called the Copland-Sessions concerts, in which much new music was performed. As a teacher in institutions ranging coast to coast, and now concentrated at the Juilliard in New York, Sessions' pupils have included such composers as David Diamond, Paul Bowles, Leon Kirchner, Milton Babbitt, and Hugo Weisgall.

For a change of place, if not necessarily of pace, the career of the singularly talented Charles T. (for Tomlinson) Griffes might be recalled. A composer cherished for such works of imagery and expressiveness as "The White Peacock" and "The Fountain of Acqua Paolo" (two segments of his *Roman Sketches*), Griffes's catalogue includes *The Pleasure Dome of Kubla Khan* (a conversion into orchestral terms of Samuel Coleridge's Kubla Khan) and settings, in one form or another, of texts by Oscar Wilde, Rupert Brooke, Fiona Macleod, Walt Whitman, William Blake, and John Addington Symonds. Not much evidence of Germanic influence there. But this all happened *after* his return from studies in Berlin with Engelbert Humperdinck (1903–07).

The metamorphosis in Griffes's career can be credited to Eva

Gauthier, a Canadian-born, French-educated soprano, who encountered him after he had settled (1907) into his lifelong occupation, teaching at the Hackley School for Boys in Tarrytown, New York. A fine recitalist (she was born in Ottawa in 1885, and died in New York in 1958) and possessed of a decided flair for the unusual—Gauthier was the soprano who persuaded George Gershwin to accompany her in a Town Hall recital that included his "Do It Again" in 1923—Gauthier saw in Griffes something musically uncommon. It was, alas, aborted by his death at the age of thirty-six in 1920.

The formidable fact is that between 1870 and 1920, the biography of almost any American composer of note (let alone distinction) includes a period of study in either Germany or Austria. Do you remember the name of Henry Hadley, for many years an associate conductor of the New York Philharmonic, by which his works were regularly, if not repeatedly, performed? His road to immortality was by way of Munich. Horatio Parker, whose *Mona* was produced at the Metropolitan in 1912, was a product of Rheinberger in Munich, where he spent the years from 1882 to 1885. He became chairman of the music department at Yale University in 1894. During the twenty-five years of association with it that ended with his death in 1919, he conveyed a high sense of scholarship and purpose to many students who came his way, including (1894–98) Charles Ives.

One could discern, in some degree, the charms of Dresden and its porcelain in such long-lasting works of Ethelbert Nevin as *Narcissus*, *The Rosary*, and *Mighty Lak' a Rose*. He lived there in 1877 and 1878. For that matter, Rubin Goldmark, "mentor" of Copland and Gershwin, did not *bring* a background of European scholarship and training in a quest for a home in the New World. He was born in New York (1872) and studied at the Vienna Conservatory from 1889 to 1891.

What impelled the Americans who came to musical maturity in America during the decades identified above was more than a preference based on locale or language. It was part of a conviction in the English-speaking world that the best music was German, hence the best training for being the best kind of musician was to be found where German was spoken, verbally as well as musically. As an instance, it was a hard blow for Edward Elgar to learn, in his twenties, that his father could not afford to underwrite the years in Leipzig that young English musicians of the 1880s and 1890s felt were essential for "professional" status. Without the nature of the thinking to which others—Americans as well as English—were exposed, the kind of training which was, for the most part, imposed, and the consequences, in purpose, to which they were disposed, Elgar remained much more "English" than he might have been otherwise.

By comparison, the Russians of the Five (Moussorgsky, Rimsky-Korsakov, Cui, Borodin, and Balakirev) in much the same time period—1860, 1870, 1880—were exposed to comparable forms of indoctrination, and rejected them. The indoctrination came to them not by contacts with pedagogy, but with the music itself. In their thoroughgoing, painstaking way they made a social pastime as well as an intellectual exercise of the symphonic literature of Beethoven, Schubert, Schumann, Mendelssohn, and others by means of four-hand piano versions, which they shared in performance.

On one occasion, Moussorgsky reacted to his first contact with the E flat symphony of Schumann (No. 3, "Rhenish") by exclamations of pleasure and delight with the thematic ideas as they accumulated. "But now," he said in a disapproving manner, "comes the mathematics"—an apt term for the "working out" of the themes, the breaking of them into bits or inversion of one part against another, in the hands of a composer such as Schumann who lacked the forceful manner of a Beethoven but felt obliged to work at it nevertheless.

Tchaikovsky, who tried with all conviction to apply himself to such problems in his six symphonies, nevertheless—honest man that he was—worried that "his seams showed." In other words, that the transitions, contrasts, and interconnections to make the texture smooth were roughly formed and ineptly stitched. And the Five, honest men that *they* were, rejected Tchaikovsky as being "too Western" in his emphasis on such practices.

Questions of "mathematics" or annoyance with "seams" were not worrisome to most of the Americans of the nineteenth and early twentieth centuries who went to Germany or Austria to "learn how to compose." Their prime objective was to write a performable symphony, concerto, or something else in what was called a "large form." To have it praised in the press as "well written" or, perhaps, "skillfully orchestrated" was the kind of recognition that meant much. Few ever conquered the distinction, and difference, that Rimsky-Korsakov brought to bear when someone praised his *Scheherazade* for its "orchestration." "No," he said in effect, "it is not a work that is well 'orchestrated': . . . it is a skillful composition for orchestra" (meaning that the orchestral detail was inherent in the compositional scheme, rather than being added afterward to something that had *not* been "orchestrally conceived"). American composers of this period continued, largely speaking, to "orchestrate" pieces composed at the piano rather than writing compositions for orchestra.

For them, too, matters of temperament, of impulse, of design, concept, and character that made a symphonic structure the only outlet for the ideas they had in mind were largely lacking. They had their performance—and rarely more than one—collected their credit for having the piece described as "well written," and looked elsewhere for the market in which this credit could be spent. If all went well, they might earn positions in a conservatory or university school of music, to "teach" others what they had not really mastered themselves—how to express themselves musically (see page 54).

IV

The change in objective from one side of the Rhine to the other, in circumstances which related less to judgment than to lack of an option, cannot be regarded as a triumph for wisdom and reason. Paris is, in any circumstances, a seductive place to be: studying there has many reasons for being preferable to Berlin,

Munich, or Stuttgart, with or without regard for what is being learned, academically.

Even without the geographical factor, French thought, French taste, French preference for enterprise rather than conformity have mighty values to commend them. The Russian Five, for example, derived from the two visits of Hector Berlioz—one in 1847, the other not quite twenty years later—the breath of air, the spirit of liberation, the embodiment of artistic freedom they found infinitely more compatible than Germanic restraint. The results were historical.

All these abstractions, philosophic and ethnic, were confirmed and verified in the person of Nadia Boulanger—plus the stimulation and liberation to be found in Paris itself. Not one, but two generations of American musicians put their future in her hands, and found it safe, guarded, and nurtured into growth. But there had to be a first time, a first year, a first *one* to open the way for what followed.

What commended her to Copland was, as he has said, "such enthusiasm and such clarity" as he had never found in a teacher before. That he puts "enthusiasm" in a place of priority is as true an expression of the speaker as it is about the person of whom he was speaking. Copland has been an enthusiast all his public life, with a range of response that speaks for itself. What was there to be kindled, at twenty-odd, did not lack for a response that has been lifelong.

Boulanger has never spoken at length about what she perceived in Copland: she put into action one expressive commitment of belief that outweighs words or encomiums. In 1924, Walter Damrosch, whose part in the creation of the Fontainebleau venture has been mentioned, invited Boulanger to make an appearance as a soloist with his New York Symphony Orchestra in an Aeolian Hall concert. She decided that the occasion would be embellished by a new work for her to perform as soloist, and asked her first American student to write it for her.

The ivory tower to which Copland retired to create the new work was a summer resort in Milford, Pennsylvania, where he was earning a few months' respite from city life by playing in a trio. The work, which eventually became an addition to a literature best known for a work in C minor by Camille Saint-Saëns, was given the title of *Symphony for Organ and Orchestra*.[11]

The material chosen by Boulanger for her introduction to America foreshadowed the kinds of programs she preferred on visits to follow: a work of the eighteenth century (in this instance, Handel's D minor organ concerto), something representative of her sister (this time *Pour les funerailles d'un soldat*), and something more contemporary in which she was the soloist.

The program and its aftermath might have passed as a generous endorsement by Boulanger of her faith in a talented pupil had not Damrosch, who had something of a reputation as a talking conductor, made it historical by saying to the audience which had just heard the novelty: "If a young man at the age of twenty-three can write a symphony like that, in five years he will be ready to commit murder."[12] In later years, when Copland had won his place of prominence in American music, Damrosch explained that the words came out differently than he had intended. But there they were, and there they are . . . a red badge of identity by which Copland was to be characterized for years to come.

In any case the implications were not sustained in the opinions in the next day's press. One penetrating comment was under the name of W. J. Henderson (*see* "The Man Who Rebuked Heifetz," pages 69 ff.). His first words to the reader were of a work "singularly interesting and astonishingly uneven," a form of characterization *and* penetration at which the writer was plurally adept. The first movement (an andante) he commended for "a well defined mood" of which some segments were "captivating." Taken together, the movement was "skillfully sustained throughout." The scherzo and finale appealed less to the critic, but he saw

---

[11] His first extended composition while working with Boulanger was a ballet, *Grohg*. Later in the twenties he recast it into the score that became the (unnumbered) *Dance Symphony*. See page 179 in re the Victor Talking Machine Company competition.

[12] Berger, op. cit., p. 12.

in Copland "a real talent," who, given the valuable benefits of growing older, "may produce something of lasting importance." In totality he described the symphony as "bold and vigorous and sometimes it is almost beautiful."[13]

Boulanger's belief in Copland was further demonstrated when she appeared in Boston on February 20, with Koussevitzky conducting. The immediate effect was to introduce the symphony and its young composer to an audience both discriminating and responsive; of longer consequence was the introduction of Koussevitzky to a composer for whom he had an immediate affection and an everlasting enthusiasm.

Neither man was quite aware of the importance of the event. Still in the first of the twenty-five seasons he would spend in Boston, Koussevitzky had been given an unequivocal answer to a question he had posed on arrival aboard ship in the port of New York a few months before: "Who are the new American composers?" In Copland there was not only, instantly, such a one; he was a young composer with a particular, unexpected adjunct. He was so instinctive a protagonist for other composers in whom he believed that as soon as he found one, the way to Koussevitzky was open.

Taken together, the weeks of January–February 1925 were not merely enormously fruitful ones for Copland; they were a harvest of success, and promise, for Boulanger. They were also a turning point in the history of music by Americans, and for Americans. Down the road was a conjunction of Copland as creator, Koussevitzky as re-creator, and Boulanger as an instigator of unmeasurable consequences to follow.

Behind this, in a curious way, was Walter Damrosch, whose invitation for Boulanger to visit America set the whole improbable sequence in motion. Well before any of it came about, he was well acquainted with Boulanger and her accomplishments. Recounting his experiences in France during the beginnings in Chaumont that led to the consequences in Fontainebleau, he wrote (in a book published even before her first American concert): "Among women I have never seen her equal in musicianship and,

[13] New York *Sun*, January 12, 1925.

indeed, there are very few men who can compare with her . . .
She is one of the finest organists of France [in 1918 Boulanger
had shared the stage with Damrosch as conductor and herself as
soloist in a Paris performance of the Saint-Saëns C minor symphony, in the presence of the composer], an excellent pianist, and
the best reader of orchestral scores that I have ever known."[14]

In these words of decades ago, a highly qualified observer put
into print what could hardly be said more prophetically of the
qualifications that Boulanger brought to her career-to-come as a
teacher. In an additional citation Damrosch observed: "I have
seen her take up a manuscript orchestral score, sit down at the
piano and brilliantly read it at sight, transcribing it for the piano
as she played along . . ." What an attribute for a teacher of composition!

But as her career unfolded, year by year, it brought to light
more than qualifications and aptitudes. From the basic two of
Copland and Thomson (who told Boulanger, after hearing the
Copland symphony, he had "wept," and when she asked why, had
responded "because I had not written it myself"[15]) accrued a sequence of successors as remarkable as it was varied. To each of
them she imparted not only a means of expression, but a means of
self-expression.

One of the first was Roy Harris. Born in Lincoln County, Okla-
homa (prophetically, on February 12, 1898, which gave him lifelong access to a "rail-splitter personality"), Harris was educated in
California. He came to New York in 1926 and, through private
patronage, was provided with means to go to Paris for a year's
study with Boulanger. He stayed four.

Totally opposite in background and character was Walter Piston, who originated in Rockland, Maine (out of a family background whose name, Pistone, proclaims an Italian origin). He was
tempted to a career as a painter as well as a musician and did not
graduate from Harvard with a degree in music—*summa cum laude*

[14] Damrosch, Walter, *My Musical Life* (Charles Scribner's, New York,
1923), p. 238.
[15] Thomson, op. cit., p. 71.

—until he was thirty (1924). His time with Boulanger covered 1924–26.

In a panorama of names which mark the coming of age for American music between 1920 and 1940, the name of Boulanger recurs with the frequency of "Nevermore" in Poe's *The Raven*. A selective survey would include Douglas Moore (*The Ballad of Baby Doe, The Devil and Daniel Webster, The Wings of the Dove*), David Diamond, Robert Russell Bennett (who added, as arranger, jewels to the crowns of musicals from Jerome Kern's *Show Boat* to Frederick Loewe's *My Fair Lady* and dozens in between), Alexei Haieff, Gail Kubik, Louise Talma, Marc Blitzstein, Ross Lee Finney, and Elliott Carter (two of importance who did not come her way were Samuel Barber and William Schuman). And as an instance of the forming "second generation," there was Leonard Bernstein, who found his channel to Boulanger through Walter Piston at Harvard, as did Harold Shapero, symphonist and head of the music department at Brandeis University.

The outstanding distinction of these names, together with those of Copland, Thomson, Harris, and Piston, prompts a quest for a common denominator, a linking likeness, a Boulanger thumbprint. As with any good workman's product, thumbprints are carefully erased from Boulanger's work. But in addition to the overpowering individuality that emerges (already discernible in the unlikeness of Copland, Thomson, Harris, and Piston), there *is* a quality in common—quality itself.

They are, almost without exception, composers whose musical manners are never crude or unrefined, save when invoked by creative needs, and then, most likely, crude and unrefined in a highly refined way. In every case, the palette belongs to the individual— as early as Thomson's *Symphony on a Hymn Tune*, Copland's *Music for the Theater*—rather than the one who was, for a time, a mentor.

Least of all is there any evidence of a Boulanger who was a composer (second Prix de Rome, 1908) before she discovered she did not measure up to her own standards for creativity. Asked why she ruled herself out, she said: "My music was less than bad. It was useless."

V

But what she lacked as a creator of her own music she evolved into a creative force in the music of others. Her procedures as an educator were almost as remarkable as the results themselves. Her home at 36 rue Ballu was, year after year after year, the scene of many hourly sessions, across days, weeks, months. Boulanger was tyrannical in only one respect. Promptness was mandatory. A new-comer might be granted one misdemeanor to learn the rules. He or she was not indulged another time. Once each week, after a group class (traditionally on Wednesday), Boulanger was hostess to a tea. Unwarned, the group might discover among those present as many of their musical idols, revered masters, or perhaps favored peers as were in Paris on that day.

On one occasion, Thomson met Erik Satie, an idol of such dimensions that he had never given thought to such a possibility. On another, the very young Aaron Copland met the very old Camille Saint-Saëns. It must have been in October 1921, because Copland has said that the patriarch—aged eighty-six—died two months later (history says the date of Saint-Saëns's death was December 16, 1921).

Here the subject was, inevitably, music in all its forms, manifestations, and permutations. This related not merely to opinions and disagreements, but to performances of the very new, the moderately old, and the totally forgotten. On one occasion, it was *Wozzeck*, when Berg's work was first being heard in 1925. On another, it was a manifestation of Boulanger's passion for Monteverdi. When *Lasciatemi morire* and *Ballo delle ingrate* appeared on a 78-rpm recording in the thirties, his name as a composer was barely better known to a wide public than hers. The purpose, clearly, was to make her pupils at home in an atmosphere where music was not thought of in terms of styles or trends, but as an ongoing art, not exclusive but broadly inclusive, never ending in its unexpected infinity of affinities among vibrations.

If there was one aspect of the whole vast subject to which

Boulanger was more devoted than to any other, it was technique. She was, indeed, known to have said: "Music is technique" (an expression, in another form, of Rudolf Serkin's aphorism: "What difference does it make how much eloquence you feel in the slow movement of Beethoven's G major concerto if you don't have a good trill?"). Clearly, the composer must have the technique to set forth what is in his mind before the interpreter can be called upon to interpret it.

Boulanger's identity as a teacher is so long established that the most basic of facts about it is rarely mentioned: how did it begin? In 1904, in her mid-teens, Nadia Boulanger was assigned by her parents, both musicians, both teachers, to supervise the education of her sister, Lili, aged eleven. Thus she was devoted to the same form of intellectual discipline for most of the century.

Technique, in the Boulanger sense, had little relation to a pianist's finger facility, or the footwork to perform an organ work by Bach or Franck, Widor or Vierne (although Damrosch's encomiums leave little doubt that she was well versed in both). Her technique pertained to the kind that went into strict counterpoint, or was required to combine musical parts in a rank and file in which the inelegant double bass moved with as much agility as the flighty flute or the flexible clarinet. The by-product of such technique is, for the composer, the kind of mind-peace about details that comes to a writer of prose who has a fair assurance about how a sentence, once begun, is going to end.

Boulanger had a lifelong devotion to Stravinsky and his works, a very prime reason being the kind of technique he had learned, in the usual way (hard work), to leave no doubt of exactly what he meant in every measure he wrote. Vis-à-vis such a question as "trends" vs. "vogues" she would reply: "Trends are always interesting, but the result depends on who is handling the tools." In other words, music is in the man, not in the method. Many questions in compositional practice could be answered by reference to Stravinsky. They had an affinity not merely in musical tastes and preferences, but in blood lines: he was Catholic and Russian, she was Catholic and half Russian. The mother to whom she had so long an attachment had been Princess Mychetsky before she met

Ernest Boulanger. Both taught at the Conservatoire, as had his father.

After decades of association with young people, she told an interviewer: "They change very little. There are serious people and there are frivolous people. What would trouble me is if the young people lost their enthusiasm, their concentration, their power of choice and selection." She observed, from the study of her cat, the innate quality of selection in animals. When it wasn't hungry, it didn't eat. Humans are not always that selective. "Each period is different," she insisted. "But there is no progress in Beauty. Beauty is Beauty, where or when it occurs."

During her visit to New York in 1924, her performance with the New York Symphony was followed by an evening in which she gave a discourse on the then contemporary scene. A piano was readily available for demonstration as she talked about the extension of harmonic resources, the inclusion into the everyday vocabulary of music, of devices previously considered exceptions from order, or even causes of disorder.

She sensed some discontent in the audience (mostly amateurs) because they were looking for the latest, the newest, the extremest in experimentation as it then existed. Her calm response was: "We must not judge art by the last six months." Years later, in another kind of discussion, she invoked the same line of reasoning to say: "Like most rare and precious things, the exquisite quality of a work is not to be discerned all at once. It must be discovered."

Among those who knew Boulanger as a student, retained an acute impression of his experience of it, and recalled it to mind when he attained a world respect for mastership was Elliott Carter. The recollections are not "written" in a customary sense, but conveyed verbally, at some length and in detail.[16]

As previously noted, Carter came to her early in the thirties, after graduating from Harvard, where his instructors included Walter Piston, and so he was, to some extent, indoctrinated in what to expect. But apparently not to the extent (Copland-like)

[16] Edwards, Allen, *Flawed Words and Stubborn Sounds. A Conversation with Elliott Carter* (W. W. Norton & Company, Inc., New York, 1971), pp. 50, 51, 56.

of being prepared to study harmony. "I must say," he tells Edwards, "that though I had taken harmony and counterpoint at Harvard and thought I knew all about these subjects, nevertheless, when Nadia Boulanger put me back on tonic and dominant chords in half notes, I found to my surprise that I learned all kinds of things I'd never thought of before."

Among those "things" were voice leading in Bach chorales, and how the seemingly "inevitable" details were arrived at by highly sophisticated *election* of one note in a chord rather than another. What value did this have to the "student composer," as Carter was at the time? "It brought me a full consciousness of the importance of the very smallest details of a musical work and of the way that these can influence the expressive character of the whole." The Boulanger who said "Music is technique" was also saying, in a way that Carter comprehended, that "technique" and "aesthetics" are not merely interrelated, but inseparable.

She unlocked many secrets of contemporary works, says Carter, then twenty-four and avid of education (1932). He and the other members of the group at that time had to all but memorize Stravinsky's *Symphony of Psalms* (first performed in 1930), along with learning Bach cantatas to sing at a Wednesday tea. None of this was conveyed in a sharply defined separation of pedagogue and pupils, but with a personalized process of *discovery*, as though some startling insight was as new to her as it was to them. If—as demonstrated by Carter and Diamond at the Juilliard; Moore at Columbia; and most conspicuous of all, Piston at Harvard— Boulanger pupils became outstanding teachers as well as composers, it could be because they had subtly been learning principles of pedagogy as they were learning principles of composition.

In her own way, Boulanger repeatedly gave insights into her practices when she was interviewed—provided the interviewer knew the right questions to ask. One of the most revealing of recent date was an exchange with Vivian Perlis.[17] Her view of herself is contained in such statements as:

"The teacher is but the humus in the soil. It is the product that counts . . .

[17] New York *Times*, September 11, 1977.

"As a teacher, my whole life is based on understanding the other, not on making them understand me. What the student thinks—what he wants to do—I must try to make him express himself and prepare him to do that for which he is best fitted . . ."

VI

Could a Boulanger have flourished elsewhere than in Paris? The question can be raised to be refuted, but not to be ruled out. She was, after all, half Russian. She enjoyed the status of Maître de Chapelle to the principality of Monaco, where, in 1967, an invited audience of friends numerous enough to fill the opera house of Monte Carlo participated in an eightieth birthday in her honor. Doubtless facilities could have been provided to welcome her students there. Indeed they might have been taught, physically, as they were in Paris (minus, of course, the Wednesday afternoon teas). Spiritually, however, the result could in no way have been comparable to what they learned in Paris.

Even for the earliest of them, consequently the oldest in the long sequence, awareness of the difference between what they were taught and what they had learned took some time to be absorbed and utilized. This is comparable to visiting a friend's home, observing the way he lives and makes his way, taking it all in, admiring it, and then failing to absorb, or emulate, anything from the experience, until "later."

The variety of possibilities, the diversity of responses to such a French experience is readily at hand, whether in the portable form provided by Hector Berlioz, or the home form embodied in Nadia Boulanger. One might cite differences of degrees of talent, and immediate responses in purpose, to the effects of Berlioz on the Russians. One immediate consideration that also comes to mind is that in Mikhail Glinka, the Russians had a forebear who made all who followed—whether the Five or Tchaikovsky—keenly conscious of a folk heritage that was their common vocabulary. The Americans had no such prototype. Their folk heritage, into the thirties, had so many dialectical differences that there was perhaps more embarrassment about using any one of them than an awareness of communal riches.

Generically speaking, however, the generations of American composers trained in Germany had been conditioned to believe that they had been given the means of becoming composers of consequence, providing they used them properly. The newer generation of French-trained Americans was given no such guarantee, nor were they so rigidly formed to a pattern.

As Boulanger has said so eloquently, it was her task as teacher to understand "the other," and accommodate her teaching to his needs, rather than to make the student responsive to a binding, pedagogic formulation.

Nothing could more clearly define the difference, philosophically, between the French approach to the individual and the German treatment of the mass.

Between the philosophic and the practical, however, there were worlds as different as the classroom and the street-corner cafe. I have already noted (page 157) the divergence in direction in the early thirties during which Copland was back in the States, "securing his reputation as a composer," and "Thomson's career revolved more and more around Paris." That the two things should, after a time, tightly interact, was as improbable a fantasy as either could imagine.

One prophetic happening that could be isolated and described as indicative of what did, in fact, come about, remains vividly in mind because I was not only present, but to some extent, a participant. The year was 1932, the period of time, end of April and beginning of May; the place was Saratoga, New York, specifically the mansion built by Spencer Trask and endowed, after his death in 1909, as a refuge (under the name of Yaddo) for writers and composers in need of quiet in which to live and work. From time to time, it might also serve as a gathering place for a weekend discussion or, as in the present instance, for concerts of unfamiliar American music. In those days, if it was really contemporary, it was also unfamiliar—there wasn't any other possibility.

Something more than seven years had elapsed since Copland's

Boulanger performances. He had profited from Koussevitzky's enthusiastic response to the *Symphony for Organ and Orchestra* to compose for him, and to have performed, his *Music for the Theater* and Concerto for Piano and Orchestra. He had also entered into a competition sponsored by the Victor Talking Machine Company the score of what had become known as his *Dance Symphony*. He won the competition, but the recording that was promised was "deferred" because of the Depression. A series of programs of new chamber music in New York under the title of Copland-Sessions (1928–31) had attracted attention in the press, but little among the general musical public (see page 164). Thomson had completed both his *Symphony on a Hymn Tune* and *Four Saints in Three Acts*. Neither had been performed.

I had, in spring 1932, completed my first seasonal activity as a newspaper reviewer. This meant that I was unemployed, and quite happy to be present in Saratoga as a reporter, at space rates, for a New York newspaper. The programs promised much. Included was the first performance for a general public of Copland's massively crafted Piano Variations; a group of songs by the all but unknown Charles Ives; and sundry works by a variety of little-known young American composers. The programs had been organized by Copland; he was the activist who made what happened happen.

What happened to the music on the three programs of that 1932 weekend has now all been sorted out, filed, and not forgotten. What was more immediately stimulating and now all but forgotten was a midday outdoor meeting on Sunday in which Copland "chaired" (he was standing up most of the time) an informal discussion among the composers, performers, and listeners on the state of the American composer among his fellows. Not good.

Among those present was a reporter (name still unknown) representing the Associated Press. He also misrepresented the meeting, in an effort, no doubt, to make a furor of a forum. The opening paragraph asserted—without citation of a source, or the identity of a speaker—"Professional music critics were given to understand by contemporary composers of chamber music today that the world would be a better place without them."

This was a rendering, for running and reading purposes, of what

Copland had set forth in a series of comments on the treatment of American music generally in the daily press, and, specifically, the lack of coverage by one prominent New York paper of the previous day's Saratoga concert. It had, however, cabled coverage of the same day's happenings at a concert in the Württemberg (Germany) Festival. In making mention of this, Copland said: "Frankly, under such circumstances, I consider daily newspaper criticism a menace, and we would be better off without it."

I had, by a blend of good journalistic indoctrination and inherent curiosity, set down a running record of what was said. When the circulation of the openly inaccurate Associated Press report aroused complaints from those who had been present, the New York *Herald Tribune*, for which I had been providing day-to-day capsule comments on the concerts, was delighted to publish, in a subsequent Sunday issue, a correction and elaboration from my notes, including the quotation above.

What was, and is, of more lasting importance is a résumé of some of the more pertinent other things that were agitating Copland's mind in 1932: "A composer cannot write in a vacuum—somehow, in America, a composer is regarded as a menial . . . little place is reserved for him in the scheme of things . . . a composer must have a sense of belonging, of being intelligently listened to . . ." and then, farsightedly, "My idea of the ideal critic would be one who would have not merely a passive interest, but who would believe in American music, or what it is leading to. Edwin Evans said to me at Oxford last year: 'I wish I were young enough to come to America and do what I did for English music in 1905 . . .'"

Central to Copland's contention of neglect was a statement of conviction which supersedes all else: "For years American music has not been very good and everybody knew it. Now, however, the situation is different: our composers have craftsmanship, and it is time for critics to drop their prejudices against American music based on the works of twenty years ago and work with us to improve it." (May 8, 1932.)

These words locate precisely where Copland and his colleagues believed they stood a dozen years after their first encounter with

Nadia Boulanger and the developments that had flowed from it. But the earlier words about a "vacuum" and the need to be known to their countrymen conveyed a side of the dilemma apparent to few others at the time: the influential critics were not interested, and the interested critics were not influential.

Above all, it was Copland's profound perception that if the public and the critics would not come to the American composer, the American composer would have to go to them. If the ivory tower in a Milford, Pennsylvania, had produced a work to which some part of the press and public had responded, perhaps a different approach would produce a more inclusive response. This would require not merely some works of different substance, but also a practical application of what they observed in France—"the arts prosper in a society in which artists make them prosper" (page 158). In other words, as much as Copland, Thomson, et al. had been taught about music in Boulanger's studio, they had to apply what they learned about promotion in the corner cafes of the Latin Quarter.

Even as he spoke in April 1932, two supports to his contention of "craftsmanship"—a modest, *provable* claim that did not rant about "inspiration"—were in being, and soon would be in circulation. Copland's Piano Variations was, without question, the best piece of music written by an American to that time. It deserved, and received, performances by others than the composer himself. Thomson's *Four Saints* was finally presented by a group of sponsors looking for a work of quality with which to attract attention to the opening of the Avery Memorial in Hartford, Connecticut, early in February 1934, as a preliminary to the long-sought premiere in New York. The all-Negro cast (Thomson's innovative brainstorm after an evening in Harlem not long before) stirred a response that no white group, however gifted, could have equaled: the Gertrude Stein text, the Florine Stettheimer decor (with cellophane hangings!), and Thomson's enchanting score were a packet of pleasure such as "serious" American music had never known before. Needless to say, it had all been conceived, created, and completed in the only place in the world appropriate to it—Paris. Following its opening at the Forty-fourth Street Theater later in February, *Four Saints* played a total of six weeks on Broadway, an unprecedented, impossible, unforgettable accomplishment for an American composer from Paris by way of Harvard.

The economy was depressed, but not too depressed for President Franklin D. Roosevelt's New Deal to underwrite its WPA (Work Projects Administration), which dribbled, rather than poured, money into the arts. Even so, it was more than Washington had ever provided previously to the theater, music, and dance. The "humus to the soil" of which Boulanger had spoken enjoyed the financial irrigation and sprouted results never before known to amply talented, underprivileged artists of all colors and backgrounds.

Despite economic pressures, the common sense of nationalism engendered by common problems prompted an awareness of the depressed and deprived that prosperity had never provided. An interest in the "American spirit" prompted CBS to commission Copland to write a work whose title would be determined from a poll of its listeners. The winning submission, *Saga of the Prairie*, informed Copland that he possessed command of a generic idiom not known to him, but he did not reject the allusion, or the power of communication it implied.

Another aspect of federal funding brought into play the abilities of Pare Lorentz as a cinematic documentarian, and the unique capacity of Thomson to provide, through folk idioms skillfully utilized, works of musical art as scores for such films as *The Plow That Broke the Plains* and *The River*. They touched not merely chords of response, but the hearts of other Americans.

Nor can the appearance (one can hardly call it a reappearance of an art briefly seen in America twenty years before) of ballet be ignored. Tentative in its offerings, limited though the response was, the Ballet Russe de Monte Carlo aroused latent memories, generated new involvements, and implied the possibility of participation on a domestic level. Lincoln Kirstein persuaded George Balanchine to make his home in New York (if not, at once, in America) and though the way was slow at first, the inevitable came about: ballet needs music, and the best ballet music has, since Delibes and Tchaikovsky, been written by composers of special talent.

Thomson proved to be one (*Filling Station*), and, perhaps as a result of his *Saga of the Prairie,* Copland found a "Western" idiom for *Billy the Kid* (1938). When, in 1942, he produced *Rodeo,* in what he now calls his "easy" style, adaptability and productivity were no longer at issue: the man who had written *The Cat and the Mouse* BB (Before Boulanger) had matured into a master who could think small as well as big.

To be sure, this was far from the whole story of the enfranchising of American music. But Copland and Thomson provided a double-pronged probe into the resistances and the rejections which made the way much easier for their immediate followers: Roy Harris and Walter Piston, Samuel Barber and William Schuman, Gian Carlo Menotti, and others who, whether specifically American or not, became a part of the new liberation that prevailed in American attitudes.

The vacuum had begun to fill with the oxygen of approval. More energy was available to power the minds and hearts of those who needed it. Best of all, very little was specifically imitative of what others were doing. All too easily, however, the open chords and empty sonorous spaces that had caused a specific device of Copland to be called "Western" prompted others, empty of originality, to use similar means to evoke obviously emptier spaces. Those who could write symphonies did so. Those who couldn't, didn't feel obliged to prove that they couldn't and risk the worry of having their "seams show."

The arrival of enfranchisement in its fullest form can be dated to October 11, 1939, when the first article by Virgil Thomson, as successor to the late Lawrence Gilman, appeared in the New York *Herald Tribune.* What had begun at 36 rue Ballu and at the corner cafe, and continued in the salon of Alice Toklas, likewise Gertrude Stein, spread out, nationwide, to distribute waves of French influence long withheld from the American interior. With infrequent exceptions, prior press musical criticism in New York had been German-schooled, German-dominated, German-determined in values and attitudes. Thomson's predecessor was a man of grand, broad culture, in whose work from day to day one might readily find a quotation from Swinburne or Coleridge, and he had his responses to Maeterlinck and Debussy. But the household gods were still Wagner, Strauss, and Brahms in a long line of connection to Bach, all of which chimed as much in Gilman's prose as in his heart.

Thomson's prose was the bell of a different cat, one with as much disparagement of long-cherished symbols as promotion of little-known alternatives. Works of Satie and Milhaud, Fauré and Chabrier, Poulenc and Sauguet found a place, front and center, on Thomson's stage in the *Herald Tribune*. Soon enough it found echoes elsewhere, in younger minds and other locales.

Promotion, in the manner of Jean Cocteau and *les Six*, became a way of life, sometimes a way of living . . . with, eventually, inevitable consequences. All the promotion in the world will not achieve an enduring result if what is being promoted doesn't deserve it. What is seen by the rocket's red glare may appear to be the dawn of a new artistic day, but if there is no afterglow when the glare dies, all that is left is the barren stick, which falls to ground.

But the totality of the enfranchising and the en-Frenchising was as enduring as it was productive. The time had not yet come for Americans to make a credo of "doing your own thing." But on one broad art front, music, any American composer could be what he was, do what he would, live, artistically, as he wished. And even when the wave had swept away all in front of it, for the time of the bird to be past and the voice of Schoenberg to be heard in the land, every option still remained open.

For the whole marvelous moment, Gertrude Stein had the words to say it best: "It was not so much what France gave you as what she did not take away."[18]

Little wonder, then, when Nadia Boulanger died in Paris on October 22, 1979 (aged ninety-two), a Memorial Mass of commemoration was held at the Corpus Christi Church on New York's Morningside Heights on Monday, November 5. It was ar-

[18] Thomson, op. cit., p. 74.

ranged by Louise Basbas, the church's director of music, a Boulanger pupil, with whom she had maintained a long correspondence.

As a perspective of Boulanger's musical interests and the way in which they were communicated to those who cherished her, the contents of the Mass, and those who performed it, have been perpetuated on the following pages.

The small structure was all but filled. When I arrived, I observed Aaron Copland in a pew to the right, near the front. Before the service began, Virgil Thomson came in, and took a seat in the center pews.

They were, of course, after nearly sixty years, in the forefront of those who cherished her.

CORPUS CHRISTI CHURCH
MEMORIAL MASS FOR NADIA BOULANGER (1887-1979)
Monday, November 5, 1979

Prelude: Chorale Preludes from the Orgelbüchlein and Chorales J. S. Bach
- "Da Jesus an dem Kreuze stund"
- "Es ist genug"
- "Christ lag in Todesbanden"
- "Ich ruf' zu dir, Herr Jesu Christ"
- "Jesu, meine Freude"
- "O Mensch, bewein' dein' Sünde gross"

Introit Antiphon: Requiem aeternam   Mode 6

> PRIEST: The grace of Our Lord Jesus Christ and the love of God and the fellowship of the Holy Spirit be with you all.

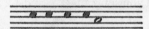

> PEOPLE: And with your spi-rit.

Kyrie: Mass for Five Voices   William Byrd
Gradual: Requiem aeternam   Mode 2
Alleluia   Mode 7
Offertory: "Komm süsser Tod"
"Bist du bei mir"   Bach

Hugues Cuénod, tenor

PRIEST: The Lord be with you.

PEOPLE: And with your spi-rit.
PRIEST: Lift up your hearts.

PEOPLE: We have lift-ed them up to the Lord.
PRIEST: Let us give thanks to the Lord our God.

PEOPLE: It is right and just.

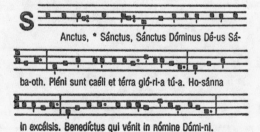

Anctus, * Sánctus, Sánctus Dóminus Dé-us Sá-

ba-oth. Pléni sunt caéli et térra gló-ri-a tú-a. Ho-sánna

in excélsis. Benedíctus qui vénit in nómine Dómi-ni.

Hosánna in excélsis.

PRIEST: Through Him, with Him,...forever and ever.

PEOPLE: A - men.

(The congregation then stands.)

THE LORD'S PRAYER

PEOPLE: Our Fa-ther, who art in heav-en, hal-lowed be Thy name; Thy king-dom come;

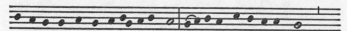

Thy will be done on earth as it is in heav-en. Give us this day our dai-ly bread;

and for-give us our tres-pass-es as we for-give those who tres-pass a-gainst us;

and lead us not in-to temp-ta-tion, but de-li-ver us from e - vil.
PRIEST: Deliver us,...our Saviour, Jesus Christ.

PEOPLE: For Thine is the kingdom, and the power, and the glo-ry for ever and ev-er.
PRIEST: Lord Jesus Christ...forever and ever.
PRIEST: May the peace of the Lord be always with you.

PEOPLE: And with your spi-rit.

Agnus Dei	Byrd
Communion Antiphon: Lux aeterna	Mode 8
"Pie Jesu" from Requiem	Gabriel Fauré
Brenda Fairaday, soprano	
"Ave verum"	Byrd
"In paradisum"	Fauré
Postlude: Fantasy in g minor	Bach

Richard Morris, organ
Louise Basbas, director of music

MC
Cosmopolite

Born in America, educated in Greece, musically per-
fected in Italy, traveled on a Monaco passport. Died in
Paris.

I

As Parisian addresses go, the only one to which I can claim a contemporary affinity, other than 36 rue Ballu, is, by rather spooky coincidence, also numbered 36.

My access to 36 rue Ballu is purely fanciful, on behalf of its innumerable lifelike associations.

My association with 36 avenue Georges Mandel, Paris 16ᵉ, is
factual. This was the house in which Maria Callas lived from
1967, and in which she died in September 1977.

A reasonably unpretentious building on a tree-lined thor-
oughfare in a reasonably unpretentious neighborhood—the adjectives relate to the practicality that people with the means to afford
such peace and security could be considered to be, on the whole,
reasonably unpretentious—36 was stone, weather-worn, perhaps
eight floors of flats in all.

Following instructions given to me in our telephone conversation following arrival in Paris, which I passed on to the cab
driver, we went along the Seine for a certain distance, turned right
near the Trocadéro, and were shortly at the destination.

The house was sufficiently withdrawn from the center of Paris
to be out of the crunch of traffic. But it was also close enough to
the Etoile to reach major objectives with no difficulty. So much
for money and the burdens of it.

Unlike 36 rue Ballu, where visitors had to toil up flights of stairs to reach the Boulanger studio, 36 avenue Georges Mandel had a typical Parisian elevator (open cab, in a cage) with a surrounding staircase.

When I reached the designated floor, I found no door bearing the name of Callas. I did find a door with the number she had mentioned, and pressed the bell. In a moment I was admitted by a maid (Bruna, who accompanied her to several continents, and who was to find her collapsed on the floor not much more than a year later).

Almost instantly, Maria sauntered in, smiling, casually dressed (it was a midsummer Sunday afternoon of a famously hot spell), but with the elegance that characterized her for most of the twenty years of our acquaintance.

The apartment was spacious enough to merit a "Come, I'll show you around." I made some reference to the absence of her name on the door. She laughed. "If you look carefully," she said, "you will see a plate with the name of the prior tenant. I particularly left it that way to discourage unwanted visitors."

A suitable word for the darkish, homogeneously furnished surroundings would be "restful." Not quite luxurious, but certainly costly. The apartment fitted Maria, and Maria fitted it, as a self-made woman of accomplishment, of self-possession, indeed self-position.

When I made some comment on the carved, solidly built, and carefully waxed furniture, she told me that most of it had been brought from Italy, that she had acquired it after her marriage to Meneghini, lived in it until her marriage broke down, and brought it with her when she decided that Paris was where she wanted to live. Sometime later, it occurred to me that the surroundings were curiously similar to those of another residence I had once visited. There too, the lady of the house had been a soprano, Frances Alda, who had brought furniture from Italy to furnish a home in New York where she lived with her husband, Giulio Gatti-Casazza, general manager of the Metropolitan Opera between 1908 and 1935. When that marriage also ended, she used it to furnish a hardly restful, more than luxurious home on Sands Point, Long Island.

Having taken note of the drawing room and the formal dining room which adjoined it, we passed through a large, ornately furnished area whose antique bed clearly proclaimed its purposes.

Then into a casual sitting room, where Maria motioned me to a chair, settling into another, for a talk.

"What do you think?" she queried brightly. "How do you like it?"

"I like it fine," I answered. "It just suits you."

"I got the key [French expression for purchase of an apartment] for ninety thousand dollars. It's worth a lot more now," she added proudly.[1]

As may be suggested by the huge estate she left (estimates ranged from $10 million to $15 million pending disposition of property she owned, and the size of her bank accounts in Paris, New York, Palm Beach, Florida, where she liked to visit, and London), Maria Callas was shrewd, well aware of her worth, and not disposed to be taken advantage of.

Some weeks prior to my arrival in Paris, she had tangled, legally, with a newspaper. The reason? She had arranged for daytime use of a nearby theater, to work and rehearse with a view to resuming her concertizing (this was three years *after* her disastrous tour of Europe, America, and the Far East with Giuseppe di Stefano).

A photographer for one of the Paris tabloids (abetted, no doubt, by someone with privileged knowledge of Callas's routine at the theater) secreted himself without her consent or observation, and took a batch of pictures which appeared under some such title as "Diva Struggles to Regain Her Voice." "I sued them," she said with more than a little venom. "We just got a judgment. Not a bad amount, I'll tell you."

There were, as there are to so many things, two sides to this story. One was simple pride in privacy and her determination to preserve it at any price or effort . . . especially when she had been exploited for someone else's profit. The other was, that despite all the realistic, indeed anguishing evidence to the contrary, she still thought of herself as a singer and was making plans, even then, to return to public view.

[1] Information circulated after her death established that the apartment was owned under the name of Trenton, the money was Aristotle Onassis', and she paid the maintenance fees.

"I was going to give a concert in London a couple of months ago," she continued, "but decided not to. Now I'm looking forward to one in the fall, with Gorlinsky" (referring to her longtime manager-promoter for English business).

"Maria," I said, "how can you? After all that you went through, in the States, with di Stefano."

"That was different," she argued; "just with piano. This time it will be with orchestra in back of me. You'll see."

"See" or not (the concert never came off, of course), the proposed "date" brought to mind all too vividly an episode during the winter (1971–72) she spent in New York working with young singers at the Juilliard. More important to her (I think) was the large studio with which she was provided. Here she could work on her own vocal regeneration with the well-schooled, musically demanding Alberta Masiello of the Metropolitan Opera's coaching staff.

The weeks also marked the time during which I had become reasonably well acquainted with her. Even before she came to America in the 1950s, mutual friends, with a high regard for her artistry, told me I would profit much from knowing her. But in keeping with a long-standing resistance to knowing people I had to write about, I avoided a meeting.

It eventually came about in rather special circumstances, after she had been "fired" by Rudolf Bing (November 1958) in a disagreement relating to scheduling, repertory, etc. She had also accepted an engagement to appear in Carnegie Hall in Bellini's seldom heard *Il Pirata* shortly after the turn of the year. In conjunction with her Met appearances and the Carnegie Hall concert, I had set aside six pages of the *Saturday Review*'s month-end January (1959) issue for the publication, for the first time in English, of Teodoro Celli's still unexcelled study of Callas as the *soprano d'agilità* of old, whose like had not been heard for decades.

The article had been expertly translated by the late Herbert Weinstock, set in type, and was ready to run. The question at issue was: now that Bing had "fired" Callas from her winter's work in New York, would she, indeed, appear in *Il Pirata?* The only one who could answer for Callas was Callas.

Through Weinstock, a date was made, and an hour set at the Hotel Drake, where Callas would be staying on her return from Dallas, Texas. She was hardly the elegant lady she became very soon after, of whom I said, in remeeting her in Paris, she bore herself as she had "as long as I have known her." I didn't *know* her in New York in 1959, though, I am told, she regarded me as a "friend" (meaning I had written well about her as an artist).

She was much disposed to rough talk on Bing and his "rude" way of dealing with artists; to derisive comment on her perpetual "rival" Renata Tebaldi, though, as time passed, they shared less and less artistic terrain; to the Metropolitan itself, as a shabby likeness of an opera enterprise (in its old Thirty-ninth Street and Broadway building) compared with the "art" she and her friends in Dallas were achieving. To my countercomment that she was much too important in the world of opera to be bothered by, or concerned with, what Tebaldi did or said, she answered—in effect and with some pique—"That's the way they [Tebaldi and her clique] talk about me, so that's the way I'll talk about them."

I also ventured the hope that she might study and perform the role of Donna Anna in Mozart's *Don Giovanni*, to which she replied: "Mozart is boring" and she couldn't stand it. My answer was, "We don't want you to 'stand it': just to study and perform it." In any case, she affirmed her intention to sing *Il Pirata*, as well as she could. The way in which she said it left no doubt of her intentions, so I departed, leaving Meneghini a few feet away, his back to the discussion, writing checks to pay bills, sending letters, or whatever else one does at a desk in a hotel room. He took no part in the conversation whatsoever.

Pirata she performed, and well. I don't think I spoke to her again for ten years or more, though we had an occasional exchange of letters on this or that, including arrangements for an interview in Paris after the death of her mentor, Tullio Serafin, in 1968. I assigned the interview to Jan Maguire, a free-lance writer who did her work well.

But as of fall 1971, Maria was no longer a performer (in my opinion, if not in hers). Her qualities as a person, an artist, a public personality, an apt participant in a Juilliard project that would benefit its students, and a woman who had reshaped the operatic repertory, were worth whatever time she was willing to give me.

On one occasion, when she was talking of her work at the Juilliard, and how much she had learned about her own problems from listening to and analyzing the shortcomings of the young vocalists in her "class," she talked about singing again in public.[2]

My well-meaning suggestion was: "You should go someplace out of the way and see how it goes."

Her answer was both decisive and revealing: "I will look the lion in the eye. I will go to London." Five years later, the will was still strong, whatever the happenings in between.

II

As B follows A in the alphabet, especially in Greek (English, French, and Italian were her usual languages, but she loved to talk in her "native" tongue whenever possible), so the answer was a successive step in a lifelong artistic sequence. Unfortunately, the life leaped from L (for London) to Z long before it should have, which was, perhaps, a consequence of her judgment—which was not notable for caution. Or, perhaps, impulse and risk were deep in her nature, bred as she was in what she called her "trapeze parts."

The image is as apt as it is uncommon. Nobody wants to commit suicide, even artistically. That is why, perhaps, a whole file of operas—great in beauty, eloquent in expression, fastidious in workmanship—had all but ceased to exist in public performance between the 1840s and the 1950s. They are the ones which, for lack of a leading soprano skilled in the "trapeze part," were simply not heard. The phrase, in the Callas usage, refers to a role in which a

[2] Few things irked her more than allusions, in the press or on television, to her having "lost her voice." She contended that her problem stemmed from a "ruptured diaphragm" which weakened the muscles urgently required for breath support in singing. A doctor (Dr. Stanley Mirsky) queried on this doubted that the ailment she described would seriously affect muscular support.

vocal miscalculation, a difficulty fuzzed or fudged, can leave the performer aloft in midair, or more probably, flat on her . . . face.

The dates defining the hundred-year (plus) period have not been elected arbitrarily: they have been selected because they "happen" to conform to the time lapse between performances of *Il Pirata* at the high temple of Italian operatic art, La Scala, Milan. Italian operatic tendencies being what they are, the probability is that something not performed at La Scala in a hundred and ten years has, very likely, not been performed elsewhere on the peninsula.

The specific detail, as it relates to Callas, is: the outstanding *Cronologia* of La Scala (1778–1963, edited by Carlo Gatti) identifies a production at La Scala in November 1840 (none of the singers were of historic note); the next reference is to May 19, 1958, when the Imogene was Meneghini-Callas, and the cast included Franco Corelli and Ettore Bastianini, Antonino Votto conducting.

The reference to *Il Pirata* is not so much because it represents a great, neglected masterpiece: the closing mad scene is stupendous Bellini, in its demands and in its rewards, but there is much else in it that is second-rate. Rather, the work has a special place in the Callas constellation, the most distant star to which she aspired, the lengths to which she would go to accept a challenge. It is the "even" or outer limit within which her mastercraft was exerted.

Less extraordinary, but nevertheless on the borders of the improbable in their vocal demands, was her willingness to perform not only Elvira in Bellini's *I Puritani*, but Anna in Donizetti's *Anna Bolena* (a work still not performed at the Metropolitan Opera, and absent from the stage of La Scala between 1876 and 1957). From such deeds derived the will of another American-born soprano, who made her debut at the New York City Opera as Rosalinde in *Die Fledermaus* in 1955, to undertake the *whole* of Donizetti's "Tudor *Ring*" in the early 1970s. That was accomplished by adding *Maria Stuarda* to her repertory of *Roberto Devereux* and *Anna Bolena*. Would Beverly Sills have risen to the heights of her climaxing years without the mark of Callas to aim for? Some might disagree, but Sills would not be among them.

In his basic text on the subject[3] Celli states: "The voice of Maria Callas is that of a dramatic soprano *d'agilità*: It has all the characteristics of extension, virtuosity and simultaneous emotion. It even has the characteristic that seems a defect to some ears accustomed to modern singers: lack of homogeneity of texture." Celli defines her range (when the voice was at its most responsive) as including A below the staff (for Verdi's *Un Ballo in maschera*) to E flat *in alt* (Donizetti's *Lucia di Lammermoor*), with E natural as an outside possibility (for Rossini's *Armida*). In other words, as Celli puts it: "She has, that is, about the extension that Malibran had."

Very likely when Callas began her historic adventure with the great Tullio Serafin in 1947, she had no knowledge of what a *soprano d'agilità* was. Her early training in Greece had pointed her in the direction of a relatively conventional repertory: Santuzza in Mascagni's *Cavalleria rusticana* at the age of fifteen (1938), Tosca (1942), Leonore in Beethoven's *Fidelio* (1944). Even when she first came to the attention of Serafin, it was as Gioconda for a production of Ponchielli's *La Gioconda* in the Verona Arena in 1947.

Doubtless the big broad sound also enthused him as the material from which an Italian Isolde in Wagner's *Tristan* could be fashioned (Venice, December 1947) or Brünnhilde in his *Die Walküre* (also in Venice, January 8, 1949), as well as Turandot in Puccini's *Turandot*, Leonora in Verdi's *La Forza del destino*, Aïda, and Norma in Bellini's tragedy of Druids and Romans in Gaul. The gravitation to *Norma* by Serafin (who had taught the role to Rosa Ponselle at the Metropolitan in the 1920s) suggests, to me, the direction of his thought.

Ahead, for Serafin in 1949, was not only *Die Walküre* (*La Walkiria*, actually, as both the Wagner works Callas ventured onstage were sung in Italian) but Bellini's *I Puritani*. Few of the best-informed students of the Callas career know, or care, who the soprano scheduled to sing Elvira was.[4] But the world is in debt to

[3] Celli, Teodoro, "Great Artists of Our Time—I Maria Meneghini Callas," *Saturday Review*, January 31, 1959, pp. 40–44, 60–63.

[4] It was Margherita Carosio, a well-known, underrecorded soprano of the time.

her for the circumstances that forced her to withdraw from the production and put Serafin in a dilemma barely short of *in extremis*. His *cul de sac* was Callas's open door to a destiny that beckoned to her as a *soprano d'agilità*. What Serafin had heard of the Callas with whom he had been working for a year and a half had persuaded him that she was capable of singing Brünnhilde in *La Walkiria* at night (between January 8 and 19) and rehearsing Elvira in *I Puritani* by day.

Callas is better on the subject than anyone else. Speaking to Jan Maguire, she recalled the sequence thus: she "read the opera at sight for him. The next morning he called her early, insisting that she not bother to dress but only slip on a robe and hurry down to see the director of the Fenice [the historic theater in Venice, with its famous entrance for gondolas, where the season was being given]. They asked her to do the part. She thought they were crazy. She protested that she was not a light voice—and besides, she did not know the role. Maestro Serafin assured her: 'You are young. I know you will make it. I gamble on you.' "

"When that kind of maestro gambles on you," continued Callas, "you say, 'OK, I'll try it.' " What did she have to lose? Only everything.[5]

What Callas referred to as "that kind of maestro" is, alas, an apparition of the past whose like, I can say with certainty, will never come again. The dogma in that sentence is not "an arrogant expression of opinion" (as the word is sometimes defined).[6] It is a mere matter of practicalities relating to Serafin: date of birth (December 8, 1878), nature of conditioning (orchestral violinist), length of major career (1900–66), occupation (student as well as conductor). Unlike some other conductors of high rank, who divided their time between opera and concert repertory, Serafin conducted nothing but opera, except the Verdi *Requiem* (an exception that might be considered a difference without a distinction).

Unlike some contemporary students of the Rossini-Bellini-Donizetti period, whose information is derived from reading

[5] Maguire, Jan, "Serafin, Callas and Bel Canto," *Saturday Review*, March 30, 1968, pp. 47–49.
[6] Concise Oxford Dictionary, p. 363.

books or from studying the markings in scores once owned by illustrious divas of the past, Serafin came early enough on the musical scene of Italy in the nineteenth century to learn from those
who had done it. By that time, some of the *practice* had degraded,
rather than perpetuated, the precepts derived from the composers
and their chosen interpreters. But Serafin was a musician capable
not merely of learning from the best, but rejecting the worst, as
his two volumes of operatic history, published late in life, clearly
proclaim.[7]

Such capacity to make distinctions is one of the precious attributes that made Serafin's relationship to Callas of such importance. The literature is, God knows, sufficiently susceptible to
abuse not to be further complicated by ignorance. Moreover, a
singer with the instrument, and the command of it to sing the
notes with ease, can still make a mockery of musical sense by
failing to give the *words* a proper place in the combination conceived by the composer. If this brings to mind an Australian soprano of some prominence, so be it.

In her tribute to Serafin, Callas recalled: "He opened a world
to me, showed me there was a reason for everything, that even the
fioritura [a descriptive word, for what is often miscalled *colora-
tura*, which means "flowering"] and trills . . . have a reason in the
composer's mind, that they are all the expression of the *stato
d'anima* of the character—that is, the way he feels at the moment,
the passing emotions that take hold of him."

She also distinguished clearly the difference between Serafin,
the teacher, and Victor de Sabata, the fiery interpreter, whom she
also held in high regard: "Serafin seldom had a fit of temper, but
I have seen de Sabata actually spit on the first violins. Serafin was
gentle but strict, like a father. If I forgot a word, he would treat
me roughly and I would cry. 'Keep on singing,' he said, 'you will
have to sing many a time when you are crying, so you'd better get
used to it.' I was a sponge—Serafin told me everything, and I took
it in."

The "sponge," as she called herself, was more than "an aquatic

[7] Serafin, Tullio, and Toni, A., *Stile, tradizioni e convenzioni del melo-
dramma italiano del Settecento e dell'Ottocento* (Milan, 1958–64).

animal of low order." She was such a powerful instrument of impulse and intellect that, after a mere half-dozen years of working together, Serafin inscribed a photo to her in words that, during my visit to her a year before she died, she still regarded as "the greatest compliment I had ever received":

> "A *Maria Callas, voce unica, artista che sà dare tutte le emozione, creatura a me particolarmente care che a afrontato tutte le difficultà, le lotte per la carriere artistica con la fede soltanto in se stessa nel suo valore, con l'affetto di sempre, Tullio Serafin 1954.*"

> ("To Maria Callas, a unique voice, an artist who knows how to give every emotion, a creature particularly dear to me, who faced every difficulty, all struggles for an artistic career, with faith only in herself, in her own worth, with affection always, Tullio Serafin 1954.")

III

Maria Callas was not an intellectual. Great singers rarely are. Let us not forget that she was singing Santuzza at fifteen (in this respect, she beat Malibran's record by two years: that "ritarded" prodigy did not make her official debut until 1825, when she sang Rosina in Rossini's *Il Barbiere di Siviglia* in London at the age of seventeen). For most of the thirty-eight years of life left to Callas, what she had sung the day before, or what she would sing several days, a week, a month, a year later, was uppermost in her mind.

She had, to be sure, a wide range of interest for her spare time—friends, diversions, pleasures—but it was, eminently, "spare" time: what she could *spare* from the overreaching thrust of being a superb performer.

I have referred to her (page 200) as an "instrument of impulse and intellect." Both existed, of course. The impulse was fragmented into many things: friendship, emotion, liking, disliking, going, coming, living, loving. The intellect was almost wholly concentrated on being the best performer she could be. A mezzo at the Metropolitan who died all too young (the late Jean Madeira, of cancer, at fifty-four) once implored me to give her a few minutes to discuss the state of her career, with which she was dissatisfied. I agreed, and responded to her overture for an opinion on artistry by saying: "Miss Madeira, you often sing too loud." She looked at me, somewhat abashed, as though a secret had been found out, and replied: "Mr. Kolodin, when I go out on that stage I just have to show that I've got the biggest damn voice in the company."

The Callas compulsions went into quite different directions. Thanks to Serafin, or whomever, being *quietest* ranked as high, or higher, in her mind than being loudest (sometimes it even attracts more attention). The first time I ever heard her live was on the memorable day of November 1954 when she made her debut in the country of her birth in *Norma* at the Chicago Civic Opera. In my comment, I described her as "an electric figure on the stage, charged with a sense of dramatic fitness, and alternating currents of fury and repose producing a very direct result on her listeners."[8]

For much of the early part of the evening (after the early-on "Casta diva" for Norma) the performance belonged to that great artist Giulietta Simionato, who was performing her usual kind of superior Adalgisa—disciplined, lovable, fiery. Did Callas rise to the bait of contesting the greater impression that her colleague was making on the audience, and exceed the marginal dividing line between what Norma should do and what a Callas could do? She did not: she stayed precisely within the characterization as Bellini and his librettist, Felice Romani, had formed it, fully aware that, as the action matured, and Norma's part in it became dominant, her appointed time would come.

On another occasion, in Cherubini's *Medea* (which she never sang in New York), my exposure to her appearance in Covent Garden was clouded by a comment on it that I had heard a few days before from Sir Thomas Beecham. "If she is going to sing it that way," he more than opined, "she should act it differently. And if she is going to act it as she does, she should change her vocal conception." Perhaps I was an easier mark than Sir Thomas

8 *Saturday Review*, November 13, 1954, p. 37.

for the simply stupendous. As the evening progressed the effect of her effort counteracted any intelligent resistance to it. Fury hot and fury cold were the gamut of Medea as Callas played her, and the triumphant note of horror she achieved at the end, after she had struck down her children, was when Maria was most Medea.

The mind lingers on the governor within the artistic machinery which must be invoked in the playing of two such like, but unlike, roles as Norma and Medea. Crudely speaking, the situations are alike: a mother and two children. But the climactic point of one is precisely opposite to that of the other. Norma is the mother whose impulse to the maternal overrides everything else. Medea is the mother whose impulse to the satanic breaks every bond. How is the governor set to turn a passion to tears, or to tyranny? Whatever way it has to be done, Callas knew it, intuitively. Perhaps she also knew that "governor" comes from the Greek *kybernan*, meaning "to steer."

The instances cited above should not be construed as including impeccable (whatever that means, musically) execution of the vocal line. The Chicago *Norma* was, in that respect, nearer infallibility than the London *Medea*—it was, after all, six seasons (1954 vs. 1959) earlier (and probably several hundred rehearsals, performances, and recordings younger) in her career. But the drive, the intensity, the *variety* of the effort were of a quality that beggared perfection. Zinka Milanov sang a more vocally *perfect* Norma than Callas: but it was not a more Bellini-Romani Norma, nor indeed, a more Norma-Norma, than hers. As for others of more recent date, a curtain is the most kindly kind of comparison to be drawn.

The curious obsession that some operagoers—professionals included—have with "perfection" puzzled me for a good many years. Was I so much more "lenient" in my response toward a great artist of opera and *Lieder* like Lotte Lehmann, or so superb an interpreter (and violinist) as Fritz Kreisler simply because I was "taken in" by the qualities of communication they achieved?

It came to me after a while in quest of music—"a while" including the years before I had begun to spend some time, annually,

with students at the Juilliard School in a seminar on criticism—
that leniency had nothing to do with it, but lack of understanding
(on the part of others) might. The catalyst here, too, was Maria
Callas. For purposes of illustration, I was using a recording of Elvira's "Ernani! Ernani! involami" ("Ernani! Ernani! fly with me")
in three different versions: Callas, Leontyne Price, Joan Sutherland.

This is a perfect example of a three-part operatic *scena*, written
in 1844, when Verdi was thirty-one and still worrying about "classic" perfection as practiced by such predecessors as Bellini and
Donizetti. It opens with a recitation (*recitativo accompagnato*,
meaning that the orchestra participates in the background) of Elvira's mental state as she confronts the prospect of marriage to the
elderly Don Ruy Gomez de Silva (of whom she is the ward)
rather than to the young, vigorous Ernani (with whom she is in
love). Follows then the *cavatina* (slow air, this one in ¾ and
decidedly waltzy), in which she voices her plea that Ernani rescue
her from the dilemma; and, finally, the *cabaletta* (fast, galloping
conclusion), in which Elvira expresses the joy she would feel were
such a miracle to come about.

Basic distinctions were readily recognizable: Price had by far
the most voluptuous sound, Sutherland unquestionably the
greatest agility, and Callas—well, Callas wasn't always pitch-per-
fect and maybe there was a little slurring here and there. After
discussing the situation with several successive annual groups of
students—all were provided automatically with copies of the
music and translations of the text—it came to me that they mentioned the *imperfections* in pitch and the slurs because, quite literally, that is *all* they could find to say about her performance.

What about the mood and dramatic inflection of the *recitativo?* Nothing. How about the fervor and longing in every word of
the *cavatina?* Didn't notice it. And the tone painting, as Elvira de-
picts the "Eden" it would be. (The word, beautifully embellished
by Verdi to give the indoctrinated soprano every opportunity to
caress it with the voice and to make full use of the open A sound,
was "AY-den" in the Italian pronunciation.) A somewhat more

subtle point than the average enrollee could grasp. Now and then, a vocal student of the right conditioning would take it all in, including the joyful *cabaletta*, and sigh rapturously—but that was not to be counted upon.

All too many colleagues (especially younger ones) forget that the basic meaning of "critic" is to pronounce a judgment—another one of those Greek words, *krites* ("judge")—not to find fault. And for that matter, the common conception of the public is much the same—"Don't be so critical," I hear from time to time, when, in all good conscience, what I have heard I have judged to be inferior. I often feel that I am more "critical" (to borrow the *mis*application of the term) when I have heard something so fine that what lingers is the rare miracle of re-creation, with or without regard for the paltry "fact" that a trivial deviation from impeccability is a reminder that the performer is, after all, a human being, not a machine. Of course, if the reminders are recurrent, the only conclusion can be that the performer is all too human, and his/her place is not on the stage.

That chilling realization finally came to pass with Callas. But the place was Carnegie Hall in 1973, not the Metropolitan Opera House in 1964, when she made her final New York appearances in opera. The two March evenings were devoted to *Tosca* (which, as I have mentioned, she had sung for the first time, as a teenager in Athens, more than twenty years before). Sinuous, volatile, capable —in Act I—of an instant change of temperature from torrid to frigid in her scenes with Cavaradossi, Callas was, on those two evenings, more Tosca than any other performer of the role I had ever experienced (perhaps I was not wise enough to appreciate the artistry of Maria Jeritza years before). The Callas voice was certainly not in good order, but a tape I have of her last operatic performance in America (March 25, 1964) contains more to learn about performing Tosca than any other document of which I have knowledge.

There was still a hope that the career could be salvaged as late as 1971–72. She had done her work at the Juilliard diligently, faithfully, unfailingly, on behalf of both her students and herself.

The work was divided into two periods: the fall months, following which she went back to Paris for the holidays, and a spring sequence. When the end of the formal aspect with her class was approaching, she estimated she was 95 per cent of the way that *she* wanted to be vocally. A properly qualified musician (in every respect, including collaboration with Callas) to whom I mentioned this at a chance encounter a few days later shook his head when the estimate was passed on. "If she isn't 100 per cent," commented Leonard Bernstein, "she shouldn't sing again."

In the weeks that elapsed during her Juilliard work, she seldom let one pass without a call at the end of a day: "It's Maria," was the inevitable announcement. "What are you doing tonight? How about dinner?" When possible, the suggestion was acted upon, for dinner in one of the public rooms at the Plaza (where "expenses" —on a Callas scale, and far from negligible—were all the compensation she received from the Juilliard for her work) was only an incident in long, sustained conversations. On one occasion she reported that she had had a really good working day, that she was singing "much better than when I did those Toscas at the Met." When she was reminded that these were in the stream of an ongoing career, and carried the dramatic momentum still in effect, that it was the theatrical results that were inimitable, not the vocal means at her disposal, her response was a negative head shake. For Callas, the argument didn't hold water.

At length, the work came to an end, and she announced that she was going back to Paris, with the understanding that she would be coming back to New York in a matter of weeks, pick up the work she was doing with the ever responsive Masiello, and see it through to the end. She didn't.

Rather, one heard from time to time of a venture into operatic staging (at Turin), which included the participation—apparently as a means of regenerating confidence by recalling their triumphs together—of tenor di Stefano. As di Stefano was never more than a voice wrapped in ego, that did not promise well for any artistic venture together.

Least of all did it promise anything more productive when word began to circulate, toward the end of 1973, that she was actively preparing a "comeback" by way of a concert tour with him. In an article titled "What Makes Maria Sing?" I reviewed some of the possibilities that entered into her "judgment," if such an emotional decision could be described by that word.[9]

Money, she didn't need. She had proudly told me, during her New York work at the Juilliard, that her "records were selling as well as ever" (if not that Aristotle Onassis had assigned to her, as a parting gift, the income for life from one of his tankers). Occupation she did need, because the stage and the impulses it engendered were as much a part of her bodily chemistry as alcohol to an alcoholic, and nobody had yet organized an AA on behalf of Artists Anonymous.

Tightly woven into the warp and woof of her ambition as then (1971–73) textured was a deeper motif, a not visible but intensely audible thread of purpose that guided much of what she was doing at the time. Prompted one night, by her description of a day's work with Masiello, to venture a square question, I said: "You have had every kind of recognition, enough to last a lifetime. Why drive yourself?" Her reply was: "I've got to prove he was wrong." "Who was wrong?" I queried. "Onassis," she replied. "He said I was washed up as a singer, and I should leave the stage to marry him."

A week before the American tour was to begin in Carnegie Hall, the artistic Gemini (di Stefano and Callas) arrived in New York. A press conference (arranged to bolster the sale of tickets at "gala" prices to benefit the Metropolitan Opera Guild) had been arranged. My name was on the press list, so I was invited but didn't attend, because the venture was foolish, unwise, and could only be detrimental to her reputation.

Toward evening, the phone rang. When I picked it up, a familiar voice was right at me. "Where were you?" she queried. "I was looking forward to seeing you."

"As you probably know," I answered, "I thought this tour was a bad idea and said so in print."

[9] *Saturday Review/World*, February 9, 1974, pp. 53–55.

"What's that got to do with it?" she cross-queried, rather impatiently. "You're a friend, aren't you?"

IV

To that question I could not readily reply, but Callas hardly expected an answer. My status was deeply etched on her mind and would remain so, permanently.

My ascent to that place of honor occurred slowly during the sixties, when she had all but stopped singing in America. So far as I can recall, the first intimation came as a holiday greeting—the reproduction of the infant Jesus and mother, painted by Veronese. The internal inscription was duplicated from a plate, but it was a pleasure to have in any case.

That could have been late in 1962. Earlier in the year, though she had no professional commitment in New York, she came to participate in a combination birthday greeting/fund-raising affair in the old Madison Square Garden for President John F. Kennedy, whom she greatly admired. It was a Saturday night: she sang the "Habañera" from *Carmen*, not very well. I had been advised that Callas would like to say hello and would call the following afternoon around four. The time came and passed. Also four-fifteen and four-twenty. As I was leaving the phone rang. No question it was Maria, but I went on my way, being already due elsewhere. When she returned to Europe, she sent me a note, half chiding, half apologetic. Not at all unreasonable.

Dear Mr. Kolodin:
I called and called on Sunday before taking the plane back but no answer. What happened? I had kept the afternoon free for you before leaving . . .
Anyway I was most unhappy and I wish you were here for the Medea! (hoping they will go well).
After, I'm recording Tosca (28–30 of June) but I don't think anyone can replace De Sabata! So I'm quite unhappy about it, but I must repeat it stereophonically.

Please let me hear from you, and remember that I have a very long memory . . . You respected and admired me years ago. I don't forget easily.

My very best to all friends like Weinstock, etc.

Yours most sincerely ————
Maria Callas

May 24, 1962

For the while, exchanges were of the "How have you been, hope you are well" variety, though now and then something musical would creep into the content. In the latter part of 1963, I heard that her record company (Angel) was anxious to record a *Carmen* with her, but she was resistant to the idea (she never sang the part on the stage). The essence of her hesitation was that Carmen was a mezzo part, and people would say she had lost her top notes if she took it on.

I sent her a note mentioning that among past Carmens were such ladies as Rosa Ponselle, Maria Jeritza, Geraldine Farrar—even Emma Calvé, who liked to sing Marguerite in *Faust*—and none of them was exactly a mezzo. I didn't have an answer: the answer came in the form of the recording that was issued the following year.

Perhaps my introduction to the real Maria came in the latter part of 1968, when her breakup with Onassis made international news. Much of it was rumorous and rancorous, including statements that she had "held up" Onassis for a settlement of a million dollars. Through it all she held both her peace and her temper.

In the latter part of October I expressed my congratulations to her for good, patient behavior, and cited Ernest Hemingway's characterization, for character, in terms of "grace under pressure" . . ."especially," I continued, "as I do not doubt that the inward emotions are rather at variance with the outward control . . ."

The response must have been written almost as soon as my letter arrived.

It reads (in part):

If ever a letter was gratifying and beautiful it was yours . . .

I am proud that so many people and friends appreciate my qualities, if any . . . and your letter will remain engraved in my mind and soul forever, dear friend.

I will write of future plans or decisions later.

Now I'm trying to hold myself and heal my broken cartiladge among other things.

Yours most affectionately

26/10/68

This was quite a different person from the one of only fourteen years before who responded to process servers at her American debut in Chicago (on behalf of a manager who claimed some earnings based on a prior plan for appearances in that city, which never came about) with imprecations and denunciations.

Was it all now contained, tightly suppressed within her, or had some armor accrued from absorbing Norma and Medea, Isolde and Elvira, Alceste, Armida, Anna Bolena, Violetta, Lucia, and the other ladies of operatic lore with whom she had lived, and died, in such close communion?

Certainly there had come about a unique fusion in her as an artist, with the dream world of the nineteenth century, its breadth of expression and depth of musical meaning (as communicated to her by Serafin and others), and the opportunities available to her in the electronic age in which she found herself. And, from the squat, nearsighted, heavy-in-the-legs person who came back to America from wartime Greece in 1946, there had emerged, through hard work, an insistent drive for self-improvement, and a richness of nature rarely lavished on a human being, a woman truly of the century's memorable few.

There is little question in my mind that the grand passion that united her to Onassis was love as she knew it, felt it, understood it. The casual affair was not in her line, to judge from one marriage (in a fatherly fashion) that lasted more than ten years, and the sunlight of self for which she left Meneghini.

How she felt about the separation from Onassis came to my attention all unwittingly in the fall of 1971 when she accepted Peter

Mennin's invitation, as president of the Juilliard School, to share her time and views with its vocal students.

She had left a message for me to call her, which I did. When she asked me what I was doing, I said I was going, the next day, to the opening of the John F. Kennedy Center for the Performing Arts in Washington, D.C., and added, mischievously: "How would you like to come along?" "What!" she said venomously. "To a place with that woman!?"

To know Maria Callas was not necessarily to love her, but to respect, admire, and value the qualities she possessed as a human being as well as an artist. The two things may or may not be interrelated—too often, they seem to be almost arbitrarily unrelated. But when they are interrelated, the belief that art has, to use a sometimes overworked phrase, some redeeming social value has to be considered at least a possibility.

Considering the distance that Callas had traveled in the relatively short period between Chicago, 1954, and Paris, 1976, the possibilities that were extinguished by her sudden collapse and death (September 16, 1977) were inestimable.

Needless to say, these did not relate to possible further performance as a singer. Before I left Paris for home, we had a long conversation in which I suggested that she drop the whole idea of singing again, and apply herself to something else. "Like what?" she queried.

"The theater," I said. "You should spend three months with a coach like Stella Adler, and see how it goes. Find out what you have to do to convert your production from singing to speaking."

"That would take a lot of money," she said. "You need a producer, and so on, and a play."

"You already have a subject," I said. "You have done it on the opera stage. And as a film. Now you should do it as a play."

"You mean *Medea*?"

"Of course," I said. "There is a wonderful translation by Robinson Jeffers, which served Judith Anderson so well (and vice versa) —Medea is Medea is Medea. You can do it in English one night, and in Greek the next. As far as a producer is concerned, you say you'll do it, and I can guarantee you one the next day . . ."

I cannot say that the suggestion stirred Callas to instant rapture. But she did not reject it. On returning to New York, I put together some further ideas, including a reference to the success of Ezio Pinza *after* he had learned how to overcome the problems that bothered him in speaking the lines of Emile de Becque (in *South Pacific*).

The answer was not long in coming.

> Paris August 19 1976
>
> I came back beautifully bronzed [from a Mediterranean holiday she had been contemplating] full of health and read your lovely letter.
>
> We will talk about everything when I see you in New York. I hope to be there in autumn if not sooner.
>
> In any case I really will be very happy to see you as always and we will continue our conversation soon.
>
> All my love and friendship
>
> > Love
> > Maria

She did not come to New York in the autumn of 1976, or ever.

POSTLUDE

Letters are, of course, the property of those who write them, and legally remain so.

But who owns the rights to letters written by a person who dies without leaving a will?

And, more particularly, when the estate is contested by two parties to whom the deceased would not give so much as the time of day?

In mid-1978, after much negotiation, the contest for the estate of Maria Callas was settled by a division of assets between Evangelia Kalogeropoulou, the mother from whom the artist had been estranged for decades, and Battista Meneghini, the husband from whom she had been divorced ten years before.

The formula for settlement was devised to avoid a costly court contest, and in consideration of the age of the two contestants. Both were more than eighty.

Cause of death was pronounced, by medical authorities of Paris, to have been a coronary, though she is not known to have had such a history. It is possible that it was the result of medication she had been taking for hypertension. Sir Rudolf Bing, out of his close connections to her, antagonisms with her, and observations of her, told me recently that he believes she committed suicide.

It will be recalled that Celli, from all his comparative studies, believed that, vocally, Callas was very close to Maria Malibran.

It is not commonly known that Maria I, for all the legend and lore that attached to her great career, died on September 23, 1836, at the age of only twenty-eight, after a severe fall while horseback riding. Not a tone of that voice has been heard in nearly a hundred and fifty years, but the mystique endures.

Maria II, who was fifty-three when she died in 1977, was, as I have said, a unique fusion of nineteenth-century impulses and twentieth-century opportunities. Not only did she record a considerable part of her mature repertory, but there has accrued, since her death, an astonishing quantity of issues of live performances. Among them is a hair-raising reproduction of her Kundry in *Parsifal* as she sang it on a broadcast in Italian, in Rome (1950).

Rest in peace, Maria.

Alfred

I

To include Alfred A. Knopf in a book which relates, however indirectly, to an angelic company will impress some who know him as either whimsy or satire. Alfred, assuredly, is company. But angelic? That can hardly be a less than facetious summation of his reputation over years of professional prominence.

But it may be added that God (whose name he seldom invokes, except scoffingly) gave him a long life in order to show, in the latter years of it, that under the crust of his never humble pie, he is a man of considerable warmth, even of kindly impulse. That he was a publisher of eminence has nothing to do with such added insights. But one might speculate that he perhaps concealed, much of his life, the qualities that came to the surface later, in order not to be considered a softy, hence, one to be taken advantage of.

My introduction to the possibility that his bark is more menacing than his bite came early in our relationship, and thus served well in later circumstances. He had, at the suggestion of Herbert Weinstock, then music editor for the firm, agreed to publish, in 1952, an updated, extended version of *The Metropolitan Opera* identified by the subtitle *1883–1950* (two previous editions produced by the Oxford University Press had brought the history to 1940). The timetable set forth in my contract of several years before seemed reasonable—what timetable in a contract doesn't?—until, near the end, I was in need of a further payment to fund the summer months of work that would see the book to conclusion.

This request I put into a brief note.

This is his reply, dated May 14, 1952:

Dear Mr. Kolodin:

I hope you won't mind me saying that I think that the request you made in your letter of May 10th was an extraordinary one. After all, we have been waiting a long time for a book that would comply with the terms of our agreement and the two thousand dollars we advanced in January of 1950 is not hay.[1] Even now you propose a book that will exceed the contractual maximum by perhaps as much as fifty thousand words which will again substantially increase the amount of our investment. Finally, there is no possibility of our getting a manuscript now in time for publication in the autumn, which is the time when this particular book ought to make its appearance.

Nevertheless, having said all this, if you feel that you can honorably promise me the final manuscript by August 1st, I will be glad to advance you another five hundred.

With kind regards, I am

Yours sincerely

That was, at its most graphic, the stern rejoinder before the gracious concession. First, he would exercise his annoyance, sometimes elevated to a high work of art, in denunciation and finality. Then, having put the recipient in tears and trembling, he would show the generosity of which he was capable, and come through with what was wanted, even though it was, as of the moment when the reply was formulated, "extraordinary."

The mixture of kindness and indignation was similarly shown on a later occasion, all unexpectedly (it was almost always unexpected, because the context was completely Alfredish). This pertained to the publication, under the Knopf imprint, of a collection of mostly brief pieces entitled *The Musical Life* which arose at his suggestion.

Everything went well this time: no delay, no request for an additional advance; it was a wholly manageable book to write (and rewrite). The time for perusal of the dust jacket arrived, with a copy in the mail. The blue and gray treatment was both attractive and imaginative, with only one reservation. The descriptive matter

---

[1] The sum referred to bought considerably more hay, also provisions for the family table, in 1952 than it does today. The book also bears the publication date of 1953.

about the author was pitched a little higher than I thought "he" (myself) merited. Taken altogether, the praise struck me as likely to arouse the resistance of other music critics, who might be inclined to review it.

Later in the day I called him, told him I liked the design, and that I had only one objection to the whole jacket.

"What's that?" he queried.

"The blurb on the inside front flap," I said. "It strikes me as a

© 1948 THE NEW YORKER MAGAZINE, INC.

Some Random Recollections

little high-pitched, and likely to arouse resistance from some potential reviewer."

"Listen," he said imperiously, "I wrote that myself. Now shut up!"

This instance of Knopf's participation in the coming to birth of a project that, in the perspective of a year's publishing schedule, could only be called minor is by no means atypical.

He was, in the very first instance, an enthusiast about two things: publishing and music, or, some who knew him better might say, music and publishing. When publishing and music were *combined*, the result was his particular pleasure . . . to work with, to have to do with.

That, perhaps, is the underlying reason why I have the particular kinds of recollections of him that I do. Others could, in all truth and sincerity, tell a wholly different account of their dealings with Alfred Knopf during the same period (from 1950 until 1975, when his day-to-day participation in the affairs of the firm which he had sold several years before dwindled). He had his views on any and all subjects, especially authors (including his own). His collected letters, when published, will make rich reading.

Those authors fortunate enough to have their manuscripts read and pencil-marked or more formally edited by Alfred Knopf were indebted to him for a service to which only one who really needed it could take exception. I have in mind one young author who was fortunate to have his manuscript gone through in this manner, and, in high dudgeon, rode off to another publisher. Curiously, he never had anything so readable published elsewhere.

Nor was Knopf of the opinion that his firm's processing of manuscripts in which he did not have a hand was uniformly better than that of other publishers. "Too damn long" was a favorite comment. "Could have been cut fifty pages and made a better book." He cherished reference books, having many years ago published one of the best: H. L. Mencken's *The American Language* (the first edition appeared in 1918).

To have been, in his time, a "Knopf author" was a mark of distinction as well as accomplishment, not unlike the cachet that attached to having a book published by the Oxford University Press.

There was, however, one significant difference.

It was somewhat difficult to get to Mr. Oxford to talk over with him something about a book. Mr. Knopf was always approachable by telephone (an instrument he has frequently denounced for having caused the decline of letter writing). And, for editorial problems, an appointment was always readily available.

One of the more pressing problems of such a relationship was to render unto Alfred what was Mr. Knopf's due, in a proper senior-junior status. After a few years—which could be paraphrased to read "after a few books"—the next phone call might be opened with the words: "This is Alfred." My response on that occasion was: "Mr. Knopf, how are you?"

"Don't call me Mr. Knopf," said Mr. Knopf. "Call me Alfred."

The privilege was hard to take in, all at once. But eventually I realized that about the only people who say "Mr. Knopf" to him in public are maître d's: so that formality was readily abandoned.

Among the infinity of distinctions—plaques, awards, honorary degrees—that Alfred owns is one that has to be unique.

On the back of the dust jacket of the most recent edition of *The Metropolitan Opera* (subtitled *1883–1966*) is a panoramic photo of the audience gathered for the final opera gala in the old theater before the demolition scheduled for the end of May. To my knowledge this makes Alfred the only publisher to be included in a news photo on the jacket of a book he published. There he is, only a few rows from the stage, waiting for the curtain to go up and the performance to begin.

II

Waiting for the curtain to go up and the performance to begin is a posture which Alfred Knopf has assumed so often (literally thousands of times since his student days at Columbia University, pre-World War I, which he marks as the beginnings of his serious interest in music) that one can hardly know where else he would be on April 16, 1966, than in the Metropolitan Opera House.

Each present occasion is more than an extension of habit: it is the external, visible evidence of an inner, invisible enthusiasm that has prevailed for nearly seventy years. Above all else, it is an enthusiasm that has benefited the world on a scale that few other music-loving publishers have approached.

My own experience with "Mr. Knopf" began, fittingly enough, when the firm occupied offices at 745 Fifth Avenue, then (1932) known as the Heckscher Building. A friend,[2] several years older than I (then twenty-four), and living in Europe, had an idea for a pioneering book about classical recordings. The content would be critical and comparative, arranged alphabetically by composers, a format that distinguished several later books, including one of my own, but which was then unavailable. He had sent me a batch of manuscript pages to show to publishers, in the hope of finding one interested enough to encourage him to go on listening and writing.

As a sample of the Knopf receptivity, I had made a prior approach to several publishers, without raising a response. But when I called the Knopf office and told his secretary the nature of the project, she found a time on his calendar, and entered my name. When I presented myself, the familiar figure (familiar from pictures in *Vanity Fair* and similar publications of the day) was seated at a large table (no office I ever saw him in had a desk). A few words of identification (I had just started work on the *Sun*) and he said something like "Let's see what you've got." I produced the sheets, and he examined them carefully, as anyone interested in music and records at the time would have.

"Interesting idea," he said, after a while. "I'd pay ten dollars for a copy, but I don't want to publish it."

As far as I can recollect, I thanked him and left.

Whether my first venture with Knopf was a success or not—and clearly it wasn't—my interest in his musical publications, and the year-to-year announcements of new ones to come, never faltered. As perusal of bookshelves in private, as well as public, libraries be-

[2] C. G. Burke (who died in 1975), known for writings in *High Fidelity*. I met him in the twenties in, of all places, a Doubleday bookshop, Newark, New Jersey.

came more extensive, so did my acquaintance with such names as Bodley Head (John Lane of London), Drei Masken Verlag (Munich), and Larousse (Paris). But Knopf appeared and reappeared, with impressive regularity, plus the greatest promise of interesting comment on all aspects of music. In a recent conversation, he mentioned: "My *beau idéal* among publishers at that time was William Heinemann. He not only published Galsworthy, but engaged Constance Garnett to make translations, as a result of which Dostoevski, Chekov, and other Russians could be read properly in English for the first time. S. Fischer Verlag of Berlin was another on which I modeled myself then."

A composer's name followed by the words "as Man and Artist" has become one of the most shopworn clichés of musical biography. But *Wagner as Man and Artist* was the first combination of these words to attract my attention when Ernest Newman's study appeared in 1924. (I still have the volume, minus cover, proof that pages sewn together endure longer than glued board covers.)

Pursuing the blood lines of books bearing the leaping dog (Borzoi) on the spine (the first appeared in 1915), I was soon into Rimsky-Korsakov's *My Musical Life* (this one so well produced it hasn't come apart fifty years later), J. W. N. Sullivan's *Beethoven: His Spiritual Development*[3] (1927), and J. B. Trend's *Manuel de Falla and Spanish Music*, a still unsurpassed treatise on an inexhaustible subject.

In many instances, awareness of a new book's existence came not so much from visits to bookshops, as by paying attention to the weekend newspaper columns by such men as Lawrence Gilman, Pitts Sanborn, Olin Downes, and, of course, Henderson. Writers of this quality, and the columns they produced, have steadily declined in American newspapers, as the newspapers themselves have even in such a metropolis as New York. For the eager young mind of today, such stimulation is far less readily available, least of all in newspapers and magazines.

Nothing so reveals a publisher's character, and the products in which he takes pride, as a list of books published as back matter

[3] Knopf acquired this great study as the result of publishing Sullivan's scientific literature.

in one of his own publications, to entice reader interest. The random list for a Knopf book published in 1929 reads:

TITLE	AUTHOR
Arturo Toscanini	Tobia Nicotra
Moussorgsky	Oskar van Riesemann
Franz Schubert's Letters etc.	Edited by Otto E. Deutsch
Correspondence Between Richard Strauss and Hugo von Hofmannsthal (1908–1918)	
Music: A Science and an Art	John Redfield
Chopin	Henri Bidou

There were, of course, publishers of books on music for the American market before Knopf joined them in 1916 with Carl Van Vechten's *Music and Bad Manners*. I would especially honor Charles Scribner's Sons for a list that included sixteen volumes of James Huneker's writings (a "list" in itself); also D. Appleton, Doubleday, and Macmillan, later Simon & Schuster, Random House, and most productively in recent years, W. W. Norton & Company.

But why did not one of them produce such long-inaccessible classics as Henry Chorley's *Thirty Years' Musical Recollections* or Hector Berlioz's *Evenings in the Orchestra* before they appeared with the Knopf imprint in the twenties? Perhaps because no other firm had so perceptive a musical adviser as Ernest Newman, or an owner with so avid an interest in music as Knopf himself. His correspondence with Newman began as early as 1912, when Knopf was still an employee of Doubleday, Page & Company, at the Country Life Press, Garden City, L.I. He wrote to Newman, suggesting he write a book on Berlioz. "Were you acquainted with him then?" I inquired. "No," said Knopf, "but I had read his early books and liked them. I first met him when I went to England in 1921. He made many suggestions, as did Henry Mencken and, of course, Van Vechten."

Far-ranging as the Knopf list of musical books may be, they

have (for the most part) several elements in common: almost every title on the list represents a distinctive approach to its subject matter, the literary quality tends to be above average, and it is likely to interest an educated layman as well as a well-informed musician (not necessarily a tautology).

You can work backward or forward through a list totaling nearly one hundred and fifty titles—which is to say, either from the last in the sequence or from the first—and come away with the same conclusion. Behind every book Knopf published on music is a man who knows music, who wants to know more *about* music and is determined that the experience be enjoyable rather than tedious—which is to say, Knopf himself.

In my assemblage of persons hitherto enumerated—conductor, pianist, novelist, critic, composer, pedagogue, opera singer among them—Knopf holds a place of honor: without his like, all their efforts would be in vain. He is a *music lover* par excellence, whether or not he was also a publisher. He has sat before musical performers for a longer period than anyone known to me personally. It is a sequence challenged for durability by only one other person—known to me only by reputation—who happens to be another publisher: the late Victor Gollancz. He had the extraordinary experience of hearing Joan Sutherland's first recital in London as a celebrity and being able to say, as he stomped out: "She's as great a bore as Nellie Melba."

Not unexpectedly, running through the inner circle of authors (I never heard him refer to a Knopf client as a "writer") whom he took particular pride to "publish for"[4] is a pronounced predilection for music. Thomas Mann, who became an adornment of the Knopf list very early, reflects such an affinity from *Buddenbrooks* (1924) and *The Magic Mountain* (1927) to *Dr. Faustus* (1948) (see page 46). Indeed, in a preface to his *Stories of Three Decades* (1936) Mann remarks of *Tonio Kröger* (1903): ". . . its musical affinities may have been what endeared it. Here probably I first learned to employ music as a shaping influence in my art."

Others of high priority to Knopf as persons to "publish for" were Willa Cather and H. L. Mencken. In *The Song of the Lark*

[4] I have never heard any other American publisher use that phrase.

(published by Houghton, Mifflin before Miss Cather became a Knopf author), the former created one of the first, best fictional studies of a singer (Olive Fremstad) ever put on paper; and the latter, with his enthusiasm for Bach, Beethoven, Brahms, and bock, was as much a part of the Borzoi lore as the Russian hound's rear paws. It is also known that, to invert a cliché, some of Knopf's best friends were performers, including Arthur Rubinstein, who, late in life, rewarded Knopf's patient wait for a book of memoirs by producing half a one in *My Young Years*, which became a best seller.

I discern in all of this a lifelong, rampant affair with sharps and flats, tones and timbres, tenors, sopranos, altos, mezzos, baritones, and basses (Feodor Chaliapin's *Man and Mask*, detailing the craft of one of the greatest of basses, was published by Knopf in 1932). He also likes pianists, violinists, and cellists, but conductors interest him even more.

He tolerates them for personal shortcomings as well as occasional virtues, providing the music they produce at the podium or in the recording studio lifts his spirits. Now that Serge Koussevitzky, Leopold Stokowski, Thomas Beecham, George Szell, and several dozen other perennial favorites have died, he takes a deeper participatory pleasure in the music of Herbert von Karajan than of George Solti.

Knopf has maintained a lifelong interest in recording in all its forms, from single- and double-sided 78 rpms, acoustic, then electric, LPs mono and stereo, but never quad. He is guardedly of the opinion that the disc may have outrun its utility and cassette may be the wave of the future, for convenience as well as quiet. He agrees with me that banishment of the stylus, hence suppression of surface noise, may be the greatest boon to mankind since whoever it was enabled a TV user to look at the picture on his set with the sound turned off.

He never published a word of James Huneker, not for lack of admiration, but because that encompassing critic, as I have noted, was a house pride of Scribner's. Included among Huneker's interests were Picasso and Prokofiev, Strindberg and Schoenberg, Duse and D'Annunzio, in most cases before any other American writer knew their names. He also invented a word that well describes not only Alfred and myself, but many others hopelessly attached to music.

We are, in Huneker's fine resonant word, *melomaniacs* (a title he used for a book of 1902). Virgil Thomson more recently described the same segment of society, in a contemporary analogy, as addicts. I like the Huneker term better. Addictions can be acquired easily—merely by overindulgence—whereas to be a melomaniac one has to be born one.

III

There may be thousands—nay, hundreds of thousands—of melomaniacs in the world at one time, but identification and classification of them can elude ready public recognition. As a person who has pursued this innocuous form of vibratory response for most of a lifetime, I know the telltale signs are by no means uniform. Unlike addicts of the non-Thomsonian order, the arm is not pitted with evidences of the needle, the "fix" is acquired invisibly, and even the cost of the "habit" is relatively modest. I have not yet heard of any true melomaniac snatching a passerby's purse in order to buy tickets to an all-Bruckner program—severe as his need may be—nor is the average householder in danger of having his premises rifled for a piece of property that can be pawned for the price of admission to *Parsifal*. The hunger can be keen, but it is rarely converted into asocial behavior.

To recognize a person as a melomaniac takes a good deal of observation. In the common cant of thieves, it takes one to know one. The mere fact that one person in a particular profession may be a melomaniac does not mean that his colleagues also are. Hector Berlioz, as an instance, was unquestionably a melomaniac as well as a great composer. It did not show in the music he wrote, rather in his prose. No one not so infected could have attended the quantity of concerts and operatic performances Berlioz did as a critic, and have written his kind of witty prose about so many of them, were he otherwise. Perhaps it was the duality of his gifts that brought about his schismatic expression of them: I can hardly think of any other professional composer so curious as Berlioz was about the music of others. Liszt? Perhaps. But I would credit the abbé's far-reaching curiosity about the music of others—Grieg to Borodin, Smetana to Edward MacDowell—to *egomania* rather than melomania. I think he enjoyed being thought of as broad-minded and hospitable.

In the ranks of professional performers, the symptoms crop up, like guilt, through association. In his great, long prime as a performer, I have seen Rubinstein, Arthur (especially in the years when he spent his Christmas holiday in New York) at a Metropolitan Opera performance (when the cast was choice), in Carnegie Hall (to lend his attention to a Sviatoslav Richter), even to a recital by a young pianist in Town Hall. That the performer's name was Eric Heidsieck may suggest that the great pianist-gourmet etc. was more motivated by fondness for the family that produced so fine a champagne than by an attachment to their young offspring's performance of Chopin.

Eugene Istomin I would characterize as a pianist with an advanced case of melomania. That would relate not alone to the time he takes from a solo career to perform trios with Isaac Stern and Leonard Rose—both practicing melomaniacs—but also to his predilection, Rubinstein-wise, for opera. Time and opportunity are both restricted for one with his yearly schedule of travel, nor is he likely to put himself out for the next *Rigoletto* or *Tosca* he might encounter on a night off. Change the bill, however, to Moussorgsky's *Boris Godunoff* or Beethoven's *Fidelio*, and Istomin might even stand to participate.

Times, of course, change circumstances. Some years ago I measured the depth of the true melomania in a friend (who had nothing to do with the professional world of music) when he began to salivate at the prospect of hearing a *particular* piece of music. He was a writer celebrated (in suitable circles) for his wit in a column that appeared several times a week in the New York (Jewish) *Forward* (*Vorwärts*).[5] He was also a record collector of such formidable appetite that I took to calling a music store in which we met,

[5] Villard, Oswald Garrison, *The Disappearing Daily* (Alfred A. Knopf, Inc., New York, 1944), pp. 209–15.

day after day, Finkel's Cave, in tribute to his family name as well as his affection for the music of the man (Mendelssohn) who produced the great *Fingal's Cave* overture. He occasionally visited me at home, where I listened professionally to new releases in the thirties and forties, in the hope of acquiring a discard before it reached the shops. One day—and the content dates the occurrence as pre-LP—he listened enviously to the final measures of a Beethoven overture as he was admitted to the apartment.

"*Fidelio* overture," he exclaimed. "That's something!" In 78-rpm days it was indeed a find. Today's LP catalogue would show *six* versions not only of the overture, but of the whole opera. But then, Ben Finkel's day would have been ruined if he couldn't take the *Fidelio* overture home with him and play it as often as he wished. So, when he left, it left with him (his need being greater than mine).

In the larger reaches of melomania which can only be surmised, not proven, are literary works in which the author's references to musical works is decidedly suggestive. The *Ulysses* of James Joyce is replete with references, through Buck Mulligan, to Mozart's *Don Giovanni* and to Meyerbeer's *Les Huguenots*, among other operas. These allusions, plus the biographical data that link Joyce's early ambitions as a singer to the career of John McCormack (who was born in Athlone two years after Joyce was born in Dublin in 1882), leave little doubt that he had a feeling for music comparable to that of another Irishman and lover of *Don Giovanni*, G. B. Shaw.

In addition to lecturing such a winning singer of the 1890s as Victor Maurel on how to sing Don Giovanni, Shaw converted his esteem for Mozart and the Don into the blood and bone of *Man and Superman*. The factors were so pervasive a part of one visit of mine to the same Covent Garden in which Shaw had sat as a critic (in London they don't close down an opera house after a mere eighty-three years' use as they did in New York with the original Metropolitan) that a residual element came my way after a performance of *Don Giovanni*.

Though I have long been indoctrinated in the practice of avoiding communication, either spoken or written, with other reviewers before I put my own thoughts in order, nobody had ever suggested that this should apply to those from a fellow practitioner actually deceased. In any case, curiosity got the better of me, and this is what I read (there had been the usual dress rehearsal forty-eight hours before) from a wad of paper pushed into a hinge between the seat and the back behind me as I have deciphered and transcribed it:

> *Don Giovanni* is not only Mozart's best opera, it is opera at its best. Here is a welcome sign of the good things I have been hearing [astrally of course] about the emergence of a new school of native British singers. All the tiresome Italian mannerisms I had to endure from Signor this and Signora that are, apparently, as dead as I am. They have—I would say "Thank God" save that my time in the afterworld has given me no cause to change my mind about the non-existence of such a divinity—been succeeded by people named Evans and Glossop, Burrows, Howell, even Jones. They are better to look at and decidedly better to hear than those who tried my patience in the '90s. Not that good looks are a guarantee of good Mozartian manners. How often I scolded the lovely Emax [the name was hard to make out[6]] with her gem-like tones, for the slovenly way she strung them on a golden strand of a total misconception.
>
> By comparison with one performance I then attended, Miss Gwyneth Jones did not omit Donna Anna's "Non mi dir" nor did Stuart Burrows opt to give "Dalla sua pace" a miss. Much of this could doubtless be attributed to that youthful tidal wave of directorial power, Colin Davis. He conducted as though he were, indeed, facing Mozart, rather than the inanimate score on the music desk. My mother in Dublin used to say that if you could sing such a phrase as "Là ci darem la mano" properly you could apply the same sense of line, of climax and of drama to everything else in *Don Giovanni*. Davis could, and did.
>
> I would, however, have admired Davis more had he acquired some of the authority that pervaded the work of Hans Richter (sometimes!) or of Toscanini (unfailingly!) when he visited London for concerts with the BBC Symphony in 1938. If Davis had, he would have cut short the audience's enthusiasm for Burrows' good singing of "Il mio tesoro" in order to get on with Elvira's "In quali eccessi." I could see Davis fretting at the desk as the

---

[6] Doubtless the reference was to the fair-faced Emma Eames. See page 95.

applause continued, muttering to the orchestra leader that the public, even in London, is an ass—but one cannot have all the good things at once, save perhaps in *Man and Superman* or *Pygmalion*, which, I have heard, is now called *My Fair Lady*, for some curious reason.

I observed, from a pre-performance glance at the list of performers in the program held by the lady who had actually owned the ticket [for the seat Shaw was also occupying, as astral bodies can adapt themselves to any physical formation] that the knighted member of the cast, Sir Geraint Evans, played Leporello, the Don's servant.

That is entirely in order, for the servant class in Britain has regularly surpassed, in tact, sensitivity, and mode of behavior, its masters. That Sir Geraint is also Welsh is fair assurance that he would be a good singer. Indeed, this cast had the rare distinction of having three principal singers of Welsh origin: Burrows, from Pontypridd, a performer with a straightforward manly style and none of those Italian affectations beloved of Slavic and Germanic singers of Mozart; Evans; and also Miss Jones, out of Pontnewynydd. She has a stately manner as Donna Anna, no doubt derived from her place of birth.

Now, then, to the Don. I wish that young Peter Glossop, who has a fine figure, a lovely voice and a courtly manner, would read my *Man and Superman* (I could hardly expect him to read what I, as a musical critic, was writing in the 1890s about Maurel, entertaining as it was). He would then know something about the Life Force and how not to squander it.

But would a Don who plays the part so much for sexual virility have thrown away all those lovely visions of the future—he had a whole ballroom-full of them in his castle—just to make a debating point with the Commendatore, when he comes to visit him as a stone statue? Losing the debate cost the Don not only his life, but cost him eternal damnation—and, as an expert on the subject, I can tell you it is more eternal than damnation, and damnably boring. Glossop's Don should have temporized a little, taken an oath at the Commendatore's knee about virgins such as Donna Anna, just to go on being a bit more of a bastard . . .

Even though the note from GBS, on a night off from damnation, was incomplete, there could be no doubt that, on the whole, he thought well of the Mozart at Covent Garden in the late years of the twentieth century. His jottings suggested that the Mozart of the 1970s was decidedly more suitable to its sources, musically, than what had been heard when he was a young critic, "Golden Age" though it was reputed to be. At least, in this performance, he did not hear the performer of Zerlina sing the last note of "Batti, batti" an octave *higher* than Mozart wrote it, as he mentions in his comment of May 13, 1891.[7]

Such an intimation from so celebrated a bygone melomaniac as Shaw gives welcome reinforcement to those who consider Mozart, in this period, to be much better served in *totality* than he was, sporadically, at any prior time.

If the astral excursions of GBS include the privilege, now and then, of dropping into a bookshop and perusing its contents for mentions of his name in contemporary publications, I should amend the prior paragraph. While he was indeed a melomaniac, he had his own way of referring to it. As both a critic and playwright, Shaw made no secret of his limitation. Like mine, it pertained to knowledge of foreign languages.

In one of his sequence of *Self Sketches*, he states: "As to languages and mathematics, my qualifications are negligible." He professes the ability to "read French as familiarly as English," and that he can "gather the news from the local papers" in Italy and Spain, and "guess" his way through "most of the letters" he receives in German. But, he says, "As a linguist in conversation I am hopeless."[8] This is altogether in keeping with his other dictum that learning to use English well is a sufficient life's work to keep a man from learning other languages.

Such being the case, I am not startled to observe, in Hesketh Pearson's biography, that in speaking of the problems that arose when he banged away at his favorite selections from Wagner's *Ring*, which drove "his mother nearly crazy," Shaw writes: "If I had to live my life over again I should devote it to the estab-

---

[7] Shaw, Bernard, *Shaw on Music*, edited by Eric Bentley (Doubleday & Company, Inc., Garden City, N.Y., 1955), p. 70.

[8] Shaw, Bernard, *Sixteen Self Sketches* (Dodd, Mead & Company, New York, 1949), p. 117.

lishment of some arrangement of headphones and microphones
. . . whereby the noises made by musical maniacs should be audible to themselves only."[9]

I respect Shaw's right to use the English form of the term, if
that is his preference, but I do not feel that it is anywhere as near
expressive as melomaniac.

IV

The remarkable thing about all those of the clan of recent date
(including myself) is that we are all better-informed melomaniacs
than we might have been otherwise, because of a Lebanese mystic
named Kahlil Gibran, and his place in the life and fortunes of
Alfred A. Knopf, Inc. "I met him in the Village," Knopf has recalled, "at a lunch given by [Harold] Witter Bynner. We published several of Gibran's books—one I think was called *The
Madman,* and another was a collection of drawings—that lost rather sizable sums of money."

In 1923, Gibran produced the now universally known "prose
poem" (Gibran's title) called *The Prophet.* Unlike some other
publishers who have given up on unprofitable authors one book
too soon, Knopf was, and is, publisher of *The Prophet.* "It sold
about twelve hundred in the first year," commented Knopf, "and
stayed about that way, then doubled. It began to climb but stayed
around ten thousand a year, then climbed again. The first million
took a while: and the second, even longer. The third million was
not quite so long."

As to the suggestion that this was akin to "having a license to
print money," Knopf has noted that *The Joy of Cooking* has had
a comparable sale. The outcome has not been spelled out to me,
in dollars and cents. But the impression I have gathered over years
is that a substantial number of the hundred and fifty books on
music that have been published during Alfred's time as head of
the firm have been made possible by the flow of money from the

[9] Pearson, Hesketh, *G.B.S. A Full Length Portrait* (Harper & Brothers, New
York and London, 1942), p. 36.

firm's backlist. This has, over decades, included such authors as Thomas Mann, Willa Cather, Sigrid Undset, Albert Camus, Catherine Bowen, and, of course, Gibran.

If this latitude was invoked on behalf of Ernest Newman's four-volume biography of Richard Wagner (published in separate volumes dated 1933, 1937, 1941, and 1946), a near impossible task has never been funded from so unlikely a source. By a curious perversity of publishing, the thick volumes languished during much of the remainder of Newman's life (he died in 1959) in mute, dormant non-glory. Thanks, however, to newer techniques in publishing, the four volumes have become both more visible and more viable in the 1970s than ever before. This includes a paperback form that provides the essential information at a much more appealing price.

To dwell further on the manner in which Knopf's personal love for music has rendered an impersonal but irreplaceable service to the art over nearly six decades would be laboring a point by now self-evident. He has himself, from a retrospect of an octogenarian, seen it in a vista hardly possible for anyone else.

"Put me down as an old man who grows more radical year by year," he says. "Let's face it. Our firm was a one-time shot. It never happened before and it couldn't happen again. We had a free hand and could do what we wanted to do. If we ran into trouble my father was there when we needed help. When he died [1932] we had a couple of tough years. We never had any 'real' money until the sale. Of course we lived well and had everything we wanted before that, but we lived up to what was coming in."

In a rare burst of continuous comment, he went on: "I get furious when I read about 'Blanche Knopf, wife of the publisher.' Blanche was a damn fine publisher. She was also a partner from the very first. She was altogether responsible for our 'French connection,' Camus, Sartre, Beauvoir, and so on. Everything to do with Elinor [Wylie, author of *The Venetian Glass Nephew* among other novels and books of poetry] was hers, and many, many other things too." When the late Herbert Weinstock came on as music editor (1944) the list of books on music expanded significantly, including his trilogy of the I's: Rossini, Bellini, and Donizetti.

The "sale" to which Alfred referred in this conversation of June 4, 1979, crystallizes much about the arts and their inseparable ally, the private sector, at this period of the twentieth century. The impact of a Charles Scribner's Sons has been perpetuated unto a Charles Scribner III; Doubleday has its line of succession. Schott und Söhne in Germany persists as one of the great music publishing enterprises of modern times, like Boosey and Hawkes, and Ricordi in Italy. In each instance, the name defines an identity, an interest, a guarantee of quality carried forward from generation to generation.

As presently constituted, the trade name of Alfred A. Knopf, Inc., suggests another such dynasty in the grand tradition, flying a house flag (the bounding Borzoi), renowned for excellence, responsive to its heritage of quality to provide a present related to the past and to the future, not only by blood lines, but by similar aspirations and objectives.

The unhappy truth is that it is nothing of the kind. Nearly twenty years ago, having arrived at a point of life when he was approaching seventy, Knopf says, "Physically speaking, there was only one Alfred A. Knopf. I had one son. He had left the firm and started a business of his own [Athenaeum]. This prompted some queries from other publishers. Bennett Cerf, of Random House, an old friend, was among them. You must remember, at that time, that Random House had floated a few shares of stock at a price that just went up and up. The age had begun when getting money from Wall Street bankers for the purchase of a well-known profitable publishing firm by another well-known publishing firm was no problem.

"One day at lunch, in the Cub Room of the Stork Club [original site, East Fifty-third Street] I finally said to Bennett: 'Why don't you make a proposal?' He said: 'Can I see your books?' to which I answered: 'Well, certainly.' A couple of weeks later," Knopf went on, "there met in my office on Madison Avenue, Bennett, his partner Don Klopfer, Blanche, and myself, and an agreement was reached. We soon [1960] became a part of Random House, with the stated agreement that we would preserve our own complete editorial identity, advertising, sales, publicity, and all. It was a perfect union."

During the decade that ensued, several things happened. Blanche Knopf died in 1966. Cerf's own ambition (characterized, by one who knew him well, as a desire to sit on the board of RCA) brought about Random House's absorption by the giant conglomerate. Shortly after [1971] Cerf died. Knopf and Klopfer lived on in a new, somewhat less than perfect union. During the seventies much talk circulated about a take-over by the Times-Mirror Syndicate of Los Angeles, but it did not occur. In 1980, however, a sale by RCA to the Newhouse Newspapers did. The interests of S. I. Newhouse, son of the founding father of the enterprises (of the same name), promise well.

My interest in such an accommodation to the conglomerate concept (which rules American life, as cartels rule international life) has nothing to do with who owns a business, or why. Rather it points a fairly unsteady finger of discontent with a practice all too commonly encountered in the arts today, and constantly on the rise, namely: "Whose name means what?"

When a business is called not the Oxford University Press but Alfred A. Knopf, the public has every right to assume that it is Mr. Knopf who is responsible for the merchandise sold in his name, not Mr. Oxford. Likewise such names as G. Schirmer (in music publishing), Avery Fisher of Fisher Radio (once one of the proudest names in audio), or Steinway (in the making and merchandising of pianos). The latest of these is somewhat marginal, for there still are Steinways in that business.

But the forebears—known widely as Theodore or Uncle Billy to the musical world they adorned—who gave them the proud possession of a multistoried building at 109 West Fifty-seventh Street, would be appalled to discover that not only has the firm name been erased from its façade (to be replaced by that of an insurance company) but that the frieze commemorating the muses of music has given way to a bas-relief of the Statue of Liberty encircled by the words: Manhattan Life Insurance Company.

Now and then an offshoot of such a liaison may benefit an art rather than misserve it. When the proud name of Fisher, which once (1940–50) identified the highest quality of radio and recorded music reproduction in the American market, was sold to a purveyor of production-line merchandise, the contract of sale provided a substantial quantity of stock in the buying firm. Eventually it was shared by its owner with Lincoln Center for the Performing Arts to a degree that made possible the rebuilding of the acoustically deficient Philharmonic Hall.

This was a community service of true distinction, one that gave high credit to the name of Avery Fisher. But, I would say, my preference would have been for Fisher, as a practicing melomaniac (chamber music branch, home party variety), to have insisted that the hall continue to bear the even prouder name of the Philharmonic which inhabits the hall. It could even, like some of his best audio merchandise of old, bear the designation: Mark II.

Perhaps if I were a balletomane rather than a melomaniac, I would have less regret for the second-generation Borzoi who bounds on the back of some fine balletic picture books. They are often quite handsome. And the substantial biography of Anton Webern by the Moldenhauers does the family line credit.

But, taken together, somehow they just don't *sing*.

Willie

Among the many melomaniacs known to me, from Alfred A. Knopf to Ben Finkel, almost all pursue their interest as an avocation. There is, however, one who pursues it as a vocation as well as an avocation. This makes him happy as a hummingbird—a winged creature whose sound he could probably produce in recorded form on demand—while making for him a more than passable income.

Everyone is, of course, versed on the effect, influence, and social impact in our times of the counterculture. But how many reckon with the magnitude and diversity of the under-the-counter culture?

Put this way, it suggests that, if I share with you, the reader, the whereabouts of his operation, I should say that you approach a certain number on a certain street in New York's mid-forties (west side), knock twice, and ask for Willie. Such is hardly the case anymore, because the under-the-counter culture has so flourished around the world that, in at least one country, a code of legitimacy has been contrived that can only make practices in other countries appear to be outmoded and unrealistic. As the country is Italy, a highly important source for much of the most desirable output, the implications are far-reaching.

A good two thirds of the merchandise which Willie Lerner cherishes a) for his personal pleasure, b) for the personal profit derived from making it available for the pleasure of his clients, has a factor in common. That is a "superior" performance of something which has originated on the stage of an opera house. I utilize the questioning quotes around "superior" because what causes one customer's blood pleasure to rise might have the same effect on another's gorge. That is to say, an incredibly sustained high (or low) note may be the exceptional experience that one melomaniac considers priceless, and another, merely bad taste. But that is what makes not only horse races, but melomaniacs.

More often than not, the performance has been broadcast, which means that it can be tape-recorded, whether the Italian point of origin was La Scala, Milan, San Carlo, Naples, or the Maggio Musicale in Florence. The recent legislation that is now operative provides that any live performance circulated by radio within Italy's borders enters, after a twenty-year period, public domain. Clearly this means that an enormous backlog of source material from Italian broadcasts of the forties and fifties is reproducible at will. It also means that the pursuit of copyrights involved there, or elsewhere, is far more complicated than previously.

As to the under-the-counter aspect of the culture, it brings to light a proliferation of product that now circulates in some of the largest record outlets in the country, such as the King Karol shops in many of the boroughs of New York City. The audience for it is avid, indeed insatiable. The circumstances pertaining to the appearance of some great figure, or figures, of the art at a moment in time, a given day, a particular evening, are far more appetite-inducing than another version of Beethoven's Third, Fourth, Fifth, Sixth, or Seventh symphonies. Of course, if it is the Ninth, interests and anticipations may change, depending more on the members of the vocal quartet than on who is conducting.

Willie Lerner's combination of vocation and avocation may be cited as a shining example of a barely distinguishable line between who does what, and what is done by whom, *when*. If he should, by some form of investigative magic, come up with the rarest of all *un*recorded phenomena, a credible likeness, duly authenticated, of the voice of Jean De Reszke, he would be hailed as a public benefactor. As a simple satisfaction of my own historic curiosity, I would myself be a customer for such a disc at, say, fifty dollars— *provided* it meets the criteria set forth.

The great Tristan and Romeo, Faust, Chevalier des Grieux (in Massenet's *Manon*), and much-prized performer of a dozen other roles, left the operatic stage (1902) before live recording was even a speculative possibility. Connoisseurs are well aware that Lionel Mapleson, Sr., a history-minded music librarian of the Met in De Reszke's time, rigged up a horn and cylinder device on a high point above the stage, and came away with the distant sounds of barely recognizable voices. Some now say that modern filtering devices, computerized techniques, etc. may permit a claim "That could be Jean De Reszke." But proof? By the time (1907–8) studio resources had improved to the point where great artists, such as Caruso or Edouard De Reszke (see page 76), participated, Jean had retired and had no interest in "singing into a horn."

Indeed, it was not until the mid-twenties, when the electrical method of sound reproduction was introduced (an advanced form of the analogue method, employing a microphone that converts sound into an electrical impulse, which is reconverted into sound from an amplifier and speaker), that a voice in a live operatic performance was recognizably reproduced for commercial sale. By far the most successful of such early ventures is contained in segments from a performance of Modeste Moussorgsky's *Boris Godunoff*. In it, Feodor Chaliapin's reputation as a great embodiment of the Russian Czar is sustained in sounds that are heard from the stage of London's Covent Garden.

They are extraordinary in vitality, if only moderate in volume; but there they are, more than fifty years after the performance of July 4, 1928.

Having achieved such a success with the primitive microphones then available, the presumption would be that record companies would keep closely in touch with opportunities that presented themselves in outstanding musical events of the time, to gather, systematically and live, important events in the careers of such performers as sopranos Rosa Ponselle and Kirsten Flagstad, tenors Beniamino Gigli and Lauritz Melchior, bass Ezio Pinza, mezzo Sigrid Onegin.

Anything of that *veritable* sort to be found in archives (or among reissues on shelves in Lerner's shop, those of King Karol, Sam Goody, and others in cities elsewhere) is derived, almost uniformly, from broadcasts that have been retrieved and reprocessed. The stylus-and-wax method of reproduction, for discs that could, at most, accommodate four minutes of sound, was sacred to all sorts of preconceptions and preconditions as to how a disc was made. I was myself a worshiper at the altar of perfection, in which the rigor of take after take after take in a studio discouraged experimentation. So many of the results were of such imperishable value—the Schnabel Beethoven, as an example—that criticism of the method that produced them is all but an impertinence. But there *were* other possibilities, few of which were pursued.

Periodically, *force majeure*, such as the unwillingness of an independent-minded conductor (such as Leopold Stokowski) to settle for the results that were possible in a crowded studio, prompted experiment in a concert hall. It was under such circumstances that the best results in the thirties were achieved in this country by Stokowski in the Philadelphia Academy of Music, Serge Koussevitzky in Boston's Symphony Hall, eventually Arturo Toscanini in Carnegie Hall, with the famous orchestras with which they were associated. But the point of view remained much the same: each hall became a different, larger kind of *studio*, in which the objective was hardly "realism" (frequency range was too constricted for that), but the same artificiality as before, in better sound. As is well remembered, the frustrating short time period possible with a twelve-inch 78-rpm disc prompted an effort (in 1931) by the Victor record engineers to reduce the playing speed to 33⅓ revolutions, and thus produce a "longer-playing" record (seven minutes, plus). But the turntables were unreliable at slow speeds, pitches were unbearably erratic, and the effort was set aside.

When a rare live recording did come along—such as Bruno Walter's direction of Mahler's Ninth Symphony in Vienna on January 26, 1938, shortly before *Anschluss* with Hitler's Germany was proclaimed[1]—techniques of procedure were carried over from

[1] The surprising quantity of live recordings of Mahler in this period (1930–40), including Walter's great *Das Lied von der Erde* and Eugene Ormandy's pioneering recording of the "Resurrection" Symphony (No. 2) with the Minneapolis Symphony, does not indicate a partiality to his literature. Rather, it was the most available way for a recording company to acquire such material *without* underwriting the large rehearsal costs of the sizable orchestra required.

the studio to the concert hall. I observe as much from these comments on that document (V Set 726): "So far as can be divined
by a strained attention, one could hardly hear a more eloquent,
thoroughgoing and generally penetrating performance than this
one: but the restatement of it in the recording leaves much to be
desired. There are few evidences of the audience in the concert
hall, but an irritating buzzer can be heard before the beginning of
virtually each new side, the breaks are exceedingly abrupt, and the
instrumental sound is erratic."

I'd say in retrospect that the notion of the record as a means of
purveying perfection was still uppermost in the mind of the man
who wrote those words (myself).[2] Unquestionably, what was then
issued as a record was, indeed, a *record* of what somebody had
done, rather than—as in all too many recent instances—a compila-
tion of takes edited into a performance which, as a totality, had
never existed. But I didn't make sufficient clamor to support the
value of live reproduction in a way that demanded more of it,
with improved technology. It took a war to produce the means
(primarily magnetic tape and improved microphones) that produced the under-the-counter culture.

II

What I would call the milestone occurrence in this long, undis-
tinguished, and not very productive chapter in the use of recording to the greatest advantage happened—by curious coincidence—
in the same year, the same month, and almost the same day as the
Vienna concert which produced the Mahler Ninth Symphony.
The day was January 16, 1938, the place was Carnegie Hall on a
cold, cold Sunday night, and the audience participation differed as
greatly in character as it did in distance from Vienna.

The evening marked the first appearance in concert by clarinetist Benny Goodman and the extraordinary assemblage of great
jazz musicians in his band (enriched by a choice coterie of invited

[2] Kolodin, Irving, *A Guide to Recorded Music* (Doubleday, Doran and
Company, Inc., Garden City, N.Y., 1941), p. 229.

guests). Like a near-myriad of other happenings in this great hall, it would have vanished into silence save for a Goodman enthusiast named Albert Marx, who had the interest, the means, and the foresight to arrange for a live recording (there could be no other kind!) to be made at his own cost, for his own pleasure. "Foresight" was the indispensable ingredient: there were in the hall microphone facilities maintained for the weekly broadcasts by the New York Philharmonic Orchestra. The line could be "opened" for a fee. The rest was a matter of processing, though the short recording discs then available had to be changed rapidly to cover what was going on—none of it altogether predictable.

As I have written elsewhere, I discovered all of this a day or so after the concert (in which I had a minor part as an adviser and program-note writer) when I paid a visit to Goodman and said: "Too bad, Benny, that no one made a recording." He laughed and said, pointing to a pile of shiny zinc boxes on a table, "Somebody did." I borrowed one set for an aural revisit to the occurrence, and, after absorbing it overnight, returned it to Goodman. Marx had his set, Goodman retained another, and the third went to the Library of Congress.

Why, at this distance of years, such a happening would have *already* appeared to have such a historical impact is perhaps, for readers and listeners of today, difficult to comprehend. Jazz concerts are a familiar fact, worldwide, and reproductions of them are commonplace. As the first of its kind, the Goodman concert was certainly historic. But what made it as widely remarked as it was in the days that followed?

Perhaps some part of the answer can be provided by the following editorials in New York's most prominent newspapers:

HOT MUSIC AT CARNEGIE

Benny Goodman glorified swing music at Carnegie Hall on Sunday evening, and some of those who heard him were bored. The great majority of Mr. Goodman's audience, however, vibrated in unison with the master's clarinet, and in fact did everything except dance down the sawdust trail and get prayed over by this musical Billy Sunday. There seems to be no middle group who like swing music a little. One either loves it to the point of distraction or one takes to the hills to get away from it. It is of no use to argue about it.

In this respect swing is in harmony with the major movements that are sweeping the world today. It is of no use to argue about them, either. Each has its prophet and each prophet is as unassailable as Aristotle was to the scholars of the late Middle Ages. Nor is it of any use to think about them. Their adherents don't think about them. They feel about them. Like swing, they are strictly a spinal column affair.

Yet swing differs from our other great contemporary trends in having nothing repressive about it. It gives free exposure to the player's individualism. The best things he does are not in the written score at all. It encourages a style of dance, as in the Big Apple, which has more exuberance than pattern. Perhaps, after all, it is not so much a doctrine set to music as it is a revolt against doctrine. Let those who do not like it try to bear with it. If Mr. Goodman and his colleagues take music to pieces, maybe some genius will presently put it together again. And if the individual has his unhampered say in music, he may manage to have it in other fields. Dictators should be suspicious of swing.

New York *Times* editorial, January 18, 1938, Robert L. Duffus.

SWING IN CARNEGIE HALL

Swing music has its fanatical devotees. It may not be music at all, but it has developed an immense following, and the masters of swing have invented a language containing many strange and wonderful terms—words which are so much gibberish to the old-fashioned music lover. Mr. Benny Goodman's highly successful concert of swing music in Carnegie Hall Sunday night presented a nice problem to the critics. Judged by ordinary standards, the concert might have seemed utter nonsense, and yet the hall was packed with eager worshipers of the Goodman technique, and the event became, in its way, as historic as that evening, fourteen years ago, when Paul Whiteman essayed a jazz concert with great success.

The trouble with bringing a critical judgment to bear on such a performance is that the commentator is likely to be placed in the position of a man who, upon examining an orange, remarks:

"This is not a very good apple." Thus, to be too critical of the concert would convict one of being an "alligator" (one who pretends to know swing but doesn't). But to the "cats" (experts in swing language) it was great stuff.

New York *Herald Tribune* editorial, January 18, 1938, probably Stanley Walker.

More than a decade, and a war, later, Goodman's box was discovered on an upper shelf of a closet in his suburban home by a daughter who asked, "What's this, Daddy?" Daddy took a look and recalled instantly what it was. He took it immediately, all but unplayed and virginal, to a sound studio. Both the long-playing record and tape had come into being by that time, and the union was heaven-sent. The acetate discs in the box, spotless and scratchless, were transferred to tape (in laboratory use at the time —1950—though not yet available as a home consumer product), and the recording was produced for mastering. Sales began in 1951.

The processed product brought to world attention a marvelous likeness of an unforgettable evening. The true *marvel* of it all is that rather than deteriorating with time and all the improvements in recording (including stereophony and digitality), the contents become ever more remarkable as improvements in amplifiers (or receivers) and speakers bring the thrust, excitement, and raw vitality of the playing ever closer to the ear.

The immediate beneficiaries were the jazz melomaniacs (an unaffiliated, sometimes complementary, rarely identical branch of the breed). They responded not merely with enthusiasm, but with such an outpouring of cash that Columbia OSL 160 is one of the most successful, if least intentional, productions in history. Within ten years after the records were put on sale, sales of the albums had passed a million, with a steady, unremitting interest since. Against the infinity of studio recordings of jazz before and after, it is unique in providing audible evidence of how a great ensemble (*and* its audience) sounded on a particular night and in a specific hall.

Doubtless there was enormous envy across the jazz world of the early fifties, among the Dorseys, the Kentons, and the Woody

Hermans, even among Ellington and his advisers—none had such a testament to their best days for public sale. The Ellington band had given a similar concert in Carnegie Hall in 1943, but he had no Albert Marx among his friends, and the example of the Goodman retrospect was still in the future. Such sound as has been preserved is a muffled likeness of the original (Prestige).

One of the first to react to its lesson when it was made evident in the marketplace was jazz impresario Norman Granz, whose "Jazz at the Philharmonic" (a title derived from the now bygone home of the Los Angeles Philharmonic, where the Granz series began) added foresight to accident. A paying audience was attracted by the names of the participating personnel; and the quality of music that was heard could be skimmed, from the tape that resulted, for the best of the best. In time (now more than twenty-five years) the total of jazz, rock, pop, even disco, derived from live performances has documented several successive waves of the *counter*culture as they had never been documented before.

By contrast, the under-the-counter culture has had relatively little to work with among the outstanding popular and jazz performers of the sixties and seventies. The cause for this is not lack of interest among the buying publics (each has its own idols), but the lack of need for bootlegging.

Such astute students, and merchants, of their own productivity as Ella Fitzgerald and Frank Sinatra have found it more profitable, and satisfying, to supervise the making of their own tapes of live performances. They are then in a position to sell them to the highest-bidding record outlet (often an independent rather than a big, monolithic portion of a conglomerate). This frees them from the hampering restraints of "exclusive" contracts and, in effect, makes them proprietors, as well as purveyors, of their own talent. It also gives them control of all elements relating to the appearance and production of their albums, and, even more to the point, renders unnecessary recourse to the under-the-counter market for reproductions of their best live performances. As for the unauthorized reproduction of their products in a *black* market, that is a form of piracy that afflicts all producers, regardless of the kind or color of recorded material.

III

But for all the evidences of public interest and the benefit of public returns that might accrue to those who purvey studio recordings of concert and operatic music, equivalent initiative has lagged far behind. One summer sequence (1951) of Wagner performances at the Bayreuth Festival was taken down, edited, and made available for public sale. But the new recording techniques were inadequate (tape was just beginning to be used in the field) and the cloistered atmosphere of the Festspielhaus was hardly conducive to experimentation.

Rather than persisting with its superb surroundings for live recording, Bayreuth was only occasionally utilized and not until 1967 for a *Ring* (there were, in the later fifties, taped performances of *Lohengrin* and *Der fliegende Holländer*, and in the sixties, *Parsifal*, *Tristan*, *Tannhäuser*, and *Lohengrin* and *Holländer* again, from which recorded albums were derived, and sold). By then the outstanding quality of a *Ring* achieved in the super-studio surroundings of the Sofiensaale in Vienna had established tonal standards very difficult to be matched, let alone surpassed.

The rise of such readily reproducible sound sources as the cassette (a product of Dutch engineering) and the proliferation of live performances on radio and television—including those in the "Great Performances" series (including a 1978 televersion of *Tannhäuser* from Bayreuth, distributed in April 1980), or distributed by satellite from the distant source—have enabled even a moderately skillful home engineer to serve his personal melomania in a vast variety of ways.

Formerly, the degree of aptitude in threading the tape of a reel-to-reel unit to the take-up spool required a bit of finger skill, if nothing else. But that meager kind of adroitness is obsolete with the cassette. All the mechanics are cared for within the tiny box; all that the user has to do is to place it in the receptacle (which won't take it if it is wrong side in), adjust the controls so that the "record" function of his unit is engaged, and sit down to listen to the radio broadcast or to watch the TV screen. As the sound on the latter is often conveyed in highest fidelity via FM radio (whatever the low grade of fidelity provided by the speakers of the unit itself), he has a prize worth the effort to keep. If the copy is retained for his own use *exclusively*, there is nothing in the least illegal about the process.

To dispense with one final aspect of this whole procedure: it may be useful to mention that cassettes are now available in time spans from half an hour (in one direction) to an hour and a half (in one direction). These are identified by the code number 60, for the shortest (indicating an hour for the *two* sides), or 180, for the longest (indicating three hours for both sides).

I would advise against the *shortest* for such purposes as operatic listening. It would require being flipped over, in almost the shortest act, thus losing some content. I would also advise against the *longest*, for two reasons. The longer the playing time, the thinner the tape in the cassette. At 180 minutes, the thinness of the tape may cause a malfunction in the average home unit, especially snarling or breaking of the tape. In either case, the user loses the cost of the tape and, even worse, the precious content. My preference is for the tape marked 120. This provides an hour per side, which is a median length for the average operatic act. It also enables the user to plan ahead for the longer acts, and select a preplanned lull in the action for turning the cassette. Another admirable aspect of tape, whether reel-to-reel or cassette: it's good for what it is only as long as *you* want it. When its interest has run its course, it can be erased and used for different subject matter.

In one of his highly readable books (*A Musical Motley*) Ernest Newman recalls Villiers de l'Isle-Adam's *L'Eve future*, in which Thomas A. Edison, as a character in the novel, wonders why on earth so simple an invention as the phonograph was not made several centuries before 1877. Had someone else done so, speculates Villiers de l'Isle-Adam (abetted by Newman), we might now have "the actual noise made by the Roman Empire when it fell," or "the original swan song."

Musically, opines the great English critic, if we had the sound of Farinelli, the great *castrato* (1705–82) so admired by the eminent Dr. Charles Burney, to compare with that of Enrico Caruso (or, now, Luciano Pavarotti), we might know which was, indeed, superior. In an extension of his own thoughts, Newman adds to "Edison's" own regret that the phonograph was not invented sooner his own whimsical sense of deprivation that some of the pregnant silences in history have been denied to future generations. Included among them, notes Newman, could be "the rent the envious Casca made," or "when Roland died, a great silence was through all the world," or "the vacuum that nature abhorred."

IV

No analogy more suitable could be invoked for the under-the-counter culture. Such a market exists because it has been abandoned, for the most part, by record makers. Also, it is surrounded by silence, for the Willie Lerners of the world (there are counterparts in many major cities, and at key spots in Europe) do not have to advertise. The melomaniacs who use his services are proud to have made such a discovery, and to brag about it to their fellow melomaniacs. What he has to provide becomes, thereafter, a kind of non-posted chain letter.

The "vacuum" that nature abhors is, from time to time, invaded by a record company, which then takes pride in "satisfying a consumer want." Such a "satisfaction" has to be the joint enterprise of an adventuresome company and a like-minded artist. There is no under-the-counter culture for the playing of the great, short-lived Romanian pianist Dinu Lipatti—so far as I am aware of—because the late Walter Legge had the enterprise to make himself available to record whenever the ailing artist (he suffered, and died, from leukemia) felt up to it.

Perhaps the greatest of many *coups* to Legge's credit was the effort he expended to attend, and record, the last recital Lipatti ever gave, at the Besançon Festival in the fall of 1950. Had it not been for the pride of performance in doing the impossible by which Legge was animated, there would not be today even that limited access to Lipatti live.

There is a cross section of Vladimir Horowitz live over a span of a quarter of a century because a) he has no fear of playing a wrong note now and then, b) he likes to celebrate important anniversaries by playing in public. Thus there is a Carnegie Hall concert of January 12, 1953, in which he performed the B flat minor concerto of Tchaikovsky, to electrifying results, with the New York Philharmonic under the direction of George Szell; and another in January 1978, in which the New York Philharmonic again participated, this time in the Rachmaninoff Third Piano Concerto, with Eugene Ormandy conducting. The first commemorated the twenty-fifth anniversary of his first American appearance in the same hall; the second, the fiftieth anniversary of the event. The second was taped live and has sold in astronomic numbers for RCA, Horowitz, and Ormandy; the first was not reproduced commercially, but can be purchased through the under-the-counter culture. Was this an oversight on the part of RCA, for whom Horowitz was recording in 1953? Perhaps; but it is also factual that he had recorded the Tchaikovsky with Arturo Toscanini (his father-in-law) conducting not too long before, and it has long been high among the best-selling records of both. Thus, the melomaniac has to be satisfied with the solo sound of Horowitz in 1953, by RCA LM 6014, which contains his Carnegie Hall recital of February 25 in that year.

More recently Horowitz has been represented in the shops by more than a few records made up of repertory chosen by him from recitals played here and there. I use this term because it is sometimes difficult to know which extended works (sonata, etc.) are all of a piece, or made up of "pieces." Unquestionably Horowitz is more stimulated by playing for the public and deriving records from the taped results than he is by performing in a studio or even in his own home (which has also been tried). Certainly the astonishing performance of Moussorgsky's *Pictures at an Exhibition* contained in a live reproduction of his Carnegie Hall recital of April 23, 1951, is exactly what it says it is. But the reproduction of multi-movement sonatas of more current date leave some doubt.

Perhaps this degree of dubitation is unwarranted, but there is dubiety even about that. I am thinking of another release from the same company (RCA) of a broadcast performance of Giuseppe Verdi's *Aïda*, which was conducted by Arturo Toscanini in two NBC broadcasts on March 26 and April 2, 1949. Principal roles were performed by Herva Nelli (Aïda), Richard Tucker (Radames), Eva Gustavson (Amneris), and Giuseppe Valdengo (Amonasro). The performance by Gustavson was below the level of the others, and the result of one session reduced Toscanini, that implacable exponent of perfection, to a single statement: "Poor voman" (meaning "it was so bad, what more can be said?"). But such mishaps are not to be found on the recordings "derived" from the broadcasts. Substitute passages of better quality were extracted from rehearsal recordings, and what was heard live is not what is now heard unlive.

On the other hand, one of the most famous of *all* Toscanini-NBC Symphony broadcasts—because it was his very last, on April 4, 1954—has never been reproduced for sale. This is in no way an oversight, or based on some sentimental consideration of recorded quality: the concert was given in Carnegie Hall, under acoustical conditions similar to those characteristic of the best of other recordings by conductor and orchestra. Much of this all-Wagner program is infused with a vitality, a propulsion, a degree of commitment that beggars praise, even baffles understanding as the work of a man of eighty-seven.

But it was also the occasion on which, after the stormiest, most tension-filled performance, late in the broadcast, of the Overture and Bacchanale from Richard Wagner's *Tannhäuser* that most of those present, or listening to the broadcast, had ever heard, Toscanini blacked out momentarily, and the music almost ceased. But after thirty seconds or so the players regrouped, the conductor resumed conducting, and the program went on, with the overture to *Die Meistersinger*. A priceless document of a great career, and something to be treasured.

However, the performance has never been shared with the public, very likely at the instance of the Toscanini heirs, who cannot face the mortality even of an immortal.

As a curious, personal consequence, this proscription has left me with a prime instance of legitimacy vs. illegitimacy as it applies to the under-the-counter culture. As part of my work at Juilliard, I have, for years, used a reproduction of this historic event which I had made off the air at the time of the broadcast. That is wholly permissible, as I have never used it except for my own information and pleasure, and those of my students.

After a dozen years of careful, guarded usage, the acetate surface began to deteriorate, intruding a good deal of surface noise, cracks, grinds, and pops, into the music of Wagner.

What to do? Lacking a commercial equivalent, there was no course open to me that wouldn't violate conscience. Had I known another melomaniac who also had made an off-the-air recording for his own purposes, I could have borrowed it, made a copy, and thus stayed within the boundaries of propriety. But I didn't.

I gave up the battle of conscience when I found that Mr. Willie had access to a good source, and ordered a tape.

When it came through, I found to my surprise and gratification that it was decidedly superior to my own off-the-air copy, in musical quality and suppression of unwanted noise. It didn't take long to arrive at the conclusion that it must have derived from an in-house, first-generation by-product of the performance itself, before it reached the air.

Any reasonable deduction is permissible.

A helpful reader might suggest that the answer to such a problem—especially for teaching purposes—would be recourse to such a repository as the Rodgers and Hammerstein Archives of Recorded Sound in the Library and Museum of the Performing Arts at Lincoln Center (only yards away from the Juilliard building in which I do my teaching). The suggestion is brilliantly logical, but, unfortunately, inoperative. Under the provisions of its charter, the contents of its holdings may not be taken out of the building, for whatever good reason. Further, its property cannot be copied, even by one who gave it to them in the first place (including, in my own instance, a largish collection of Benny Goodman and

Duke Ellington discs which I deposited there a decade or so ago).
The only access to *all* its property is by earphones to a record or
tape-activated source, four floors below in the enormous, many-
shelved storage space.

Some years ago, a young collector named Richard Stryker organized an alternative to the Rodgers and Hammerstein Archives
which he called the Institute for Recorded Sound. He rented a
spacious, high-ceilinged studio in Carnegie Hall, in which he
lived, worked, and collected. Whether he was truly a melomaniac
or not, I never really determined. He was, for certain, a *disco-
maniac*. His aspiration was to shelve as many sources of sound
as he could command and afford, and build booths in some auxil-
iary space, in which the public, by becoming contributing members of the Institute for Recorded Sound, could listen at will
to whatever he had to offer.

Stryker was youngish, vigorous, and certainly an enthusiast,
whose interests roamed across a wide range of the arts, the theater
as well as music. All too suddenly, however, the Institute ran into
difficulties. Money was short, troubles were long. Stryker died
overnight, so to speak—no known illness, and no stated cause—
and without his personal purpose and commitment, the Institute
was futureless. Or so it seemed, without immediate participation
of a person or persons unknown to the outsider, who might take
over and keep it in being.

Before such a prospect could be surveyed—indeed, if it would
have helped had it been surveyed—those responsible for the contents of the studio (mostly family) moved in, and decided that the
ready way out was to dissolve the Institute and dispose of its property.

The only accessible recipient was—the Rodgers and Hammerstein Archives. Thus, it only added to its hoard, on which it sits,
Fafner-like, in the well-stocked basement, to the detriment of the
only idealistic effort in recent years to establish an intelligent, alternative sound source to the under-the-counter culture in New
York.

This should in no way be construed as an indictment of David
Hall, the curator, as library terminology goes, of the Rodgers and

Hammerstein Archives since they came into existence in 1960 (when the space in Lincoln Center became available, thanks to funding provided by Richard Rodgers on behalf of his late lyric-writing partner). Hall's knowledge of records, enthusiasm for the preservation of them, and dedication to the tedious, time-consuming task of supervising the shelving of them are second to none. But institutionalism is institutionalism, whether the subject is human beings or the artifacts—such as recordings—which preserve their history.

V

The ramifications of this singular, yet multifaceted, subject, are so many-layered that a prognosis of its future would, at best, be speculative . . . drift and lack of direction may safely be predicted, if nothing else. But the year-by-year multiplication of content and the ever growing appetite for it leaves little doubt of one thing: what has been, for all these years, an under-the-counter culture gives every prospect of surfacing in shops and on shelves where it has never had a place before.

The crucial moment came, in my judgment, on the day in September 1977 when Maria Callas died in Paris. For the many who were struck with shock and disbelief, there were a few who saw a golden consummation of some long-laid plans. Within weeks, there was, in the most respectable of New York's record shops— and, presumably, in others, coast to coast—a new green-jacketed cluster of commodities. Some of them bore the names of other well-known Italian singers of the recent past—Ebe Stignani, Giulietta Simionato, Beniamino Gigli, etc.—but prevailingly, the dominant name was that of Callas.

None of these were reissues of studio records made early in her career, and distributed then under an established name such as Cetra/Soria. (The first means "lyre" in Italian, and the second identifies Dario Soria, an Italian entrepreneur who befriended Callas in the late forties. Soria saw to it that her voice was heard on studio-recorded discs long before anyone else appreciated her value. Along the way, Soria became a resident of New York, with many, varied arts activities until he died in March 1980). But as the number increased, some were ascribed to Cetra, evoking memories if not proclaiming legitimacy. The rule of the Italian road relating to material heard in broadcasts more than twenty years before was invoked as an assurance of propriety.

I shall not attempt a catalogue or a broad retrospect of them: that has already been done, by others. However, some facets of the totality bring history to life in a way that no words, however eloquent, could. There is, for example, in such a document as the performance of Verdi's *Il Trovatore* at the San Carlo in Naples on January 27, 1951, with Tullio Serafin conducting, one unlisted participant.

The label shows the names of the cast to include the venerable Giacomo Lauri-Volpi as Manrico, the slightly less venerable Cloe Elmo as Azucena, and the very contemporary Paolo Silveri as Count di Luna. The unidentified participant is the audience, which partakes of every tone and move of the singers like an American crowd at a World Series baseball game, dispensing pleasure or displeasure with every aria and top note.

As the date proclaims, this performance preceded the celebrated *I Vespri Siciliani* (also Verdi) of May 26, 1951, in Florence under the direction of Erich Kleiber. It was after this breakthrough that Callas has said: "I no longer needed an agent." But in Naples, in January, she was still just another young soprano of twenty-eight, known to some for the wildly improbable combination of roles she had sung in Venice not long before (page 198), but lacking an established identity.

Thus the response of the audience to her kind of Leonora, all heart and impulse, and sometimes lacking in vocal discipline but growing from act to act in decisiveness and dedication to characterization, is a lesson in two things: the art of expression and the walls of resistance it must sometimes overcome.

So far, the unexpected, and for that reason, overpowering privilege of reconstructing history to hear Callas before she was Callas relates to composers with whom she had a later, long-lasting identity: Verdi, Puccini, Donizetti, Bellini. Thus the difference in expressivity and power of communication is a difference in degree, not in kind. But one other echo from the past summons up another Callas, virtually all but unknown, even to those who were making the rounds of Italian opera theaters in 1949–51. This is a replay of the effect she conveyed as Kundry in Wagner's *Parsifal* in a broadcast from Rome under the direction of Vittorio Gui on November 20 and 21, 1950.

It need hardly be mentioned that Kundry is an all but silent participant in the first and third acts of *Parsifal,* so that the abridgements that enter into the two-record set marketed under the banner of Historical Recording Enterprises have little effect on Callas as Kundry. What does have an effect is the imagination and insight with which Callas enters into a part one would consider totally beyond her comprehension.

The text, of course, is in Italian—which, if anything, contributes to the illusion Callas conveys of a seductress, a temptress, a woman under a spell, directing herself to an enterprise in which she has never experienced failure: manly resistance to her womanly endowments.

All the musical phrases familiar from countless hearings in German are set forth with a fluency and singability seldom heard from even the best of traditional Kundrys. One tends, also, to associate with her singing of Kundry the appearance she conveyed as Tosca and Norma. But the "feminine appeal" of this Kundry is all in the voice: she was still in her "heavy" period, everybody was in the street attire appropriate to the broadcasting studio, and the only scenery is in the mind of the listener.

Above all else, it brings to my mind a comment that Callas made to me the day after a Metropolitan performance of *Tristan und Isolde* we had both (but separately) attended: "I'll have to learn German and show the world how this kind of part should be sung." At that moment (in the early 1970s), the remark impressed me as another Callas conceit, implying that whatever she undertook, she could do better than anyone else. But after hearing her Kundry, I'm not sure she had not performed her Italian Isolde as well or better.

Quite as startling in a different way is a replica on a single disc of an occasion (December 27, 1954) when she shared a stage in San Remo with the sixty-four-year-old Beniamino Gigli. The billing suggests that there might be, along the way, a rare blend in duets of the already legendary tenor and the nearly legendary soprano. Such, however, is not the case: the concert is a sequence of arias in groups, with Callas venturing such high-flying material as "Ombra leggiera" from Meyerbeer's *Dinorah*, "D'amore al dolce impero" from Rossini's *Armida*, and "Martern aller Arten" from Mozart's *Entführung aus dem Serail* (in its Italian form of "Tutte la tortura"). The Rossini aria was then one of Callas's showpieces, but I much prefer her version of "Depuis le jour" from Charpentier's *Louise*—a role that would have been something to hear, and see, with the by then later, slimmer Callas.

To judge from the range and variety of Callas material in the under-the-counter culture (now as prominently displayed as the latest product from Nashville), there was rarely a time, after 1951, that she performed publicly without someone, somehow, preserving the sound of it. The existence of such a reality came to my attention some years ago, after attending an all-Hugo Wolf recital in Salzburg, during the festival of 1953, in which the performers were soprano Elisabeth Schwarzkopf and, at the piano, Wilhelm Furtwängler. The afternoon ended with much applause and a sense of satisfaction with something to be preserved in memory.

Celebrated as both performers were and novel as the appearance of conductor Furtwängler was as a pianist, no company considered this event worthy of live participation, though it was broadcast. A few years later, when the death of Furtwängler (November 30, 1954) sharpened regret that nothing had been done to preserve the magical music he had created, an effort was undertaken to repair the oversight. It was sponsored by the enterprising Walter Legge (Schwarzkopf's husband, as well as the record producer mentioned on page 248).

I cannot enumerate the number of false leads that were pursued, or the amounts that were spent on advertisements in musical publications for a tape of the broadcast. I do know that some years later I received, for review, a newly issued disc of the long-remembered, non-forgotten Hugo Wolf program by Schwarzkopf and Furtwängler. A tape had turned up in Switzerland.

Included among other tapes by the same Schwarzkopf is a true oddity dated April 27, 1975. The content ranges from Schubert to Mahler, and includes, among other oddities, the seldom sung *Die drei Zigeuner* of Franz Liszt, and the three "Ophelia" songs from *Hamlet*, set by Richard Strauss. The program was artfully composed of the very familiar and the little known, with superb accompaniments by Geoffrey Parsons. The unduplicatable further fact is that this recital in Carnegie Hall brought to an end her twenty years of appearances in New York, an event certified as official, final, and non-reversible (nor subject to contradiction five years later).

The thought, and a worthy one, is that what I have is a live recording of an event well worthy of such consideration, on behalf of all those other than the few thousand who were able to crowd themselves into the auditorium. Such is not the case, nor was there a visible microphone which might have produced a tape for some overseas usage, and, from it, a recording. It is, rather, the product of a new adjunct to the preservation of live musical performance: the portable, battery-operated tape recorder, of which several versions of Japanese/German design provide decent sound.

Thus, it may be said that the machine giveth—as in the instance of the broadcast-preserved Schwarzkopf-Furtwängler-Wolf program—and the machine taketh away. To be sure, the opportunity for such expropriation was provided by the failure of the company for which she records to invest in the relatively small sum required for a live taping—a small compensation to Schwarzkopf for the money she has earned for it (as well as for herself) over a long career.

By contrast, a similar option that confronted the same company a few years before was resolved differently. When soprano Victoria de los Angeles and pianist Alicia de Larrocha prepared a joint recital in the large auditorium of Hunter College they were, by managerial effort, also provided with microphones and engineering technicians. The outcome was a recording of splendid quality, and *no opportunity whatsoever* for an under-the-counter "rarity."

Am I, as a customer for the pirated Schwarzkopf tape, in the same category as a john who patronizes a hooker? I keep thinking that if the legitimate purveyor of her services had fulfilled *his* charter, I wouldn't have to deal with a substitute, non-law-abiding alternative.

In all such matters there comes, eventually, a matter of conscience. I am beset by the pros and cons of legitimacy and nonlegitimacy in satisfying the bottom ranges of what I consider my own, baser nature (however uplifting the matter traditionally associated with it may be).

I am also aware that, like any melomaniac with whom Willie is associated—which takes in practically anyone who has ever put a foot past his doorjamb—I am well typed in his mind. My shadow is barely into his ken when I know he is mentally reviewing what particular goody (not to be associated with any other record retailer of the same, or similar, name) he has lately come upon that is just made for me.

Will it be an old Richard Tauber record not heard outside of Japan for thirty years, the sound of a childish voice reputed to be that of Callas when she appeared on a Major Bowes radio program at the age of twelve, or the day before yesterday's Carnegie Hall program in which Alfred Brendel shared the stage with Dietrich Fischer-Dieskau?

That is why I have taken to bypassing, even though it contains a convenient post office, a firehouse with a very friendly crew, and a club of which I am a member, a block on West Forty-third Street between Sixth and Fifth avenues where Music Masters Uptown is located.

Barenboim, etc.

What is a barenboim? That question has occasionally crossed my mind, especially in circumstances relating to a person so named. I am probably wrong, but I think of a barenboim as an antique, hand-held instrument, perhaps powered by bellows, which gives forth wheezes and chords appropriate to folk celebrations in middle Europe.

"Now let's have the barenboim!" I can hear an older person crying out at a high point of a wedding or christening, eager to acquaint the young people present with the traditional music that was passed on to him by his grandfather in similar circumstances.

With a capital B, however, a Barenboim may be a product of events almost as bizarre as the career which included the recording of all thirty-two piano sonatas of Beethoven before he was thirty. As he became conductor and music director of the Orchestre de Paris well before he was forty, he may—in a time when "records" for recording are almost as numerous as recordings themselves—become the first musician in history to record both the thirty-two piano sonatas and the nine symphonies of Beethoven. Of course, the redoubtable Hans von Bülow might have achieved the same miraculous feat, but there were no microphones and long-playing records available when he died in 1894.

Daniel Barenboim might have gone to the Moscow Conservatory in the 1950s, won top prize in the Tchaikovsky Competition, and now, along with Vladimir Ashkenazy (who, we know, actually did both), be vying for the honor of being the pre-eminent Soviet musical émigré of his time, save for one biological detail. That was the migration from Russia of his grandfather in, approximately, 1903.

In this respect, he was little different from the grandfather (or, in my case, father) of countless others who preferred steerage to bondage. Unlike most of them, Barenboim did not cross the North Atlantic to the port of New York. He went, instead, by way of the South Atlantic to Argentina, where he settled in Buenos Aires.

For those raised on the "Latin" films of the pre-pre-Perón period, Buenos Aires may be construed as being made up, in large part, of gauchos and tango dancers (often the same thing). Factually, it is an extremely diverse city of millions, with a considerable German and English population (well served by a Harrod's, of all things) and a famous interest in music. The Teatro Colón, opened in 1908, is, with its rose and gold interior, not only one of the great opera houses of the world, but a fine concert hall.

As an instance of assimilation, when Barenboim I produced Barenboim II, the name he gave to his son was not Sascha or Hyam, but Enrique. He developed not only into a fine pianist, but into an uncommonly creative teacher. His wife, Aida, also a pianist, also a teacher, specializes in guidance for the young.

Which one had more to do with the development of Daniel, who was born in 1942, I cannot say. I can say, through acquaintance with both parents, that it was very likely a family affair. I cannot imagine either of them being apart from the rapid rise which produced a debut at seven and a visit to Salzburg before his tenth birthday.

Something in the way of a heavenly dispensation to the Barenboims was provided by the steady traffic of world-famous musicians through Buenos Aires. One instance was the visit of the eminent Adolf Busch, violinist-pedagogue-conductor, in 1949. Things were not going well in a rehearsal of Bach suites he was preparing for a concert, when a break was declared. As tended to be the case, Barenboim senior was present with Barenboim junior at what promised to be a stimulating experience, and the concertmaster of the orchestra suggested to the parent that a little demonstration of the boy's abilities might change the atmosphere. The plan proceeded, and within minutes Busch was all attention, extolling the source of what he was hearing. And, from a man who had given attention to violinist Yehudi Menuhin at ten (in 1926) and engaged Rudolf Serkin to be his pianist at seventeen, the response was soon well known in musical Buenos Aires.

Out of this encounter came a strengthening of Enrique Barenboim's belief that his son would benefit from two things: being closer to the source of the musical mainstream than Buenos Aires, and being part of a community in which Daniel was a member of a majority, rather than a minority. This, he says, was philosophical and psychological, rather than ethnical.

A further step toward the eventual realization of his plan came about a few years later when the Russian-born, Paris-based composer-conductor Igor Markevitch visited Buenos Aires. Through his friendship with almost all of those in Buenos Aires who were both wealthy and musical (or perhaps, musical and wealthy) Enrique Barenboim was invited to an evening of home music making at which Markevitch was also present. At a strategic point, the young Barenboim was brought on to lend luster (and youth) to a performance of chamber music, with both an expected and unexpected outcome.

Surprise and pleasure were forthcoming, as hoped for, from Markevitch, perhaps with a memory of his own youth, which had included studies with Boulanger at fourteen (in 1926). But he went further: a suggestion, when he heard that the young musician had hopes of being, one day, a conductor, that the Barenboims come to Salzburg the following summer, and enroll Daniel at the Mozarteum, where Markevitch annually had a seminar in that subject.

In due course, the plan proceeded, through this unimagined stimulus, to fulfill social and educational as well as musical objectives. In Salzburg, Daniel was heard and praised by pianist Edwin Fischer and conductor Wilhelm Furtwängler, and others. Among the others was Carlo Zecchi, of Rome. He suggested that Daniel would be welcomed at the Accademia di Santa Cecilia of that city (to which he was attached) whenever it was convenient.

When the summer visit to Salzburg and other parts of Europe was over, the Barenboims completed the final chapter of the hegira from Buenos Aires to Tel Aviv. Between late 1952, when they settled in Israel, and 1957, when the father and son made their first venture to America, academic as well as musical input was readily available. For the while, schooling had first priority. Between terms, and in the summer, one objective was Paris, and Nadia Boulanger; in another year, it included Zecchi and Santa Cecilia, where, as promised, Daniel was well received, and qualified for a diploma at the "advanced" age of fourteen (in 1956).

On January 20, 1957, Barenboim made his Carnegie Hall debut in a Symphony of the Air program conducted by Leopold Stokowski. The concert followed closely on the death of Arturo Toscanini (January 16). Many members of the orchestra, still trying to perpetuate their long attachment to the venerable maestro by sustaining the ensemble set adrift when the NBC Symphony was terminated in 1954, had a strong sense of personal loss. Thus there was more than ceremony in the playing, under Stokowski's direction, of the "Funeral Music" (for Siegfried) from Wagner's *Götterdämmerung*.

As the program also included Stokowski's version of Bach's C minor passacaglia and fugue, the debut of a teenaged Israeli pianist was almost, if not quite, overshadowed. My own comments on Barenboim's playing of the Prokofiev Piano Concerto No. 1 was something more than reserved, something less than ecstatic. Or to quote "something" of my own, it was "something more than a fourteen-year-old's performance. This is a work of rather slight expressivity which limited Barenboim to a display of technical facility, which is considerable, and rhythmic instinct, which is arousing. He did well enough to prompt curiosity about further hearing in more demanding repertory."[1]

As quickly as a year could pass, the wish was fulfilled, again in January (1958). This time the broader comment suited the more demanding repertory:

> He has found time, in barely more than fifteen years, to learn incredible quantities of music, travel in Europe, win several competitions, and otherwise occupy himself spiritually, while growing strong, straight, and fairly tall . . . So far his piano skills are more athletic than oratorical, but he has a sound sense of musical

[1] Kolodin, Irving, *Saturday Review*, February 2, 1957.

design as Bach conceived it ("Chromatic Fantasy and Fugue"), and of musical drama as Beethoven conveyed it ("Waldstein" Sonata, opus 53, in C major). He may also be commended for virtuous failings, which is to say that his inclination to rush tempi is an expectable—even a welcome—indication of adolescent musical normality, reassuring evidence that his pulse is controlled by a variable, human heart, rather than an unvarying, inanimate metronome. Given a proper opportunity for development, Barenboim should achieve a conspicuous mark either as a pianist or conductor (a career for which he has already shown some inclination).[2]

This seeming clairvoyance about a performer in his mid-teens whose career might attain "a conspicuous mark" either as a pianist *or* a conductor was owing to something more than intuition. The *cause Barenboim* had by then been espoused by the London-born, New York-based James Grayson, confirmed melomaniac. His enthusiasm for being a part of the musical world has taken him far from the business in which he prospered. Grayson became the founding father of Westminster Records, and foster-father of such young, talented people as guitarists Julian Bream and John Williams, pianists Jörg Demus and Paul Badura-Skoda (as well as Barenboim), and the Amadeus Quartet. He found them, loved them, and lost them, when their reputations were made, to larger companies with bigger bank accounts.

That Barenboim excelled them all in potential earnings and career possibilities made him all the more vulnerable to comparable temptation. A profound admirer of Edwin Fischer, Grayson doubtless pursued the *path Barenboim* from a studio in Salzburg to a dressing room in Carnegie Hall. What is more to the point is that Grayson assured those who would listen (such as myself) that Barenboim could be as good a conductor as he was a pianist, if such a career became the total object of his attention. How, and when, and in what circumstances it might come about, could not be foretold.

That Barenboim recorded the opus 106 sonata (in B flat, "Hammerklavier") three times before he was thirty is a matter of

[2] Kolodin, Irving, *Saturday Review*, February 1, 1958.

record. The third was, of course, in his tour of the cycle of thirty-two (as noted). When he might perform and conduct all or as many of the Mozart piano concertos as suited his taste was only a matter of time.

II

This sketch of one artist's background is not designed to glorify a single performer or his multiple accomplishments, formidable though they are. Rather it is cited as a specific instance of a generalized phenomenon which, musically, makes the second half of this century different from any other.

For decades, musical pundits made much of music as "a universal language." Among them were Hubert Parry and W. H. Hadow, who were products of the same nineteenth-century society which prided itself on being part of the empire on whose flag "the sun never set." However, the earliest combination of the words I can find is not by an Englishman, but by Henry Wadsworth Longfellow (1807–82), in whose *Outre-Mer* may be found the statement: "Music is the universal language of mankind."[3]

Perhaps if the understanding of the language common to Beethoven, Schubert, Brahms, and Sir Arthur Sullivan was restricted, between Suez and Shanghai, to entertainment at tiffin or along with high tea, such universality could be claimed. But it was not until many countries on which the old flag never set were hauling it down and putting up one of their own that the fantasy of music as a *universal* language began to have some validity.

One need not labor the place that Barenboim now occupies in music, worldwide, to measure its effect on Israel's high culture. Jews have been music lovers before there were Barenboims, and so they will be forever. As is not unknown, Israel is the only country in the world where a symphony orchestra has to play the same program in several cities several times to satisfy the demand for live music. But the sequence which gave rise to the development

[3] Bartlett, John, *Familiar Quotations*, Christopher Morley, editor (Little, Brown & Company, Boston, Mass., Twelfth Edition, 1948), p. 440.

of such violinists as Itzhak Perlman and Pinchas Zukerman in the immediate aftermath of Barenboim's rise to prominence cannot be wholly accidental. It has, certainly, overtones of "What he did, so too can I."

The particular trait that makes Barenboim different from contemporary colleagues is not his ability as a virtuoso pianist, or as a flamboyant conductor, or even as a virtuoso-flamboyant pianist-conductor. He is, rather, a superb musician whose mastery of both repertoires is as pervasive as it is uncommon. When one recalls such other pianists as Ossip Gabrilowitsch and José Iturbi who became conductors, the distinction is at once apparent. I heard Gabrilowitsch conduct (with the Philadelphia Orchestra in New York) one of the finest performances of the Schubert C major symphony (No. 9) that it has been my good fortune to encounter; and Iturbi had his moments in a certain segment of the orchestral repertory. But it is my belief that neither started to conduct as early in his pianistic career as Barenboim did, or had any such vista of growth, length, and mastery as he does.

The same kind of capacity restricted to a man living among the 2.9 million citizens of Buenos Aires might have pleased a small group of fellow melomaniacs. The same infusion of excellence in Tel Aviv (population on the order of 300,000) is close to a national phenomenon, especially as both senior Barenboims continue to live and work there.

I have information from an unimpeachable source (the individuals themselves) that the Russian blood brought by Barenboim I to Argentina has remained pure. But I sense in them certain temperamental traits, musical and personal, that are a fusion of some elements native to Buenos Aires. Perhaps it is, merely, that (as previously noted) the given name of Barenboim II is Enrique. Being called that many, many times a day for decades cannot fail to have a shaping effect.

Both of my parents, for example, were Russian-born. But having been born in New York and grown up less than a dozen miles away in Newark, New Jersey, I certainly reflect the country of my birth much more than the country of my parents' birth. Similarly, the combination of elements in the Barenboim mixture makes of their son a schizoid not uncommon in Israel's artistic life, and hence the more sympathetic to them. I think, for instance, of a pianist in one of my classes at the Juilliard School. He is Polish-born, of Jewish descent. He was musically educated, in the fifties, by Russian-speaking teachers; finally, in Moscow itself. Eventually he was allowed to migrate to Israel. After five years in America, he speaks English almost as fluently as he does Hebrew or Russian. (How much Polish he was exposed to during the occupation I cannot say. I doubt that much of it remains in his mind.)

The cardinal manifestation of this absorptive, blotter-like aptitude characteristic of Israel's population is the prominence within it of Zubin Mehta. Born in Bombay in 1936, Mehta was musically educated by his father, conductor of the Bombay Symphony, from whom he learned to play the violin. As his skill developed, so, too, did his involvement with the orchestra. As that progressed, with an occasional opportunity to hold a baton and stand in his father's place, the ambition to become a conductor transcended everything else.

The progression from aspiration to accomplishment was assisted no little by a sound foundation provided by studies in Vienna with Hans Swarowsky (a celebrated pedagogue of the art of conducting, in which he never attained personal prominence). For all that his career appears to be much longer than Barenboim's, Mehta is only six years older—a difference in development offset by the rapidity of the younger man's transition from pianist to conductor.

It may be noted, apropos the empire aspect of his heritage, that Mehli Mehta (Zubin's father) was educated first in Bombay, then at the Trinity College in London. He founded the Bombay Symphony in 1935, and maintained it for twenty years. When his son gave promise of a flourishing career in the West, Mehli Mehta moved to Manchester, England. In 1955, he became assistant concertmaster of the Hallé Orchestra in that city, whose principal conductor, from 1940 until his death in 1970, was Sir John Barbirolli.

Bypassing details pertaining to resourcefulness and readiness to replace other conductors under emergency circumstances, Zubin

Mehta's career may be dated from 1961 when, at the age of twenty-five, he became director of the Los Angeles Philharmonic Orchestra. Israel was one of eighteen countries in which he guest-conducted before he accepted a permanent affiliation with its Philharmonic Orchestra. Here, too, a matter of hereditary cross-fertilization may have a predisposing influence (see page 267).

The outcome has been the kind of marriage celebrated in song and story, but seldom at home—passionate attachment spiced with equally ardent dissension. Rehearsals are sometimes punctuated by disagreements, not only between conductor and players, but also between players and players. Fortunately, mutuality prevails when concerts are given. Indeed, Mehta finds himself so much at home in this home which is *not* a home that he has pledged lifelong devotion to the Israel Philharmonic, despite any other affiliation elsewhere. As an instance, his present contract with the New York Philharmonic, which extends to 1985, provides for open weeks, at several intervals each year, which he will devote to the Israel Philharmonic, or its tours.

To finalize the present status of Mehli Mehta, he became a resident of Southern California during the sixties, and has conducted the orchestra of the University of California at Los Angeles, the Pasadena Community Orchestra, and similar organizations. In all he has achieved results of an order rarely encountered in such restricted circumstances of time and talent. Some think him a better musician than his son.

Taken together, the example of the two Mehtas focuses attention on an aspect of life in the subcontinent that rarely comes to the attention of outsiders. Yehudi Menuhin, who has made repeated visits to India, describes the Parsees (to whom the Mehtas belong) as "the Jews of India (but who are in fact Zoroastrians, self-exiled from Persia) whose monotheism has bred a judicious, pragmatic race."[4] Artists of the quality of Menuhin today, or Arthur Rubinstein in the past, have been cherished visitors when they include Bombay, Calcutta, and New Delhi on their tours.

[4] Menuhin, Yehudi, *Unfinished Journey* (Alfred A. Knopf, Inc., New York, 1977), p. 255.

Given the attainments of the Mehtas, there can be no doubt that there is, among the many millions of Indians, a cadre, a core of thousands to whom Western music has no forbidden secrets. The recent popularity of Ravi Shankar, superb master of the sitar, has overshadowed the prior accomplishments of his famous (older) brother Uday Shankar, whose powers as an embodiment of the dance of his country magnetized as many in the thirties and forties. Indeed, lurking in the memory of some who see Ravi Shankar today are recollections of him as a child, romping in and around the rituals performed so well by Uday Shankar. And in the background of Uday Shankar was a time when he spent part of his career on tours with one of the greatest of Russian ballerinas, Anna Pavlova.

Clearly there are currents and crosscurrents that influence the perceptions, and the comprehensions, of an art so varied as Western music and its many derivatives. King Phumipol Aduljej of Thailand cultivated a fondness for jazz (acquired, along with a Harvard degree, during his student days in Cambridge, Massachusetts) which expressed itself through the clarinet in a well-publicized meeting with Benny Goodman at the royal residence in Bangkok.[5] And the famous history of Anna Leonowens and the King of Siam, as re-created by Margaret Landon, made several kinds of history of its own, with and without the music of Richard Rodgers and Oscar Hammerstein II.

Another kind of royal affection for music was expressed by the truly aristocratic Maharaja of Mysore, who became so dedicated a devotee of Western music that he invested more than a nominal amount of his royal exchequer's wealth in recording, and distributing, a comprehensive survey of the music of Nikolai Medtner. The brown-colored clothbound container, with the concerto in C minor (No. 2) played by the composer, also piano pieces and songs (which I still possess), doubtless did much for the *amour-propre* of Medtner (1880–1951), if not so much for world opinion of his music.

"Zubin Mehta, music director of the New York Philharmonic

[5] Feather, Leonard, The Encyclopedia of Jazz (Horizon Press, New York, 1960), p. 230.

Orchestra" is a formidable collection of syllables. If it has not added a continent to the conquest of Western music, it has, within recent years of this century, added at least a subcontinent, whose potent force for the future never had so powerful a symbol.

III

The temptation to equate Seiji Ozawa of Hoten, Manchuria, with Zubin Mehta of Bombay, India, is readily present: and should be as readily rejected. To be sure, Ozawa did not have a father who was the conductor of a symphony orchestra. To that extent, his course was a more difficult one than Mehta's.

On the other hand, he grew up as part of a society which made a state philosophy of promoting an interest in Western music (Hoten, Manchuria, was a part of the Japanese empire when Ozawa was born there in 1935—a year before Mehta). The current music director of the Boston Symphony Orchestra is a living example of the extent to which such conditioning can lead to extraordinary results.

In its essence, the promotion of Western music in Japan has been a typical instance of the systematized pursuit of quality, as a pre-condition to equality, which has governed the country's practices after it was "opened" to the outside world in the 1850s.

Having surveyed the European models which merited attention —which was the best? which was the most desirable of emulation? —the Japanese rightfully selected the German. It not only had the best names—Bach to Brahms—it also had a system of schooling (the Leipzig Conservatory, as an outstanding model) to which many of the world's most talented young musicians aspired. Such a system was imported to Japan by recruitment of German teachers.

By the first quarter of the twentieth century, the Japanese were able to prove that their pursuit of quality had brought them, in some respects, to equality. The Tokyo affiliate of Columbia produced, in 1927, the first recording of the vocal version of Haydn's *Seven Last Words of Christ*, thus proving a point, even if the name of the conductor, Charles Lautrup, was patently not Japanese. Its worldwide circulation made international news (in America it was C-set 297). Such sopranos as Tamaki Miura and Hizi Koyke gave nightly praise to Giacomo Puccini for creating *Madama Butterfly*. In turn, they earned his (and his publisher's) thanks for adding something to it, visually, that no Italian soprano could. Hidemaro Konoye, sometimes described as Prince Konoye (born in 1898, died in 1973), made many appearances in the West as a conductor (in America in 1937 and again in 1957). Professionally, he was regarded more as a curio than as a colleague.

Even to this time, Japan Victor (founded as an offshoot of the American, but since 1937 a wholly Japan-owned company, though still with some hereditary links in this country) circulates discs long out of print elsewhere. In the decade of the 1970s (see page 1), incredible quantities of yen were spent by Japanese music lovers on a lavish collection of Toscanini records. And Japanese technicians have produced transfers to tape of materials recorded in the 1920s (including a superlative version of Strauss's *Ein Heldenleben* performed by the New York Philharmonic Orchestra under the direction of Willem Mengelberg) which have astonished discriminating listeners of today with their power and realism.

Beginning in 1930, Japanese educational practices have digressed considerably from the German-oriented procedures of earlier years. The world of music has learned to respect the name of Shunichi Suzuki, born in 1905 (Nagoya) of a father who operated the biggest violin factory in the world. The idea of an instrument carried to classic heights of productivity—by such masters (of Cremona) as Antonio Stradivarius and Niccolò Amati—being factory-made hardly suggests a relationship to music. But the offspring of the factory's owner was provided with a ready-made career—he would, of course, be a violinist.

Eventually, pursuit of quality led young Suzuki to Germany, where he spent six years as a student. When he returned to Japan, it was as a violinist and teacher (the business became the responsibility of a brother, who directed its wartime activity of producing floats for seaplanes).

Shunichi Suzuki's profoundly philosophic nature prompted him, somewhat in the manner of Nadia Boulanger, to meditate on his shortcomings as a teacher (rather more than is customary among other pedagogues). Japanese, he reasoned, is a very difficult language to speak. Why do children learn to speak it so easily? The simple self-question put him on the path to a productive answer. Japanese children speak their language easily because they hear it, and little else, from birth. Why not learn violin playing the same way?

One of his first experiments came with a parent of means who brought him a four-year-old child. Suzuki had never before taught a four-year-old child, and hesitated to accept the obligation. But this one presented an opportunity, as well as a challenge. Some people of today would say that the experiment succeeded because the child had great talent. Suzuki disagrees with that phraseology. He thinks all children have talent for something. Music might be it; or exposure to music may be the way to discover another talent.

The child grew up to play the violin beautifully. His name was Toshita Eto. I have written numerous reviews of his performances in Carnegie Hall and elsewhere, especially during, and after, his studies with that peerless stylist of the instrument, Efrem Zimbalist, at the Curtis Institute in Philadelphia. His phrasing was a pleasure, his command of the instrument's subtleties a joy. His tone was a little small for the biggest halls, and Eto's musical concepts tended toward miniaturization, a national trait for which many Japanese—not necessarily *only* musicians—have become famous. But his use of the instrument was invariably artistic. After some years of teaching at Curtis, and concertizing across the country, Eto went back to Japan. I heard about him most recently in April 1978, when pupils from all parts of the world gathered in Philadelphia to celebrate, with Zimbalist, his ninetieth birthday. Eto was among them.

A clear evidence of the Japanese aptitude for the violin, and of the level of quality they have attained in recent decades, is the increasing quantity of them to be seen in the best orchestras of the world (and not only American ones). Clearly, this is part of the systematic way of procedure that the Japanese apply to all their intellectual activities—to find out the most, go to where the best work prevails. Unquestionably this precept begins with Suzuki himself. His own story[6] is a work from which almost anyone interested in music can learn. The rewards of learning, from children, how to teach them, are rich in the kind of insights that only a man who has lived for his vocation could impart.

But one particular segment of that story is of the essence in marking how the "more nearly universal language" came about.

The letter is dated September 2, 1962, and is addressed: "My Honored and Revered Teacher." The text reads:

> I have just come from Berlin. When you, Professor, were here, in which neighborhood did you live? I have always dreamed of seeing this place. All of the new buildings in Berlin still seem somewhat cold. But the people differ from those of rural Cologne in elegance, refinement and politeness. Yesterday I was given an audition by the Berlin Symphony Orchestra, and appointed its first concertmaster. The conductor—Fricsay[7]—ranks at present in Germany with Karajan and Kubelik. The only worry I have now is whether I am really fit to take the position of First Violinist in such a famous orchestra.
>
> With affection and most respectfully,
> Koji [Toyoda]

Suzuki adds: "Koji [a pupil in whom he took special interest] wrote me this letter on arriving in Berlin, after leaving Cologne. Reading it, I was not only filled with emotion but surprised as well. It was the first time since Western music had come to Japan that a Japanese had won a position like this in Europe. It hardly seemed possible, for I know the high standing of the Berlin orchestra. To be this orchestra's representative is a most important position. The chief concertmaster a Japanese—Koji . . . !"

As of 1962, Ozawa had progressed to an important way station in his career. After winning several competitions in Europe, he spent a summer in Tanglewood, Massachusetts, at the invitation

---

[6] Suzuki, Shunichi, *Nurtured by Love* (Exposition Press, New York, 1969), pp. 29–30.

[7] The correspondent does not overstate the position of Ferenc Fricsay at that time. He died only a year later, at the age of forty-nine.

of its director, and music director of the Boston Symphony Orchestra, Charles Munch, who had observed him at work in Paris. There he won the Koussevitzky Prize, and was invited by Leonard Bernstein to become his assistant with the New York Philharmonic Orchestra. Where he might go with all these promising possibilities was still to be determined.

Behind Ozawa was a diversity of educational opportunities in Japan which were greater than had existed pre-Suzuki. Of primary importance was the Toho School of Music in Tokyo, regarded by many in the Western world as the final link in the chain from student status in Japan to professionalism there and elsewhere.

Following his birth in Manchuria, Ozawa was taken back to Tokyo at the age of six, and entered in the Toho School. As he progressed, his ambition was to pursue a pianist's career: however, his hands were small, and he damaged one while practicing. But there was nothing restrictive about a small hand for a conductor, and he reconsidered his objectives.

Beyond Munch, beyond Bernstein, beyond even Herbert von Karajan (who had observed his talent in Berlin and thought highly of it), the most powerful influence on the career of Ozawa has been the American agent named Ron Wilford. A native of Salt Lake City who began a managerial career in New York in 1958 with three clients, all vocalists (tenor Nicolai Gedda and baritones Cornell MacNeil and Donald Gramm, none of them then any part of the celebrities they have since become), Wilford was self-chosen by the late Arthur Judson to share the speciality for which he had become internationally famous: the management of conductors. Judson, who died in 1975 at the age of ninety-four, was famous for "managing" (or advising, or controlling) several dozen conductors of high repute in the twenties, thirties, and forties. Within the decade of the sixties, Wilford, as understudy, had improved on the example of his mentor (who disavowed him), by controlling the services of several *score* conductors, not all of high repute, and not a few merely paddings on a list. Once, when I asked why he held strings to the activities of some eighty puppets, he replied, "It leads to control" . . . a terse way of saying that when the boards of directors of American symphony orchestras need a new music director, it is Ron Wilford to whom many *have* to turn.

Though Wilford professes no knowledge of music (Judson studied the violin, played in several orchestras, and pursued several aspects of musical journalism before he became manager of the Philadelphia Orchestra, and Leopold Stokowski, in 1915), he can count the audience value of talent on all ten fingers. Ozawa was one of the building blocks in his tower of power, unquestionably because, in his first years, he looked appealingly exotic and made difficult scores appear to be child's play. His manipulation on Wilford's musical chess board, first in Ravinia (summer home of the Chicago Symphony) in 1964, then as music director of the Toronto Symphony 1965–69, thereafter in San Francisco 1969–74, produced "mate" in Boston, even before his obligation to the West Coast was finished. This is a classic succession of moves Wilford has since found difficult to match—although he has by no means stopped trying.

What his association with Wilford did for Ozawa is beyond calculation, either in time or in money. For a student, as Ozawa still was, as Bernstein's assistant in 1962, to become music director of the Boston Symphony Orchestra approximately a decade later is formidable to think about, even more to achieve. But what he has done in that progression for other young Japanese may in the aggregate be one of the most productive things about it.

I am thinking particularly of Toru Takemitsu, a composer whose music was introduced to the United States by Ozawa, two orchestras ago (in the later 1960s) when he was music director of the Toronto Symphony. In one period of weeks a decade later (January 1977), Takemitsu had performances of three works in New York concert halls. One was a brief tone painting entitled *Winter*, performed by the Philadelphia Orchestra under the direction of Eugene Ormandy in Carnegie Hall; another was *Folios*, for guitar, which had been commissioned from Takemitsu by Michael Lorimer; the most substantial was *Arc*, for whose piano part Peter Serkin was the soloist, in a program by the New York Philharmonic Orchestra under the direction of Pierre Boulez.

Arc is essentially a work of chamber music dimensions, but utilizing a wall-to-wall percussion section, including antique cymbals, xylophones, and cymbalom. To judge from the Japanese commentary (translated by Kent Stoltzman), the poetic purpose in *Arc* is cyclical, embodying birth, growth, and decline—a parable extended by Takemitsu from growing things to sound, which by any physical measurement arises, vibrates, and vanishes.

Summarized briefly, Takemitsu's score embodies a variety of recent tendencies and trends (or what I call "Trendencies") in Western music, such as Webern's brevity, Messiaen's absorption with color, Stockhausen's interest in "chance" (the aleatory phenomenon), Cage (or the nothing factor in sound), Boulez (the impalpable as the key to indetermination).

Takemitsu brings to them a freedom from restraint, a lack of conscious effort to *negate* what has preceded in Western music because he has not been reared in it, and an aesthetic independence derived from his own background. As Japanese painters view brush, paint, and surface as things to work with in ways other than Westerners do, but communicate with us nevertheless, so Takemitsu uses the coloristic resources of a "Western" orchestra (of which Tokyo has half a dozen) to achieve concepts of artistry, design, and fulfillment which bridge the intercontinental gap. Perhaps this will be recognized, in time to come, as Third-Generation Bartók (derived, aesthetically, from his *Music for Strings, Percussion and Celesta*) which engages in a dialectical discussion about the "more nearly universal language" in no need of translation.

Most recently, Takemitsu has benefited from the interest in his work identified with Peter Serkin's participation in *Arc* by the inclusion of his *Les Yeux clos* in that fine young pianist's recital of April 20, 1980, in Avery Fisher Hall at Lincoln Center. The experience was a rewarding one for two reasons: the date of the work's completion (August 7, 1979) is a welcome indication that Takemitsu is pressing on with his compositional career, and the sound evoked from subtle use of the piano's pedals is in a great tradition of Impressionism related to such paintings as Odilon Redon's (1840–1916) *Les Yeux clos.*

IV

In each of these respects—the early singers, the recent violinists, the conductor, the composer—Japan has come close to, and sometimes excelled, Western standards for individual excellence. The ensemble art, which expounds another philosophy—subordination of the individual to the interests of the group—has, until very recently, lagged. A new example and the circumstances under which it achieved success are of special interest.

If Japan was able to demonstrate, through the procedures of Suzuki, the ability to produce a string orchestra of the quality of its touring Toho ensemble (in 1964), why not a string quartet of international quality? Simply, in my judgment, because the Tohos were guided by a model to which they responded (a steady succession of symphony orchestras from abroad that have performed in Japan since 1950). The achievements of the Tokyo Quartet in recent years suggest that it has not been for lack of individual elements, but for the lack of a missing ingredient to bind them together and to achieve the necessary chemical change.

As chemistry is historically defined, the need for such a change requires not one but two bodies: an agent and a reagent. The agents were Robert Mann, leader of the Juilliard Quartet since its founding in the mid-forties, and his longtime associate as violist, Raphael Hillyer (who has since left the quartet). As of 1966, they were closely related in a chamber music workshop, by request of the United States State Department, during a concert tour to Japan.

Among those who presented themselves to Mann and Hillyer at the Toho Gakuen (School of Music) were three string players coached in ensemble performance by Professor Hideo Saito, a one-time pupil of the great cellist Emanuel Feuermann (he is also known as the man who encouraged Ozawa to make the journey to Europe that put him on the way to his career as a conductor). The three string players were so typical of the school that they had made the American tour of 1964 with the Toho String Orchestra. By acts of international cooperation and individual devotion, the three of them persisted, as reagents, to become the nucleus of the much admired, highly rated Tokyo String Quartet.

The students in the chamber music workshop became the special charge of Hillyer. He saw in them musicians not only with the technical command to reach high objectives, but also with the desire and the discipline to concentrate those objectives on chamber music. A year or so later, Sadao Harada (cellist) and Kazuhide Isomura (violist) were invited to spend a summer at the Aspen Institute in Colorado. They played in the Festival Orchestra and continued their studies with members of the Juilliard Quartet. They were offered, and accepted, positions in the Nashville Symphony Orchestra, to fund their stay in America and to continue their studies.

The following summer they were joined in Aspen by Koichiro Harada (unrelated to Sadao, except musically), who is now the quartet's leader. By 1969, all three were enrolled in the Juilliard School, for studies with three of its best-known string pedagogues: Ivan Galamian, Dorothy DeLay, and Paul Makanowitsky. With Yoshiko Nakura, a female violinist who had studied with Makanowitsky when he was a guest instructor at Toho, as second violinist, they entered and won the Coleman String Quartet Competition in Pasadena, California. Four months later, after intensive, daylong work on repertory with Hillyer, they won first prize at the International Chamber Music Competition in Munich.

If this recitation of application and dedication seems inordinately prolonged, so too is the amount of ground tilling, seed sowing, and cultivation required to produce even a moderately good quartet. Having acquired a contract in 1973 with Deutsche Grammophon—for whom Japan is a primary record market—the Tokyo Quartet members have steadily applied themselves to becoming not merely a moderately good quartet, but one of the best. In 1973, they were invited to perform at the Osaka Festival, where, in the home country they had left as nonentities half a dozen years before, they were identified as "the world-famous Tokyo Quartet." About that time, Nakura left the quartet to live in Belgium, and Kikuei Ikeda became the second violinist.

In accord with common quartet procedure, they avoid communal activity on a day-to-day basis, except when they are rehearsing, or on tour. Years of experience by their best predecessors have proven that such separation provides the fresh edge to do their top work together. As the seventies progressed, they found residences, and families, in areas scattered around metropolitan New York.

The instant identity of the Tokyo Quartet, as heard in the concert hall or from records, is announced by a phenomenally fine sound. Could they be described as disciples of Toshita Eto, with a cellist formed out of the same mold? Perhaps. But the homogeneity flows from a more particular source: four old Amatis, on loan from the Corcoran Gallery in Washington, D.C., where they have regularly performed (a fair distance from the violin factory from which Suzuki emerged). Although leader Harada is, audibly, the most brilliantly gifted of the players, the totality is the thing—continuously, unfailingly, magnetically blended into a force that pulls listener attention to it.

All fine quartets take pride in "playing the repertory," striding across the decades and the schools and the styles from year to year. But even the finest quartets have a center of tonal gravity, a composer (perhaps two or three, if they share an epoch) to whom they return with love, affection, and a strong sense of homecoming.

To the great Budapest Quartet of yesterday it was, without question, Haydn-Beethoven (or Beethoven-Haydn); to the Amadeus of today, Schubert, who is also the "home" composer of the Melos of Stuttgart. For the current personnel of the Juilliard Quartet, led by Mann, with thirty-five years of experience behind him, it is closer to the contemporary scene, especially the scene as dominated by Elliott Carter. The big robust sound of the Guarneri Quartet flourishes best in late Beethoven, especially in the "Grosse Fuge" of the B flat quartet (opus 130), by contrast with the Beethoven Quartet of the Soviet Union, which plays any one of Dmitri Shostakovich's fifteen quartets with greater authority than the later, most challenging ones of the composer whose name it bears.

For now, the playing of the Tokyo Quartet is centered in the

Mozart literature, not at all a bad place for a youngish quartet (average age: thirty-five) to be. Here is a base from which to move out to everything else, and, also, to which to return from anything else, with no sacrifice of identity.

In a summary of the quartet world as it appeared in the postwar years of the late fifties, I wrote: "That a dozen new good quartets adorn the scene testifies that four dozen musicians in Paris and Prague, Brussels, Ann Arbor and Parma have succumbed to the old enticements, measured themselves against standards as different as those of Beethoven and Bartók, Brahms and Berg."[8] To have included Tokyo in the list of places where such a happening might have come about would in 1958 have been an absurdity, not to say an affectation. Twenty years has done much for the "more nearly universal language."

It has also done a lot to revise standards of values, and the value of standards. A clever French novel by Claude Farrere, published in France in 1909 under the title of *La Bataille*, was made into a film with Charles Boyer in 1934, under the same title, and later remade in America as *Thunder in the East*. The time is the early years of the Russo-Japanese War, and Boyer impersonates a Marquis Yorisaka, commander of a squadron about to go into battle with the Russians. Sharing the flagship with him as observer for the British is Fergan, a gunnery expert whose critique of his operation in a previous battle Yorisaka would dearly love to read. All this happens in Nagasaki, prior to the squadron's departure to sea; and Yorisaka uses his beautiful wife (Merle Oberon) to lure Fergan into an assignation (to which he is by no means averse) while he searches the Englishman's belongings, reads the critique, and absorbs its content. At a critical point in the next day's engagement, Yorisaka takes charge of his gunnery group, applies the knowledge he has gained from Fergan's comments, and destroys the enemy. Then, because he has compromised his and his wife's honor, he commits hara-kiri.

Musically, at least, Japan is moving into a position of independence of outside judgments of its values and standards. Cer-

[8] Kolodin, Irving, *The Musical Life* (Alfred A. Knopf, Inc., New York, 1958), p. 64.

tainly the worldwide supremacy of Japanese audio merchandise began at home, in satisfaction of an ever more discriminating market. Internationally, Seiji Ozawa and the Tokyo Quartet are standard-bearers in any competitive market. Behind them, there must be as many who are as conscious of such a spur to their ambitions as Israelis are of Barenboim, Zukerman, and Perlman, the young pianist Yafim Bronfman, and others not yet known by name.

Most Israelis speak English, even if the official language of the land is Hebrew. In Japan, of course, the common language is that "difficult" one to learn to which Suzuki referred: "having English" is an attribute restricted to highly trained businessmen or the upper, educated classes who travel abroad. But "having English," and being able to use it for self-improvement, can be different things.

I learned this on a visit to Japan in 1975, when the Metropolitan Opera company made its first tour to the Orient. During the opening night's performance of Verdi's *La Traviata*, which was wildly acclaimed, a bilingual friend (John Rich, once of NBC, then of the New York *Times*) mentioned during the intermission that a Japanese music critic wanted to meet me. "Fine," I said, and the critic was brought over. With him was an interpreter who expressed the critic's pleasure at meeting the author of a book on the Metropolitan Opera which he knew so well.

I thanked him, and added, "How is it that he reads a book in English, if he doesn't speak the language?"

The critic's answer, as translated, was: "We can read English in order to learn things we want to know—but speaking the language, that is something else."

V

My knowledge of things Korean, though improving, is certainly inferior to the Japanese critic's knowledge of things American. But of one thing I am highly conscious: the extent to which the "more nearly universal language" extends to South Korea. I have observed it on several levels whose origins were mystifying to me; but I have come upon several links in the chain that were previously missing. One was an account of the first International Music Festival ever to be held in Seoul, during the first weeks of May 1962; the others were two happenings in 1978 and 1979.

The first occasion speaks for itself; but the date of *May* 1962 speaks for something else. Because, as my source says: "It was carefully timed to attract audiences from the just finished Osaka Festival."[9]

Here is an incident of cause and effect that projects, more forcefully than any amount of speculation, the extent to which the expanded activity in Japan causes ripples to flow across water to surrounding areas. The *first* Osaka Festival occurred in the mid-fifties; thus it was only seven years later that its effect was felt in surrounding areas.

What did it bring to Korea? Artists of the quality of the Spanish harpist Nicanor Zabaleta; the French cellist André Navarra; violinist Ricardo Odnoposoff, a pre-Barenboim Argentinian (1914–); the Italian pianist Orazio Frugoni; and, even more important than all of these, the great forerunner of Fischer-Dieskau as the peerless *Lieder* singer of a prior era, Gerhard Hüsch (1901–). In addition to public concerts in Seoul, the visitors were heard on Seoul Radio.

Continuing its account of music in South Korea, the same source says: "People unfamiliar with the nature of the New Far East will doubtless be surprised to learn that a full stage production of Beethoven's *Fidelio* was also presented, with chorus, orchestra and supporting soloists."

Thanks to the presence in Korea of Hüsch, the production directed by him was authentic Beethoven. Thanks, also, to the Osaka Festival, where they had previously performed with Christel Goltz in Richard Strauss's *Salome*, the leading performers were as authentic in their roles as the staging of Hüsch: Fritz Uhl was Florestan, Joseph Metternich was Don Pizarro, with Goltz as

[9] Stoll, Dennis Gray, *Music Festivals of the World* (Pergamon Press, Oxford, London, Paris, Frankfurt; The Macmillan Company, Pergamon Press Ltd., New York, 1963), pp. 262–64.

Leonore. Nor could the audiences in Seoul have fared much better for a conductor. He was Manfred Gurlitt, music director of the Bremen Opera from 1914 to 1927 and then heard at the Berlin Opera (also on numerous recordings) until purged in the 1933 uprising of the Nazis. He lived thereafter in Tokyo until his death in 1972.

Here is a personification of the underlying South Korean interest in Western music. It also goes far to explain some of the outer manifestations that would, otherwise, be inexplicable vis-à-vis the country's pre-wartime musical identity. I have in mind, as an outstanding performer of Western music on the highest level, the violinist Kyung-Wha Chung, who was born in Seoul in 1948.

After displaying impressive promise at home, she came to New York at the age of thirteen, and qualified for study with the preeminent pedagogue of her instrument, Ivan Galamian. Concurrently studying with Galamian at the Juilliard was Pinchas Zukerman, also born in 1948. They pursued parallel paths, even to the Leventritt Competition of 1967. This was a meeting of East and West (more properly, Middle East) hardly precedented in musical prizemanship, certainly not in musical pedagogy, something that even a *Hauptprüfung* at the Leipzig Conservatory of Schilsky's day would have found uncommon. The jury they confronted could find nothing to distinguish one from the other, even age. They divided the award between them.

A dozen years later, the two prizewinners have equal, if different, careers well in hand. Zukerman's background now includes, in the pattern of his devoted benefactor, close friend, and model, Barenboim, some identity as a conductor (especially in collaboration with his wife, flutist Eugenia). Zukerman also plays viola in the elite company of Isaac Stern, Eugene Istomin, and Leonard Rose; and he has high rank as a solo violinist.

Kyung-Wha Chung is, without doubt, the brightest new violinist to appear on the international scene in a decade. Her tone quality is pure, her use of it rarely otherwise than precisely as the composer would have preferred. To judge from her accumulating catalogue of recordings (London/Decca), the composers tend not to be in the line of Mozart/Beethoven/Mendelssohn/Brahms, but the non-Germanic Vieuxtemps and Bruch, Saint-Säens and Sibelius, Elgar and Bartók. This is not to suggest that she is disinterested in the German classics; rather, that she is not yet ready to declare herself on such subject matter in recordings.

Least of all does this suggest an unwillingness to measure herself, otherwise, on the highest level. Her performance of the violin concerto by Sir William Walton is as good as anyone has ever heard of it, even including the one by the man for whom it was written, Jascha Heifetz.

One distinctive difference defines Kyung-Wha Chung from Zukerman. He has no siblings of remotely comparable quality known to me. She does. On one recent day, her brother took part in a conducting class at the Juilliard, of which Herbert von Karajan was the visiting professor; in the evening, Myung-Whun Chung appeared in Avery Fisher Hall in Lincoln Center for the Performing Arts as pianist with his sister, the violinist, and their sister, the cellist Myung-Wha Chung. The most current address I can provide for Myung-Whun Chung is in care of the Music Pavilion, Los Angeles, California, where he is assistant conductor, in the Exxon program, to Carlo Maria Giulini, music director of the Los Angeles Philharmonic Orchestra.

This is undoubtedly an exceptional instance of interrelated musicality among several young members of the family, recalling the Busches, the Menuhins, the Schneiders, the Compinskys, the Shankars, and not too many others. It has also provoked another generation of South Koreans of high musical aptitude. They have, as I suggested previously, continued to appear in the best American schools, year after year. The Curtis Institute in Philadelphia looks with pride on Ju Hee Suh, a twelve-year-old pianist of that background. Eight years after sixteen-year-old Ik-Hwan Bae came to New York to study with Galamian and four years after he became concertmaster of the Juilliard Orchestra, he won a North American Young Artists Competition sponsored by the Denver Symphony Guild (April 8, 1979). Others of comparable quality, but not yet in their teens, continue to arrive in America.

The examples of such talent I have encountered at the Juilliard, in my own specialized work, reflect a deep desire for greater knowledge of Western music, as a means of broadening their affinity with it. They bring with them the same attentiveness and awareness of a special opportunity conferred on them that are characteristic of others from Japan and the Philippines, Malaysia and probably—as time progresses—China. And, as I have mentioned previously, the home scene continues to expand. The Metropolitan's first performances in Tokyo were offered in a new hall that had been created for a broadcasting network; when the New York Philharmonic performed in Seoul in 1978 (and in 1979) it was in a concert hall seating four thousand that was part of a new cultural center. The hall was crowded to capacity by government officials, some socialites, and many music lovers on each occasion, but there were also students dreaming, no doubt, of the day when they could hear the Philharmonic at home.

Nor need they all be of the quality of Kyung-Wha Chung. During the same year of 1979, Carnegie Hall in New York was host to the Korean National Symphony. The conductor was a man of middle years, Yun Taik Hong, a product of Eastern aspiration and Western cultivation, having spent some of his student years in Vienna. His soloist in the D minor violin concerto of Jean Sibelius was Dong-Suk Kang, also a pupil of Galamian. His performance was clean and workmanlike, somewhat shy, and of limited personality. The orchestra's playing of the Brahms Fourth Symphony was creditable to the young players and their conductor. A *Capriccio* by Soung Tai Kim used a Korean folk song in a way that spoke well for the composer's background (he was sixty-nine at the time of the performance). The work of the younger Dong Wook Park called *Contrast*, for percussion ensemble and winds, paid its tributes to more contemporary compositional trends.

These are terms of objective judgment, not inspired by kindly sentiments. But they reflect a background in which South Korea is now fluent in the "more nearly universal language."

VI

All of this presents a fascinating study in probabilities, possibilities, and permutations. Will those, worldwide, who acquire a sufficient command of their chosen craft to qualify on the highest level of prominence (and income) take roots elsewhere and forget what they have left behind? Will it be only those who *cannot* qualify on the highest level who remain at home and put the benefits of their education at the disposal of their kin?

Much, I suppose, depends on individual character. On a visit to Puerto Rico a dozen years ago, my wife came down with an affliction which, if not mortal, required immediate, skillful ministration. Good advice was forthcoming, and it produced a native doctor of middle years, who took charge and put her into a hospital.

The problem was one that required patience as well as knowledge, to dislodge from the abdomen, through the windpipe, something that was constricting it. Five, six tries did not produce the needed outcome. Finally, after tedious work during much of the night—success. The condition was relieved, and she fell asleep.

After thanks, etc., I asked him about his background. He had been born in Puerto Rico, gone to medical school in the States, and served an internship in an American hospital with such distinction that he was offered a staff position.

"It was tempting," he said, "but I decided to go back home to my own people."

To be sure, medicine is not music, nor vice versa (except in romantic poetry). However, one side of the musical equation that puts a previously unconsidered factor into the balance has come lately from Seiji Ozawa. Discussing the personal decision that confronts him after twenty years (1960–80) spent mostly in the West, he has arrived at a resolution: "Home for the Ozawas is Seijo, a village outside Tokyo." The interviewer (Flora Lewis) attributed Ozawa's statement to his concern for his children (aged seven and five at the time of their conversation) and their schooling. "I want them to be international Japanese, not Japanese-looking internationals. Music is international but blood and skin are not interchangeable."[10]

Ozawa's comment on his children sounds a curious echo of what Serge Prokofiev said nearly fifty years before, when he decided to return to the Soviet Union (in 1932) after living in the West since 1918: "First of all, I have two sons who speak French like Russians and Russian like Frenchmen. And I want them to speak at least their own language properly."[11]

Both men were about the same age when confronted with the necessity to make a decision concerning their children. On their behalf, Ozawa will continue to spend much of his time either in Boston, as music director of the Symphony, or elsewhere; but his wife and children will remain in Japan. On behalf of *his* children —and for a few accessory reasons, particularly an attachment to the Russian soil—Prokofiev spent the rest of his life in the Soviet Union. And, as time passed, with all the well-known difficulties pertaining to aesthetic freedom, censorship, humiliating rebukes, and the like.

One might say that, in the abstract, it is easier for a composer to work where he happens to be than for a conductor, and, in effect, Ozawa has said it: "I can't stay in Japan. I'm forty-three years old and learning every day. I still need to study very hard. It would be a waste of my life to go back and conduct only Japanese orchestras."

Clearly the dilemma's horns are irking the man impaled upon them. But let us honor his recognition of their existence rather than pretending that all is well, East or West. But is it necessary that Ozawa conduct "only" Japanese orchestras? Surely there can be an adjustment when he is no longer forty-three, and as for "learning every day," that is a common condition for an active, receptive mind, age aside.

Eventually Ozawa will leave Boston (very possibly *after* the centennial season of the orchestra's founding on October 22, 1881),

[10] Lewis, Flora, "Ozawa, Man of Two Worlds," New York *Times*, June 11, 1979, p. C13.

[11] Seroff, Victor, *Serge Prokofiev. A Soviet Tragedy* (Taplinger Publishing Company, New York, 1969), p. 167.

go back to Japan, and sink roots near an airport, to find a contemporary solution to his problem, and thus accommodate both purposes of his life.

That would be an instance of recognizing a qualification in music as a more nearly universal language, which Ozawa states as a *fait accompli,* but which, he also implies, is still spoken better in Boston or Berlin than in Tokyo or Osaka.

Further—and the word takes in a substantial period of soul-searching—Ozawa should recognize that he has taken *in* a considerable amount of music on an international level, and that it is up to him to give back some portion of that experience to those who helped him achieve what he is today.

The other side of this now much mooted coin may be found in Australia, where musical talent and the cultivation of it may very well be a mystery to those who haven't been there, heard what is going on, and observed some contradictory aspects of it. For many elsewhere, the big parenthesis enclosing Australia, musically, may be expressed in the names: Melba, Nellie—Sutherland, Joan. As the former's highly successful London debut dates to 1886 and the latter's prominence should endure to 1986, it takes in a full century.

For much of that time, Australians of talent—such as John Brownlee and Marjorie Lawrence of the thirties and forties, or the greatly endowed Florence Austral (born Wilson) of the twenties, and Percy Grainger before them—had little choice but to channel their musical abilities elsewhere. Operatically, the steady succession of fine singers developed in that part of the world (including New Zealand, the birthplace of Frances Alda, see page 191) had little reason to stay at home, or endure the long sea journey to return there periodically. Even as recently as 1964, when Sutherland returned home to sing in *Lucia di Lammermoor, La Sonnambula,* and other operas, she brought with her most of the surrounding principals required, including a little-known, young tenor named Luciano Pavarotti, to perform with her.

But the ground in that area was already beginning to shake under the impact of her fame elsewhere. Other singers of quality

—Marie Collier, Lauri Elms, Yvonne Minton, Clifford Grant, Donald McIntyre, Kiri Te Kanawa—were beginning to emerge. There were already the physical beginnings of an opera house in Sydney when I visited there for the first time in 1971. The Australian Opera Company was in being, even though it was performing in a shabby theater with poor acoustics.

What has happened with it since, despite the miscarriage of building that has made the Sydney Opera House more impressive from the outside than useful on the inside, is well established. There is a place in Australia for good singers, for very good singers, even for great singers. And with the added amenity of jet travel, they can be heard and admired, while they are developing and when they reach their prime and become world-famous, by an audience that cherishes them through their struggles for success, and welcomes them with pride when they return from abroad.

Not as much can be said in other respects, especially for orchestral conductors. There are, in the five sizable cities that rim the continent (Brisbane, Sydney, Melbourne, Adelaide, and Perth) orchestras supported, like the BBC in England, by the ABC (Australian Broadcasting Commission). There is another on the offshore island of Tasmania, in Hobart. In a contagion much like that which followed the creation of the Lincoln Center for the Performing Arts in America, each of the four Australian cities has in emulation of Sydney, in being or under construction, a new home for its performing arts.

If there is an Australian conductor in two of them, that is one more than when I was last there (in 1978). There is mistrust, bordering on hostility, to the idea of the ABC entrusting one of its best orchestras (Sydney or Melbourne) to a home-grown conductor (unless he has made a reputation overseas). Perhaps there have been miscalculations and poor judgment in previous choices; but errors are no excuse for a lack of enterprise.

I have in mind the offspring of Australian parents born in Schenectady, New York, in 1925 (I suspect his father had something to do with General Electric). He was brought to Australia at the age of two, and educated, musically, at the Sydney Conservatorium, with a specialty on the oboe. At the age of twenty, he qualified to be first oboist of the Sydney Symphony.

His ambition was to be a conductor, but there was little encouragement at home. So he took his ambitions abroad, to Prague, where he studied conducting, and then to London, where he found work at the Sadler's Wells Opera. He was less than thirty when he made a highly successful arrangement of Arthur Sullivan's music (mostly *H.M.S. Pinafore*) into a ballet called *Pineapple Poll*. He has since evolved into one of England's best conductors.

Could Australia have kept Charles Mackerras at home by encouraging his aspirations to be a conductor? That would not necessarily have satisfied his needs: Australia, for all its size, has a good deal of barren space (artistically as well as physically). Foreign training was undoubtedly essential. But had some government agency maintained a line of connection to what *he* wanted to do and moved in on his talent at a point where it would have suited *his* purposes as well as theirs, Australia might have profited considerably more on behalf of its home public than it does now from an occasional visit by that "international favorite" Charles Mackerras.

Here are two classic examples of the "more nearly universal language" working at cross-purposes, inasmuch as the place of birth and early opportunities are concerned. Neither Ozawa nor Mackerras could have achieved his objectives by staying at home and limiting himself to the challenges available there. Both needed to go elsewhere, to the centers of information and indoctrination.

What both of them did with that information and indoctrination is all too evident. But why wasn't there a strong line of connection to where they had come from, to derive some return for birthright, for nativity, for early education? Japan and Australia are both famous for their history in sports, especially tennis. Apparently the people who supervise such development have a keener appreciation of capabilities than those who look after music.

The least one might say is: encourage! What is there to be lost?

Apropos the "more nearly international language," "Barenboim" is a prime example of it: a linguistic oddity, it is German in origin, and derived, via Yiddish and Russian, from *Birnbaum*—or pear tree.[12]

[12] A recent (April 1980) re-meeting with Enrique Barenboim permitted me to update some information about his son's background in Buenos Aires, as reflected in the pages pertaining to that period of his development. It also extended the etymological aspects of the family name to include the following: Mrs. Barenboim, wishing to make a person-to-person call, overseas, to her son in Germany, asked to be connected with "Mr. Barenboim." Phone operator: "Is that Birnbaum?" Caller: "No. Barenboim." Phone operator: "That's what I said. I'll connect you."

Epilogue

I

Sir Edward Elgar died, in 1934, without revealing the "Enigma" of his famous variations (opus 36), of which he said: "Through and over the whole set another and larger theme 'goes' but is not played . . ." I have no comparable hesitance in letting it be known that through and over the preceding discussion another and larger theme also "goes": what will be the consequence to the arts, especially music, now that the first Scientific Century has run its course, and a second is under way?

Discussions pertaining to the arts have usually been compartmentalized in terms of the sixteenth, the seventeenth, the eighteenth, the nineteenth centuries. Each of these divisions can be associated with political, social, and economic happenings that bore heavily on the creative faculties of men, determined their direction and expression. Johann Sebastian Bach could no more have been a Napoleonic man than Ludwig van Beethoven could have been a cantor of St. Thomas's Church in Leipzig. The young man who grew up in the court of Elector Maximilian at Bonn found a new meaning in life when he learned, in Vienna, that the court itself had been swept away by the armies of Napoleon overrunning the Rhineland, in 1794.

The immediate effect was personal: the need of returning to Bonn after his studies with Haydn ended was foreclosed; the longer effect was philosophical: if that rock of tradition could be dislodged, what else could not be?

The bell that tolled the end of the eighteenth century in music may not have been precisely the one that resounds in the

"Witches' Sabbath" in Hector Berlioz's *Symphonie fantastique* (1830). But it was certainly a conception that no composer of eighteenth-century birth could have imagined, Beethoven included. As for the nineteenth century, we are four fifths of the way through its successor, and the bell that tolls the end of its influence on the music-loving world is yet to be heard.

The clear conclusion must then be that the quaint old custom of dividing centuries numerically has run its course and some new way of dating must be devised. I pose the point that there is a precedent for this. The centuries by which the rise of music to be "a more nearly universal language" came about are, after all, for Beethoven, calculated as 1770 A.D., not B.C. The ones of the practice I project should be B.E. and A.E.: specifically, Before Einstein and After Einstein.

In this calibration, A.E. would pick up on March 14, 1 A.E., with the birth of Albert Einstein in Ulm, Germany. Put into readily recognizable symbols, the New Calibration (NC) would be printed SC I A.E., or Scientific Century I, A.E. Everything prior to that would be readjusted in the terms of 1879 B.E., so as not to disturb all the vast accumulation of historical data related to the Old Calibration.

The presumption of suggesting a new system of dates pertaining to one recently deceased non-sectarian, rather than a historic personage identified with the founding of a religion, has justifications which will be set forth presently. But as a rule of thumb, what was suitable for one Jew is not unsuitable for another.

The concept of a Scientific Century became firmly fixed on the anniversary of Einstein's birth (March 1979). Rather than presenting the reason for it in my own words, I will offer it in those of a straightforward objective source: the Oxford Concise Dictionary. This is what it has to say about relativity, the one-word synonym for Einstein among the millions of the world (myself included) who know him for little else: "Einstein's theory of the universe, based on the principle that all motion is relative, regarding space-time as a four-dimensional continuum, and invalidating previous conceptions of gravitation, geometry and other matters."

As an amateur logician, I would have to say that anything related to the universe would have to relate to every part of it. That is a thought of staggering inclusiveness, and I would not pretend to assume the capability of dealing with it. But I am quite willing to look at it in the light of my own experience, and relate it to the part of the universe in which I have the greatest stake—man himself.

Among all the abstractions related to Einstein and his theories, which few can understand, there is one simple action of his life that no one can misunderstand. That was the signature he put on a letter to President Franklin D. Roosevelt in September 1939 urging that the United States proceed with all speed to develop atomic energy. The urgency is contained in the date: as of September 1939 Germany had become at war with Poland, England, and France: her scientists doubtless were at work to unlock the atom, and with it, a bomb of prodigious explosive force.

The Germans did not; and the war was won (in the West) without it.

A great authority on the subject (Robert Oppenheimer) has said: "Einstein is often blamed or praised or credited with these miserable bombs. It is not in my opinion true."[1] But another writer tells us that his (Einstein's) "time and motion equations" were the "theoretical foundation of the atomic age."[2]

I allude to Einstein's part in the new age of atomic energy not to affiliate him with the consequences as they are now known, but simply to pinpoint a fact of life—his life—which is undeniable. My purpose is to put in place the processes which produced what is now called the Scientific Century[3] (in terms of pure science and its application), vis-à-vis the things affecting the artistic community and the particular part of it pertaining to music.

[1] Oppenheimer, Robert, *On Einstein.*
[2] Stockton, William, "Celebrating Einstein," New York *Times Magazine*, February 18, 1979, p. 47.
[3] Source unknown.

II

During that century, spanning the end of the old-style nineteenth century and the dangling part of the twentieth, man has come to know more about the cosmos *around* him than ever before. He is a being on a planet from which his fellow men have launched themselves into space, and returned with evidence thitherto unavailable of life—or the lack of it—on another planet, or the moon.

The question this prompts in my mind is: how does this relate to the cosmos *within* him? As a thinking, functioning person, of intellectual capacity and emotional aspiration, how does that awareness *aggrandize* his aspiration to personal fulfillment, or diminish it? Some might contend that it really doesn't make a great deal of difference, that man is designed by nature, and his maker, with the ability to adjust himself to the world around him, that his nervous system is equipped with all the adjuncts to absorb such an alteration of status, and proceed unhindered.

This may—and probably does—satisfy the criteria applicable to a very considerable portion of the earth's population. But there is a not inconsiderable proportion which has, over centuries, produced much of the evidence of man's existence which has made life more endurable for those who came after him.

Some call them elitists. Many others, myself included, call them artists. They exist on many levels and with greatly differing capacities. Whatever they do, and in whatever medium they do it, they are putting onto paper, or canvas, or into sound, a statement of a moment which has, for that person, an importance transcending everything else. If it is good enough, it will be important for other persons. If not, he or she can always try again.

In my judgment, the importance of that inner world, to the person who was secure in it, has been the source of sustenance for the productive capacity, the quest, the energy, the emotional power by which art is nourished.

In a time when the finite world was what could be seen of it on a clear night, the in-finite world was mere theory, and the *inner* world was the cosmos inhabited by earthly man.

One of the greatest of slow movements by Beethoven is to be found in the quartet in E minor (No. 2 of opus 59). It is music of extraordinary breadth, but also of a sublime, serene composure. So uncommon is it that his young friend and disciple Carl Czerny questioned the composer on the circumstances that brought it into being, and jotted down his answer: "The Adagio, E major, in the second Rasumovsky Quartet occurred to him when contemplating the starry skies and thinking of the music of the spheres."[4] My impression is that a Beethoven of today (should there be such in Vienna!) might, in similar circumstances, say to himself: "That reminds me. I must go home and call my friend Muzio Clementi in London by satellite."

Had the present range of scientific certainty prevailed years ago, in place of speculative uncertainty, a whole literature of works now proclaimed "imaginative" and "poetic" might never have come to be.

Certainty, in place of speculation, induces a wide, almost total reconsideration of self, and status. Is science the new reality? If so, the littleness of man in his relation to the epoch-making invasions of space, and beyond, no longer challenges him to rise, mentally, above his earthly environment. It is, more likely, a reminder of the folly of trying.

Lest this strike some as an unduly harsh bill of particulars vis-à-vis science, let me spell out the bill in more particular. Science has blessed us in an infinity of ways: medical science has extended life, made it almost tolerable for some cursed disabilities, eliminated at least one source of epidemic (smallpox). In some countries (such as Israel) it has truly made the desert bloom; and, given his will, it can make man something like the captain of his soul and the master of his fate that William Henley contended he

---

[4] *Thayer's Life of Beethoven*, Revised and Edited by Elliot Forbes (Princeton University Press, Princeton, N.J., 1964), pp. 408–9. Rasumovsky was the Russian nobleman and ambassador to Vienna who commissioned the three quartets of opus 59.

could be (a sentiment pronounced in year 86 A.E. to be "meretricious,"[5] or "of, befitting a harlot"[6]).

Science has also robbed us of decision making (via computer), deprived us of the energetic pursuit of farming (by everything from seed sowing to crop harvesting); even approached the point where man's like can be reproduced by proxy (a form of sexual indulgence not recommended for the average man). Science has also fostered a means of persuading children (via the home screen) that French fries are preferable to *pommes de terre* in some other, more digestible form.

Lest this lapse into an extended summary of the cons and pros of science (of which a new H. L. Mencken could make a surpassing volume), the additions and subtractions it has brought about will be restricted to the arts, and particularly to music. Science has, of course, generated enormous benefits for those living, by choice or necessity, far from the sources of supply. Television is a major miracle converted into a horrendous blight by those who control the major usage of it for profit. But precious reservation persists. Attention to it is optimal, not obligatory. Those who complain of inadequate time for reading, listening to music, or merely meditating have only themselves to blame. Such self-diversion requires no more than self-discipline to avoid the diversion provided for others.

At best, however—and sometimes its values have been of surpassing satisfaction—what science has done in its first century has benefited the *re-creative* aspects of music, rather than the creative. This unbalanced equation has much to do with the deficiency of creative output vis-à-vis the ever growing demand for it. Techniques of execution are enormously furthered by every new means of reproducing music, whether its sound alone, or in concurrence with sight (on television as it now exists, and on video discs as they will exist in the 1980s). Our perception of how the best music *sounds* is constantly being sharpened; the general conception of how the best music is *made* is steadily being diminished.

[5] Benét, William Rose, The Reader's Encyclopedia (Thomas Y. Crowell Company, New York, Second Edition, 1965), p. 455.
[6] Concise Oxford Dictionary, p. 761.

At first, the erosion was imperceptible: people who had learned how to play an instrument well enough to participate in the performance of music at home made available the instruments they treasured to their children, made them "take piano" or "voice," or whatever. But the cost of proficiency—*practice*—which was always tedious, becomes less and less inviting as alternatives make their appearance. As the enjoyment of music became more and more possible *without* the effort of participating in the performance of it, the alternative became much more than the exception—it has, is, and will become an ever increasing rule.

How, then, is it that the conservatories are turning out instrumentalists, in this country, in ever increasing numbers? Let it not be forgotten the population of this country is *twice* what it was at the beginning of the century; let us not forget those who are being attracted, in ever increasing numbers, from the lands where the "more nearly universal language" is becoming understandable. The apparent increase in qualified technicians—don't forget that totals do not accurately represent *percentages*—doesn't mean that there are more *music lovers* in the world than there were, say, in 1920.

The increase in the *passivity* of the average has been offset, to some extent, by the stimulus to the *activity* of a relative few.

Whether this *improves* the perception of the audience at the *average* orchestral concert, solo recital, or opera performance, I tend to doubt. Volubility is not quite the same as sensibility. A warm response to the performance of a chamber music work means that the audience has perceived the merit of what it has heard; the same amount of sound in an opera house generally means that a high final note was sung louder than it should be.

I am constantly reminded, in attending debut recitals, or auditions for a grant or scholarships, of a comment by the late Mischa Elman, who died in 1967 at the age of seventy-six. On the occasion of one of his "landmark" birthdays—probably the seventieth, in 1961—the great violinist was asked by an interviewer to compare the musical world of that day to what it was, say, in 1910, when he was making his first appearances in America. After a moment's reflection, Elman said: "The standard of mediocrity today is higher than it used to be."

That, of course, is a tribute to better teaching methods, to the widespread availability of recordings, broadcasts, and telecasts. But, as Elman meant his remark to convey, it does not make the incidence of *outstanding* artistry more common than it was, nor does it add much distinction to the quality of music being written. Again, the profit has been to the re-creative aspect of music, not to the creation of it.

I am, at regular intervals, asked by interviewers and correspondents, "What do you think of electronic music?" My answer, unfailingly, is: "That is like asking me—what do you think of organ music?" Or, to put it more conversationally: "Electronic sound is a means, not an end."

Of all its latent possibilities, the most provocative in electronic music is as a medium in which the creator can bypass the re-creator entirely, by being his own re-creator. The necessities now exist in all their component parts: a sine wave, or synthesizer, as a sound source; the tape as the replacement for a score, or written expression of the composer's intent; the reproducibility of what is on the tape, either reel-to-reel or cassette, directly on the audio equipment with which many, many homes are now equipped.

The only necessity not now accounted for is the man with the imagination, the application, and the persistence to combine such components into the elements of an art form, not a plaything or noisemaker. As Edgard Varèse demonstrated in the twenties, sometimes the absence of means may drive a motivated man to achieve his objective by working *around* that lack. What he did, in desperation, by using conventional instruments of the orchestra to articulate the sounds in his mind, could now be readily done on tape, with electronic means. Perversely, we now have the equipment, but not the mind of a Varèse to make the full use of it.

An intermediary form of creation, practiced among others by Jacob Druckman, utilizes the orchestra in the concert hall as a step—on the way to an electronic outcome. Druckman, a man of considerable craftsmanship (he is now in his fifties), has been in and out of almost every contemporary mode of sound expression in the last three decades, whether or not it contains what Ansermet has described as "expressive substance."

In his present manner, expressed in a work called *Aureole*, the objective is to create a combination of sounds that will sound even better on a hi-fi set. One might ask, "Then why go to the trouble of performing it in a concert hall?" Because, as concert life is currently organized, it is easier to get a commission from Leonard Bernstein for such a score as *Aureole* (which was performed under his direction in June 1979 by the New York Philharmonic Orchestra) than it would be to get it from a recording company. *Aureole* can be described by the courtesy term of "composition" because it makes play with the instruments of the orchestra in a way that can be seen and heard. But its end objective, aesthetically, is a taped result in recorded form, rather than an enduring life in the concert hall.

Just about twenty years ago (1959), in their innocently commercial way, Richard Rodgers and Oscar Hammerstein II wrote an innocently commercial smash hit called *The Sound of Music*. A good enough title, said many high-minded people of artistic disposition, for innocently profitable commercial purposes: but what nonsense! After all, the sound of music *is* the sound of music.

Twenty years or so later, that definition is, in many instances, the fulsome sound of the past. On all sides, and in an extravagant number of contexts, what we are incited to listen to, teased into thinking provocative, challenged to accept as stimulating, even to regard as philosophically persuasive, is: the Sound of Sound.[7]

This is not without both external and internal reasons. The same time period is precisely the one in which home reproduction of music has evolved from monophonic to stereophonic. This has been the profoundest of all changes in home listening since Edison first made it possible (at almost the same time, 1877, that Einstein was born). I use that terminology because, for the vast preponderance of home music listeners, sound had always come from a single, identifiable speaker. Substituting *two* speakers for one introduced a whole new home experience.

With stereo came an enormous upgrading in the definition, dis-

---

[7] The present administrators of the venerably invaluable Carnegie Hall celebrated SC I A.E. with a campaign extolling "the Glorious Sound of Carnegie Hall." Nobody stood in line to sit in the empty hall and listen to it.

tribution, and perception of all the external factors related to music. With it, too, came a vastly stimulated dollar value of the means—mostly, by then, Japanese-made—to achieve a maximum experience, in the home, of what was contained on the ever improving stereophonic disc, tape, or cassette.

In the early phase of this historic happening—from, say, 1958, when stereo came in, to 1968, when most people had equipment that satisfied their requirements—the measurement of value was: how does this costly item reproduce the music I am interested in hearing?

But as time passed and a newer generation came into the marketplace, the factor of emphasis changed. No longer was it "music"; now the important consideration has become: how well does this costly item sound?

For those not versed in current terminology, this might mean anything from the sound of a flute in the high register to the snap of a string, on the double bass, against the fingerboard. I have no prejudice against flutes in the high register, or to a string on the double bass plucked in a way to produce such a snap. But, I contend, both should be judged in terms of a totality of greater importance: the flute as a part of Ravel's *Daphnis et Chloé*, or the snap of the double bass as Mahler wrote it in the third movement (Scherzo) of his Seventh Symphony.

The new operative vogue in music—creative as well as re-creative —tells us: whoever said the whole is the sum of its parts? In the period of time I am now describing as obsessed with the Sound of Sound, the whole is a bygone cliché, the parts the only reality.

Not gradually, but swiftly, even precipitously, the expectations of a startlingly substantial number of people who attend orchestral concerts and some recitals are the inversion of what they used to be. What they are hoping for is *not* the fulfillment of the mechanical likeness they have been hearing on their recording, but a super-likeness of it—accentuated, extrapolated, disembodied, even fragmented, in which *sound* is the margin of success.

I have at hand the brochure for a forthcoming season of the New York Philharmonic Orchestra. Does it proclaim the great repertory, the extraordinary soloists, the provocative novelties to be performed in all those enticing weeks to follow?

None of these. Subscriptions are solicited on the promise of: "That great New York Sound . . . Zubin Mehta and the New York Philharmonic . . . !"

III

In a way parallel to the invasion of *speculative uncertainty* by *scientific certainty*, what used to be called music—with all its promise of the uncertain, the tantalizingly unpredictable—has suffered a debilitating succession of attacks in which variety of creative opportunity and abundance of structural resource have steadily dwindled. Compared to the plenitude of possibilities that presented themselves to a composer when the objective was music, not the sound of sound, the listener of today is asked to make do with an ersatz synthesis which resembles the stuff of auditory life as matzoh resembles bread, in which all the ingredients of taste, nourishment, and bodily sustenance have *not* been omitted.

It is, by a prodigious scheme of self-deception, music that is without a) melody, b) harmony, c) modulation, d) recollectible form, e) collectible dynamics, f) perceptible purpose. The alphabet could be extended to include the other twenty letters, similarly indexed, but they may be held in reserve. It is an art rich in denial, abundant only in its lack of fulfillment.

It is as though writers of English were admonished to create miracles of fantasy and unlimited flights of the imagination without a) adjectives, b) punctuation, c) pronouns, d) the past tense, e) dependent clauses, f) the subjunctive. Adverbs would be permitted only on days beginning with T, and the rhyming scheme of the sonnet not at all.

The parallel postulated above has a reasonably close resemblance to the method of Arnold Schoenberg, which, in the view of Ernest Ansermet and others, became a part of Stravinsky's decline (see page 14). In the aggregate of attention attracted to Albert Einstein at the end of Scientific Century I A.E., I was prompted to look into the lore of Schoenbergiana to see what mystical attractions one might have had to the other. As it is well known that Einstein was an amateur of the violin whose deity was Mozart, the likelihood that he might have been to some extent attracted to Schoenberg is precluded. But, the other way around?

In a letter of May 4, 1923, addressed to the artist Wassily Kandinsky, Schoenberg engages in a polemic vis-à-vis whether he was a Jew or a Christian, since he had been subjected to discrimination at a resort which practiced segregation (Schoenberg was born of Jewish parents, accepted conversion to Protestantism during this middle period of his life, and reverted to Judaism in the thirties). At one point he queries: "Do you think I owe my discoveries, my knowledge and skill, to Jewish machinations in high places? Or does Einstein owe his to a commission from the Elders of Zion?"

At a later point in the same lengthy letter, he challenges Kandinsky (who didn't deny his anti-Semitism): "You are perhaps satisfied with depriving Jews of their civil rights. Then certainly, Einstein, Mahler, I and many others will have to be got rid of."[8] Clearly, Schoenberg felt that his "discoveries . . . knowledge and skill" were comparable to Einstein's.

Along with a cant of composition which has yet to produce a piece of writing that is universally agreed to be memorable, the Scientific Century has, with its new sound resources, and daily abuse of them, pre-empted subject matter held in high respect by composers in prior times.

Of particular esteem among them was the "rescue opera." In whatever language—*Rettenoper,* for example, in German—it means exactly what the word says: a work for the stage built, dramatically, around a life in need of rescue.

According to demonstrable evidence,[9] it originated in a form

[8] Schoenberg, Arnold, *Letters,* edited by Erwin Stein (St. Martin's Press, New York, 1965), pp. 91 and 93. In addition to the salient matter of Schoenberg vs. Einstein, this letter of 1923 is extraordinary for its reference, in an anti-Semitic context, to "that man Hitler" at a time when most Germans thought of him as a mere rabble-rouser (p. 91).

[9] Grout, Donald Jay, *A Short History of Opera* (Columbia University Press, New York, 1947), Vol. I, p. 308.

the French call *opéra de la délivrance,* in the 1770s. The subject matter was derived from the famous quest of the *troubadour* Blondel for his lost master, Richard the Lion-hearted, singing as he searched. And the composer attracted to its possibilities was the great French master of the later eighteenth century, André Grétry. The opportunity the story provided for songs of search and suspense, especially their appropriateness to Blondel, is self-evident. Grétry's skill in handling their opportunities contributed much to the success of *Richard Coeur de Lion.*

Plots based on searches and sacrifices, dangers and *délivrance,* flourished during the Reign of Terror, when subject matter came to attention on all sides. One of the more famous happenings of the epoch concerned a woman who, in the disguise of a young man, acquired employment in a prison where she believed her husband to be a political prisoner.

The subject was utilized by several composers, all famously non-famous (Pierre Gaveaux in 1798 and Ferdinando Paër in 1804, among them), before it came to the attention of Beethoven. His idealistic adoration for woman as a loyal being, morally superior to man, found an ideal counterpart in this story of her self-sacrifice. To heighten the drama of *Fidelio,* Beethoven and his librettists (Joseph Ferdinand Sonnleithner in the first form, G. F. Treitschke in the more successful revision of 1814) intensified sympathy for Leonore by broadening the focus of her concern. In her disguised form of Fidelio, she is clearly concerned for the *man* in the dungeon, without being sure that the particular man is her husband. The trumpet calls that resound in *Fidelio* (especially in the best-known summation of the drama, the *Leonore* Overture No. 3) lend urgency to the plight of the man who will die unless the King's minister arrives in time to prevent it.

Later in the century, Richard Wagner's devotion to some of the ideals of Beethoven formulated the suspense of the pure rescue opera into marginal likenesses of it. Senta's search for a way to rescue the sailor Vanderdecken is a prime element of *The Flying Dutchman.* On another level, Parsifal's wanderings to resolve the agonizing life of Amfortas convert the merely physical search into a form of moral redemption for himself.

Our time doesn't lack for examples of man's compassion for the lives of other men, or of organized effort to aid those in distress. What it lacks is the initiative, the emotion, the artistic compassion to rise to the occasion of such acts of heroism in a creative way, rather than to accept them merely as "news events" and pass on to something else.

Perhaps the greatest subject in decades for a *Rettenoper* on a grand scale was provided by the famous flight organized in July 1976 by the government and citizens of Israel to rescue its nationals from capture by hijackers who were holding them in the airport of Uganda named Entebbe.

Here was a perfect instance of a wholly contemporary situation, one that a Beethoven or a Wagner might dream about, but hardly foresee as an actuality. It brought together technical means against technical means, the plane as a means of transportation converted into a plane as an instrument of banditry (like a stagecoach or train of the nineteenth century), then *countered* by the plane as an instrument of rescue. Aligned against its misuse, by men striving to overcome the piracy of other men, are all the devices of communication and navigation ranging from radio to radar. Here is a situation as contemporary to a composer of today as Leonore-Fidelio was to Beethoven. What a subject to sing about!

Instead, as some may dimly remember, it became a toy for quick exploitation by two competing TV networks, which leveled the subject to dust under technological bulldozerism, and will never stir the hearts of men again.

Unless, and again I say *unless*, someone with the power to redress that ethical injustice realizes that there can be a collaboration of science and the arts on a subject of such importance, rather than merely a confrontation in which the arts are leveled and subjugated. Beethoven seized upon the subject matter of his time to treat it in a manner suitable to the nineteenth century. Why cannot it be converted, in the same way, into subject matter suitable to the Scientific Century? I think of Leonard Bernstein as a man, a musician, and a conductor-composer with innumerable instances of devotion to the ideals of *Fidelio* as one who would find a similar stimulation in the idealism of Entebbe.

The parallel becomes completely clear if one examines the nature of the two incidents and evaluates them in terms of how they relate to the artistic resources of their time. Beethoven's subject matter is ideal for the stage of its time, because the whole opera plays within the stone walls that *do* a prison make. Indeed, the play reaches its climax in a space (the dungeon) barely large enough for the people of the action (the quartet of Florestan and Fidelio, Rocco, the jailer, and Don Pizarro, the *Gauleiter* of the time) to stand in.

Entebbe could only be properly done through a kinescopic medium—using the term in its broadest sense—either film or videotape, for television purposes. Its subject matter requires airborne flight, both for the hijacking and the rescue operation; the split-second timing of a landing, rescue and departure—even to the heart-stopping, tragic conclusion in which triumph and despair are mingled in the success of the rescue and the death of its valiant commander, Lieutenant Colonel Yehonatan Netanyahu.

I say "heart-stopping" because this is no intrusion of fictional latitude, but a measure of the high risk, pyramided to almost inevitable, superhuman obligation, of one man's devotion to the mission under his command. Could the commander leave the scene while there was still one person under his command remaining behind? Was there one moment of possible danger that could be delegated to someone else, one minute detail of supervision for its success that could be set aside in the interest of personal safety?

I think not, nor did Colonel Netanyahu.[10]

[10] Netanyahu was American-born, the son of a professor at Cornell University, who delivered the traditional kaddish at his son's funeral ceremony at a military cemetery in Tel Aviv on July 6, 1976. As reported in the New York *Times* of July 7, 1976, Defense Minister Shimon Peres played on the Hebrew name of Yehonatan (Jonathan) in quoting the Book of Samuel to deliver King David's lament for Saul and Jonathan: "How the mighty have fallen." The life of Colonel Netanyahu and the compulsion that led him to return to Israel during his student days in America is told with admirable restraint by Max Hastings in *Yoni, Hero of Entebbe* (The Dial Press/James Wade, New York, 1979).

IV

We may write off Entebbe as a subject gone, wasted, forgotten, an opportunity to depict that rare happening in today's scientifically impersonal world: man as master of a machine using it to pursue an act which reflects greatness of purpose, rather than man as a servant of a machine performing some base act of violence. But there is a challenge for a rescue mission of another kind, to use the betrayal of Entebbe as a point of no return, and to say: stop here and go no farther.

I am referring to the needs of the arts themselves, the noblest expression of man's godhead, imperiled and at bay in a scientific world (even to the notion of writing music by the numbers).

This may strike some as overdramatic, but I don't feel it that way. Science, after all, is the creation of man himself. It began as a slave of his purpose, and has become a monstrous master of too much of his life.

To me, the arts are the gospel of a secular faith: they invite participation, raise the heart, and give hope to all who are responsive to them, whatever the theological differences that divide us, binding together those with a common link to a Michelangelo, a Rembrandt, a Dürer, Bach, or Beethoven. Whether or not they were men who painted as they prayed, or inscribed every note they wrote "To the glory of God" (as Joseph Haydn did), or wrote of their life's experiences in words that cursed their Maker, but were aimed, nevertheless, at some fellow man who might read and learn, listen and react, they used the medium of an art to bring us closer together.

We are all co-religionists in the journey through life that we make together. The arts are a dispensation as vital to the inner life of man as clothing to protect him, food to nurture him, or shelter to house him are to his outer being.

If some of those whose view of art doesn't measure up to the standards I have attributed to it—my answer is: they are parishioners in some other faith than the secular one I have mentioned.

The Scientific Century measures its attainments in terms of how far, how fast, how low, how high, how big—even how small. But as the lore of sports tells us, records are made to be broken. There is hardly one of these now "great" attainments not destined to be surpassed in some subsequent SC A.E., whether II, III, or IV A.E. Meanwhile we look but do not see, listen but do not hear, peruse the artistic skies around us in vain to discern anything comparable to what man has been living on, artistically, for more than two hundred years.

As the sixteenth century gave way to the seventeenth in its modes and manners of using the vibratory matter, so too the seventeenth and eighteenth lost much of their identity as the nineteenth put in motion forces that, for a time, eclipsed the eighteenth. Modern scholarship, modern access to previously neglected sources, modern talent and curiosity have returned to circulation the sense of structure and discipline embodied in such terms of musical reference as Gothic, Baroque, Rococo.

When, in all these decades and centuries, has there been a time like today, when so many composers complain of so little appreciation? They have, in the manner of other pressure groups, "lobbies" to enlist support, exercise influence, convey the conception that it is the "duty" of American orchestras to play American music. There was little such problem in the days of the enfranchising (pages 153–88), when the composers were working in an idiom to which the public was responsive. Such propaganda has had its share of success, to the extent of having a steady stream of works performed. That is *not* the problem. But reperformed? That is the problem.

On a visit not long ago to the University of Northern Colorado (in Greeley), I was talking to a young professor-composer on campus who asked my opinion of a new work by a friend, which I had heard and he hadn't. My answer surprised him, and he said: "Say that again?"

"Certainly," I answered. "I said it was a once-around piece."

"Gee," he remarked, "that's a great name for all those pieces that get heard once all over the country and never get repeated."

That, I am sure, is a phrase no composer of today would like to have applied to his work. They regularly gather in earnest groups at the end of a concert of their new music (mostly of the chamber ensemble variety, because that is what is easiest to get performed) to have a "panel" discussion of techniques and problems, in which the audience (clearly partisan) is invited to participate. But whenever the question of a *general* audience is raised, it is, more often than not, blamed on ignorance, or left unanswered.

It recalls an incident of the early fifties when RCA was trying to establish the 45-rpm disc, with its brief playing time, as a competitor, for purpose of classical music, to the LP (which outlasted it in playing time, a ratio of seven to one) sponsored by Columbia.

At the instigation of the "General" (David Sarnoff, chairman of the board of RCA), a large fee was paid to the eminent publicist Ben Sonnenberg to investigate the problem and submit a report. Six months later he produced a document stating that the principal problem with the 45-rpm record for purposes of classical music was—something hardly worth paying $50,000 to find out— "the public didn't like it."

I can say immediately, with no need for elaborate research or a fee for my findings, that the principal difficulty with most of the serious music being written by today's young composers is that the public doesn't like it.

This is somewhat different from the dilemma that beset earlier composers of the century—Stravinsky, Hindemith, Prokofiev, Bartók, Berg, Webern, and the Americans preceding the great Boulanger breakthrough—in the twenties and thirties. Their idiom was difficult and required considerable readjustment of the listener's perception. The conductors who believed in it persisted with it, to results that are now apparent: the worthwhile was separated from the spurious, and the repertory was enlarged. It was under a similar, even more concentrated pressure of conductors that the music of Gustav Mahler found its place in American concert halls.

I hear no comparable difficulty with much of the music that has been accumulating within the last few decades (1950s, 1960s,

1970s). That idiom is, by and large, not the problem: the great difficulty with much of the new music of today is not what is present, but what is *absent*—personality, conviction, motivation, provocation, not to mention originality, musical character, audience interest.

Rather than dealing with communicable content, the analysts of the new compositions—often the composers themselves—tell us about stresses and tensions, the compositional "gestures" through which they evoke this or that response, the compositional "frame" in which a nuclear element is contained. Some of them—George Crumb; Leslie Bassett, the previously mentioned Druckman—are more adroit than others, and produce well-sounding pieces. I had high hopes, a few years ago, for the obviously talented Charles Wuorinen; but he had formulated a pattern of existence in which the income from one commissioned work sustained him while he was composing another commissioned work, etc. This required the constant writing of music, à la Mozart. No further comment.

Frederic Rzewski has given promise, in another, more liberated approach to composition (as in *The People United Will Never Be Defeated*), of a dimension of thought directly addressed to listener participation. He has earned good wishes for himself, and for his very able pianist-interpreter, Ursula Oppens. David Del Tredici, also new to the national scene, has produced, in *Final Alice*, an entertaining work that several critics have described as a "masterpiece." It is an adaptation of Lewis Carroll utilizing a very high soprano (Barbara Hendricks at the premiere, in October 1978) to dispense charm, in a flattering audible costume of instrumental weave. I liked its informality, also its pleasant musical concept. Let us see where Del Tredici goes, minus his Dodgson gambit. His first step further, in the spring of 1980, was a Pulitzer prize for *In Memory of a Summer Day*.

Some great masters have evolved, of whom Elliott Carter, now in his seventies, is a father figure. He has emerged from the climate of encouragement that accompanied the rise to prominence, during his younger years, of Copland, Thomson, and the enfranchisement, to become *their* fulfillment. He is a man whose intellectual vigor and aesthetic conscience are producing works which show no signs of diminution in interest at home, and ever increasing recognition abroad.

I would put Pierre Boulez and Luciano Berio in the category of inactive but not extinct volcanoes, capable of producing eruptions which we have been expecting overlong. But I can only categorize as disappointing the recent harvests from the early crops of George Rochberg, Krzysztof Penderecki, even Hans Werner Henze and Karlheinz Stockhausen. Peter Maxwell Davies of England and his countryman Iain Hamilton have not recently circulated enough music, internationally, to define present status. Thea Musgrave has. Circulated, that is. But no clear personality has emerged from such opposite forces as a clarinet concerto and an opera to define a central force.

Is it impertinent to wonder whether there will ever be another Haydn to write a hundred and four symphonies, a Mozart to write twenty-plus piano concertos, a Beethoven to create sixteen string quartets (even Shostakovich stopped at fifteen)? A composer for whom I have substantial esteem said, in a recent conversation along these lines: "Well, you know, we can't go on writing symphony after symphony as Haydn did. We must change."

Who said so? Is he under sentence to "change" or not be performed? Is there some Great Music Critic in the Sky who has ordained such a commitment? Or is it a concession to some inner expectation that every man makes of himself?

A recent writer in the New York *Times* expressed disapproval of William Schuman's Tenth Symphony because it showed he was "out of touch with the times." Does that mean that Johannes Brahms shouldn't have written his Symphony No. 4 in 1884–85 because Wagner had "already" written *Tristan* nearly twenty-five years before?

It is such trivialization of the now and then, the heretofore and the hereafter, the modes and the manners of what is in and what is out that gives the Scientific Century its spiritual poverty and its artistic neurosis.

V

Suppose that such a man of spiritual abundance and artistic sanity as Wolfgang Mozart had been born in 1956 rather than 1756: what would he be doing today, 1980, aged twenty-four?

The question immediately arises: would he have been a musician at all? Would that fine-tuned sensitivity, swift, ready responses to sound, exceptional aptitudes, and total capacity for concentration have been immediately appreciated and encouraged? My personal belief is that he would have been tested, judged to have "genius attributes" at the age of nine, urged to become a nuclear scientist at the age of eleven, been graduated from MIT at fourteen, and never heard of thereafter.

But suppose that his organist-father in Salzburg did pass a seed of such potency that it could not have found its fulfillment in anything but music?

In the first place, a Mozart of today would have been denied the marvelous childhood that he thoroughly enjoyed, and treasured ever afterward: going to the next big town (Munich) at the age of six, to be heard by the ruler of Bavaria (called the elector). There he had an extraordinary success, because the aristocrats of the time were, not infrequently, well versed in music, and recognized something extraordinary when they encountered it.

Before he was a teenager, Mozart had visited Paris and London, and been through Holland on the way back to Salzburg. None of this was done in a matter of days or weeks: it took months, during which he became familiar with foreign languages, heard other ways of making music, met a son of the great Bach (Johann Christian) in London. In all, he was away from Salzburg for three years; it wasn't much longer (before he was fourteen) that his father took him to Italy.

Such a program at the present time would be considered child abuse, and legalities would be invoked to prohibit such exploitation. Even Enrique Barenboim had to take recourse in "educational" intentions to permit his son's early gifts to be developed under suitable "supervision." And his gifts were not creative, but re-creative.

In the early 1770s, the maturation of Mozart was, musically speaking, going on in every stagecoach he rode with his father, every roadside inn at which they stopped. As a result, he became the first truly *international* composer in history (Handel was also German-speaking by birth and spent considerable time in Italy before going to London, but he had no direct French influence).

Today, I can see Mozart becoming a participant in a festival somewhere (it wouldn't have been in Salzburg, of course), making records, appearing on television. As he was a prodigious performer on the keyboard and could, as his father has said, "have been the first violinist in Europe" had he applied himself to that instrument, he would have gravitated more and more to a career as a virtuoso. Whose music he would have performed in public, I can only speculate—but, in all probability, it wouldn't have been much of his own.

If one can imagine a world of music without the literature of Mozart, one can imagine English literature without Shakespeare, painting without Rembrandt, sculpture without Phidias (fifth century B.C.), or draftsmanship without Leonardo da Vinci.

If for no other reason than that, Mozart was a cosmological phenomenon, who gathered within himself all the kinds of music at large in Europe during his brief lifetime. As a resident of Vienna in the 1780s, he could exchange views with the great exponent of German classicism, Christoph Gluck, one week, with the great master of Italian opera buffa, Giovanni Paisiello, another. From each he absorbed a productive essence, and distilled them into that rarest of blends, formulations, and fragrances known as Mozartian.

Suppose Leopold Mozart had less comprehension of what was latent in the child playing at his feet as he went about the work required of him as a member of the archbishop's retinue in the 1760s. Let us assume that he had shirked fulfillment of the trust put upon him; that, for whatever reasons of indolence, dislike of travel, or lack of enterprise, he had not taken Mozart away from

Salzburg when he did. The growth of the child would have been different, and so, too, the history of music.

It is due in part, at least, to the pleasure that the world has derived from Mozart's existence (not to mention so many of those who followed) that what has been offered by way of substitute in these later years of Scientific Century 1 A.E. not be evaluated for more than it is. What is music, and what is the Sound of Sound, is a question for which every listener must formulate his own answer.

But more than a few performers of outstanding ability have opted for my answer, and chosen some other century—not merely the undying nineteenth, but one of the others—in which to live, spiritually, however inconvenient that may be for one forced, by circumstances, to live physically in the twentieth.

VI

Put that way, reference to "one of the others" gives rise to images of dusty abbeys, or a particularly cloistered cloister in which to pursue a preference for some of the greatest, most characteristic music ever written. That such a choice might co-exist with a talent that would attract an audience not only to a recital in a night club (the Bottom Line on New York's West Fourth Street) but also to the Hollywood Bowl suggests a divinity with an inordinate parish of co-religionists. That this might co-exist with the idea of music as the gospel of a non-sectarian faith would suit, as well as any other, the place that Jean-Pierre Rampal occupies among worldwide audiences.

A native of Marseilles, Rampal is the flute-playing son of a flute-playing father, Joseph, professor of flute in the conservatory of the Mediterranean city. As his father's son, he grew up with an aptitude for the instrument that gave him prizewinning rank in youth, but it did not appeal to him as a life work. He flirted fitfully, if not flutefully or fruitfully, with a medical career, which carried him into the 1940s (he was born in 1922). Fortunes of war

—factually, the German occupation of France—took him into the military service, and an assignment near Paris. Rather than serve under the enemy, he filed for admission to the Paris Conservatoire, and was accepted in 1942. Within a few months, his status as a prizewinning pupil kept him out of uniform. By the end of the occupation, he qualified for his first job, in the orchestra at Vichy.

Despite all, he still thought of a medical career. But appointment to the orchestra of the Paris Opéra in 1946 changed his mind. By 1958, he was its first flutist, and not long after that began to be recognized as the first flutist in the world.

There have been many great flutists before Rampal, including such fellow Frenchmen as Georges Barrère, Marcel Moyse, René Le Roy, the English Robert Murchie, and a whole school of Americans. Most of the latter were trained by Barrère,[11] who was brought to America by Walter Damrosch in 1905 as principal flutist of his New York Symphony Orchestra and taught, among many others, the great William Kincaid of the Philadelphia Orchestra. In turn, Kincaid was responsible for the training of Julius Baker, and Donald Peck of the Chicago Symphony. When Doriot Antony (now Dwyer) became first flutist of the Boston Symphony Orchestra in 1952, she opened a new career for others of her sex to follow. One of the best-known flutists of today is Paula Robison, who became, in 1970, an original member of the artists' ensemble of the Chamber Music Society of Lincoln Center.

As the attributions above suggest, even the best flutists of the thirties and forties were, for all their fame, members of orchestras in this country, or, in the case of Moyse and Le Roy, professors at the Paris Conservatoire. I have memorable recollections of solo performances by Moyse and Le Roy in New York, but they were rare occurrences (and the hall could have been as small as the one in the Steinway building, seating less than two hundred). Barrère, an extraordinarily witty man, conducted a chamber orchestra of colleagues from the New York Symphony Orchestra half a dozen times a winter (in Henry Miller's Theatre). But that was as rare a prominence for a flutist as his wit was for anybody.

Like Moyse and Le Roy, Rampal became professor of the flute at the Paris Conservatoire. But if both his predecessors may be said to have been ahead of their time, insofar as recording opportunities were concerned—Rampal has ten times as many recordings as Moyse and Le Roy combined—he is certainly possessed of

[11] Among other distinctions, Barrère, as a young member of a Paris orchestra, had the rare honor of playing the flute solo in Debussy's *L'Après-midi d'une faune* for the composer in the rehearsal, and first performances of 1894.

an attribute rare for any public performer at any time. That is a conviction in the broad, human appeal of his instrument which persuaded him to pursue its possibilities in solo recitals in Europe (1946, at the age of twenty-four) when almost all his colleagues in the orchestra of the Paris Opéra were content with their earnings in a good orchestra, supplemented by teaching.

As an instance of Rampal's serious commitment to such solo performance (his father told him it would never succeed), he chose, even then, for his associate Robert Veyron-Lacroix, a musician of high taste as well as unique versatility (he plays the piano and the harpsichord equally well). Rampal maintained that association through all the years of his slow rise to prominence, on recordings as well as in public. Veyron-Lacroix was his partner when Rampal made his New York debut in Town Hall in 1958; he was a member of the Paris Baroque Ensemble when I encountered them (the plural includes the great Pierre Pierlot as oboist and Robert Gendre, violin) in the extraordinarily beautiful Auditorio de la Reforma at mile-high Puebla, an hour's drive south of Mexico City, in June 1966; and he has pursued his partnership with Rampal as far, as wide, and as long as has suited his own tastes.

I mention these fraternal details to underscore what Isaac Stern has said of a colleague he admires greatly, and with whom he has frequently performed (in public) and recorded. In commenting on the extent to which a very general public around the globe has responded to Rampal, Stern has said: "Believe it or not, a great soloist is above all, a concept, a powerful idea. Even when an audience can't define that idea precisely, they respond to it. By the same token, I can think of certain violinists who can play all the notes in the world. But they will never make it as a great violinist because the audience senses they are too narrow, too stupid."[12]

As an observation on the audience appeal of some other remarkably successful, equally uncommon performers, Stern's comment rings true on every level. Andrés Segovia was a success, in the thirties, with the guitar—which had never been considered a *musical*

[12] Hellman, Peter, "The Most Magic Flute," New York *Times Magazine*, February 22, 1975.

instrument—because he embodied such "a concept, a powerful idea." And Wanda Landowska added the harpsichord to the honor roll of acceptable recital instruments because she, too, was impelled by a breadth of substance and a width of understanding an audience could not resist.

To say that Rampal conveys a sense of presence on the concert stage is to say that I have seen and heard him share a Vivaldi duo in Carnegie Hall with Stern, and make even that powerful performer appear to be, in rank if not in execution, playing second fiddle. Nor is this achieved by any legerdemain, presumption of undue prominence, or sly distraction from his partners.

Unlike some celebrated male dancers who have been so ostentatiously deferent in yielding prominence to a partner in a *pas de deux* that they reserve to themselves every bit of it except the tiny part on which she is standing, Rampal's artistry is excelled only by his lack of ostentation. The years he put in, during the later forties and early fifties, doing what his father said could not be done, or recording the masterpieces for his instrument on small French labels, have given him an assurance and security that convert Carnegie Hall, or any equivalent large space, into a family living room for his artistry.

Together with the "concept," to which Stern has paid the kind of recognition that could only emanate from one who possesses it himself, Rampal is undoubtedly a shrewd entrepreneur. For all the ecstasy and sense of introspection he conveys in his playing, he has been known to give a student such pertinent advice as: "Keep your head up and look at the audience, not down at your shoes," a procedure as proper in the Bottom Line as in Carnegie Hall. Though his heart is in the Baroque repertory, he draws no line at playing any part of the literature that appeals to him, whether it is Telemann or Prokofiev, or such French contemporaries as André Jolivet and Claude Bolling. Some German flute music of the nineteenth century (anything, of course, by Franz Schubert) also strikes home, but the part represented by the "romantic revival" strikes him as "virtuosity, without the feeling and goals"[13] of romanticism (a phrase that, within itself, comple-

[13] Ibid.

ments exactly what Stern has said about "a concept, a powerful idea").

His most remarkable discovery, as a stimulant to wider interest in the flute, has been a *Jazz Suite* by the Bolling mentioned above. Bottom Line or not, it has added much to the bottom line of both Rampal and Bolling. Sales of the recording were approaching half a million discs by the end of the seventies, with no indication of termination. If so many people have parted with the money to buy such a recording—some jazz evaluators contend there is as much Brubeck and Garner in the mixture as there is Bolling—it is not because they are all aspiring flutists. Rather it is because they are magnetized to hear, through such inspiring artistry, aural values of another century recast in a form not provided by many creators of this one.

Needless to say, Rampal playing Bolling is an easy form of introduction to the appeal of the flute in Rampal playing everything Bach ever wrote for the instrument, likewise Mozart, even Vivaldi. I say "even" Vivaldi, not to imply any lack of esteem for that eminent Venetian, but merely to suggest that if one of the most prolific composers in history were reincarnated for a day, there is some doubt that he would recall having written everything contained in a twelve-sided album of music for the flute.

From the Rameau Trio for Flute, Violin, and Harpsichord I heard played superbly at Puebla by Rampal, Gendre, and Veyron-Lacroix, to a jazz-flavored work performed by Rampal and Bolling *wherever*, may strike some as an artistic gulf too engulfing to be filled with equal conviction by any performer. But that is only because the lines of distinction have been too rigidly drawn by people whose minds are narrower than those endowed with the greatest of artistic gifts—flexibility.

Over the years in which Rampal's appearances in American concert halls have become occasions to anticipate, Rampal has left nothing undone for reasons of conformity, nor indulged in anything contrary to his own solid sense of good taste. Performing the solo part of the Franck sonata in A major on the flute, as Rampal did in Carnegie Hall on January 28, 1978, may strike some as presumptuous and out of order. For a lesser artist, perhaps. But as Franck allowed the same solo part to be played on the cello, the composer's sense of propriety in what is commonly called a sonata for violin and piano was hardly offended. Nor could it be said that Rampal was engaging in some form of musical showmanship. Those who were present were carried away not merely by the line of the solo part performed by Rampal with supreme lucidity, but by a seldom-equaled expression of the piano part by Philippe Entremont.

Overall, Rampal is not a man bent on exploiting his fame for personal gratification. He has not only expressed his admiration for Julius Baker by recording a collection of flute duets with him; they have shared an evening of public performance (on February 2, 1971) in Avery Fisher Hall (more recently in January 1980) that has rarely been equaled for connoisseurs of the ensemble art. With Veyron-Lacroix at the harpsichord, Rampal and Baker were heard on the first occasion in a sequence of specialities by the Bachs: trios by Johann Sebastian and Carl Philipp Emanuel, and a duo by Wilhelm Friedemann. Rampal also played sonatas by Handel and Telemann, and a sonata by Blavet of the eighteenth century.

To measure Rampal in terms of twentieth-century artists who have made the most of the unique opportunities this century has provided to the re-creative genius (if not to the creative) is to measure him against only one other: Dietrich Fischer-Dieskau (pages 93–111). Taken together, the collaborations of these two perfectionists—akin to the performance of Fischer-Dieskau and Vladimir Horowitz, in the so-called "Concert of the Century" (page 112)—could be cited as a synonym for the ultimate in impossibility. But a compatible management (both are clients, in New York, of Ann Colbert) announced such a joint appearance on February 13, 1971, in New York's Hunter College auditorium. Baroque music was the agenda, with Veyron-Lacroix as harpsichordist, and Leslie Parnas, cellist, was available wherever continuo lines were required.

Unfortunately, a few days before the concert, Fischer-Dieskau was required to return to Germany (illness was specified). In

order not to disappoint an audience which had made many con-
cessions to convenience in order to be present, a replacement program was improvised with tenor Ernst Haefliger, who was on tour
in this country, as vocalist. The audience heard Bach arias for
tenor with flute obbligato, a Lully aria, and an excerpt from Rameau's *Castor et Pollux,* in all of which Haefliger performed with
Rampal and Veyron-Lacroix. There were also works of Vivaldi
and Telemann performed by the flutist and harpsichordist.

But the idea of a collaboration of Rampal and Fischer-Dieskau
persisted, and it finally came about two years later, under the auspices of Angel records, for whom both have had occasional, if not

*"Just a minute! You don't get three years of my
life and the Dietrich Fischer-Dieskaus!"*

primary, associations. Bearing the title of *Baroque, Sacred and Profane* (Angel S36904), it is, indeed, a beautiful blend of impulses, of a rarity to challenge other discs entitled to be included in a "*Later* Great Recordings of the Century" when such a series, to extend the existing one of the 78-rpm period, is undertaken. (And the misfavored first live concert was rescheduled, and accomplished in May 1980, in Carnegie Hall.)

The recorded content, which begins with Handel and ends with Rameau, with works of Telemann and Bach in between, begins to accumulate, one unmistakable fact begins to emerge. Through the sequence opening with "Cara sposa" from Handel's *Rinaldo* and ending with "Volez, tyrans des airs" from Rameau's *Thétis*, with "Ihr Völker, hört" from Telemann's *Cantata for the Festival of Three Kings* and Bach's "Ächzen und erbärmlich Weinen" (Cantata No. 13) and "Lass', o Welt, mich aus Verachtung" (Cantata No. 123) along the way, one unmistakable advantage for Rampal begins to emerge.

He performs throughout in one language, conveyed by the wordless voice of the flute, and all the dialects of it that Rampal commands so well. Fischer-Dieskau, however, begins in Italian and ends in French, with the privilege of using his own German in Telemann and Bach. Here, let it be noted, is a professional asset for Rampal which may, in the end, enable him to surpass Fischer-Dieskau as the most recorded artist of his time (even though he began somewhat later, in the fifties, than his German colleague and friend did). One further note: Rameau's fondness for trills is more readily indulged by Rampal's flute than by Fischer-Dieskau's baritone.

As inevitably occurs when public interest is aroused in a unique speciality, in a distinctive way of doing, differently, a familiar speciality, or even in the exploitation of an unfamiliar instrument, Rampal's success has been utilized to promote an Irish virtuoso of the flute named James Galway. To say "Irish virtuoso of the flute" is to encompass almost all there is to say of this smiling, red-bearded Hibernian. He has much of the charm of John McCormack, but little of that fabulous tenor's command of style.

Whereas McCormack could utilize his fine vocal command to make Handel or "Danny Boy" sound equally beautiful in different ways, Galway uses his fine flute command to make Mozart or "Annie's Song" sound beautiful in exactly the same way.

VII

To linger over the life and lore of the French lark and his Irish echo is all too tempting, but it is merely an instance, as I have said, of the extent to which the Scientific Century has benefited the re-creators of this century and the creators of other centuries. In turn, it has benefited the world of music and music lovers through the prominence now enjoyed by a whole phylum of performers made memorable by Camille Saint-Saëns in his *fantaisie zoologique* (otherwise known as *Le Carnaval des animaux*).

For years, such men (and women) have had their artistry restricted to performance in the orchestra, with an occasional time off for good behavior in chamber music. As a result of the liberation afforded by widespread circulation of recordings and even wider-spread appreciation of their unique abilities by such a man as Rampal, more players of more instruments have been able to pursue individual careers than ever before.

Not only the specialists of the familiar instruments, but practitioners of the unusual ones—from recorders to guitars of all sizes and shapes—have been given a bright, new place in the musical sun. To some extent this has been a by-product of the ease and cheapness by which individual impulse can produce a marketable recording. But it is also a response to a much greater appreciation of the repertory they play and the qualities they bring to it. This, in turn, has promoted an audience for the live, as well as the recorded, enjoyment of the non-symphonic literature on a scale unknown in this country even twenty years ago.

I have referred to the infrequency with which such masters of the flute as Moyse and Le Roy were heard, pre-Rampal. One might also mention the clarinet. When, in the forties, such a quartet as the Budapest or the Pro Arte performed the Mozart or

Brahms quintets, it was commonly with a performer whose "name" derived from another kind of speciality (as Benny Goodman) or a principal player of an orchestral woodwind section. In the immediate aftermath of World War II Reginald Kell, of England, emerged as the best soloist on the instrument yet to be heard internationally.

Having tired of orchestral routine (largely because he found his musical judgment offended by many of the conductors with whom he had to perform), Kell came to this country in the late forties. His purpose was to organize a small ensemble with which he could tour and record, one capable of playing a wide repertory.

He assembled a group of excellent players, and set out to find an audience. It was here and it was there, primarily (outside the expectable centers) in college and university towns. But the audience didn't then (1950–60) exist in sufficient depth to support the kind of enterprise he had launched. Not too long afterward, Kell drifted out of playing the clarinet publicly, and became associated with an instrument maker. More recently, he has taken to painting, with results, I am told, that are artistically and financially successful.

Now, however, the place that should rightfully belong to Kell has been pre-empted by Gervase de Peyer, also of English birth, and doubtless in his youth stimulated by Kell as prototype. He is perhaps even more proficient technically than Kell, though less interesting or individual an interpreter. De Peyer divides his life between recording studios and concert halls in England and high-level prominence in America as a member of the artists' ensemble of the Chamber Music Society of Lincoln Center. The level of achievement he has attained is reflected in the even greater brilliance acquired by the rising Richard Stoltzman, who first came to attention as a member of Peter Serkin's Tashi ensemble. I would say that Stanley Drucker, the outstanding clarinetist of the New York Philharmonic Orchestra, could qualify on the solo level of either, could he bring himself to such a decision. So far it hasn't happened.

The kind of competitive prominence thus engendered has benefits, and consequences, far beyond those that are immediately apparent. Recordings of the ensemble classics on the highest level engender an appetite for them live. More people are discovering, every year, that the awesome name of "chamber music" has too long deterred them from enjoying music of the *same* kind that they listen to, by the same composers (from Mozart to Shostakovich), as titled symphonies or sonatas.

The proliferation of record labels here and abroad promotes greater solo opportunities for specialists of such literature in Holland and Austria, Belgium and Hungary, in addition to England, France, and the United States. When the greatest soloist on the double bass in America, Gary Karr, makes a recording of his specialities, Rodion Azarkhin (born in Kharkov) responds with a disc that begins with the Bach Chaconne and ends with Sarasate's *Zigeunerweisen*, with Saint-Saëns' *The Swan*, the scherzo from Mendelssohn's *A Midsummer Night's Dream*, Tchaikovsky's "None but the Lonely Heart," and similar made-for-the-double-bass repertory (such as "Largo al factotum" from Rossini's *Il Barbiere di Siviglia*) in between.

These are expectable fallout from launchings by the two nuclear powers.

Wholly different, but in keeping with the high sense of purpose pursued by Rampal, is the remarkable rise to comparable rank by his countryman Maurice André. He did not have the advantage of growing up under a musician-teacher-father: a substantial part of André's growing years were spent in the coal mines of the Cévennes area in the South of France. Concurrently, he was studying the trumpet. He was accepted into the Paris Conservatoire in the early fifties (in his twenties) for outstanding ability on the cornet, derived in part from army training. In 1955, after winning honors at the Conservatoire as a trumpeter, he became a member of the National Radio Orchestra.

Playing the trumpet as a solo career was even less inviting than its attraction to a flutist; but there is a difference. Even the Baroque trumpet, with its compact dimensions and high, brilliant sound, was not so much the essence of a literature as the embellishment of one. Nothing more than a mental image need be invoked: Frederick the Great was a flutist whose interest in the instrument added substantially to its literature. Can one imagine a monarch of equal musicality spending a social hour after dinner playing the Baroque trumpet?

Nevertheless, the clear evidence is that André was no more disposed to spending his life playing in an orchestra than Rampal was. He entered, and won, several competitions. The crucial, determining one was the International Competition of 1963 in Munich. This lent strength to his conviction, and energy to his pursuit of a literature even longer dormant than Rampal's. The latter had such prototypes as Moyse and Le Roy; but even so brilliant a trumpeter as Roger Voisin spent most of his time in the Boston Symphony Orchestra, or teaching.

However, as André's career has made evident, there were enough specialists of the instrument, across the span of both the seventeenth and eighteenth centuries, to prompt composers from Telemann and Marcello (both born in the 1680s) to Haydn (who died in 1809) to challenge their skills. Even the new resources of the trumpet-to-be in the nineteenth century are embodied in Haydn's E flat concerto of 1796. It is performed by André with the flourishes appropriate to one of the early keyed brass instruments.

So much of this repertory might appear to be reserved to the interests of the musical antiquarians; but when André gave a recital in Lincoln Center with a properly qualified organist as collaborator in 1975, it was an occasion that illuminated a splendid epoch of music in a way that is seldom heard. Even more to the point, the collaborative effort of Rampal-André in the complete "Brandenburg Concertos" of Bach (with Jean-François Paillard conducting the chamber orchestra bearing his name on Victor CRL2-5801) provides more than an exhilarating experience for a music lover eager to sample the best of the best: it provides a standard of excellence for orchestral players all over the world to emulate.

Some may wonder why it is only today, in the hands of such a specialist as André (and such others as Martin Berinbaum of New York, Adolf Scherbaum of Berlin, and Helmut Wobisch of Vienna), that the art of playing the seemingly impossible works of the Baroque and rococo eras is being discovered. The answer is contained in the question: they were *written* for specialists, and were brought into being for such unique performers of the past.

When a question along the same lines, pertaining to the difficulties that some horn players of today, with their keyed instruments, find in Haydn symphonies written for earlier, primitive horns, was put to Barry Tuckwell, the great master of that instrument had a cogent answer: "Those seemingly impossible horn parts were, in those days, shared. Don't forget many of the brass players in Haydn's orchestra at Esterhazy also played for the hunts. They were taught to exchange signals between one hunting group and another, and functioned in a variety of ways different than the symphony horn players of today. They developed great facility in ranges that are not much stressed in training horn players of the present time."

How the emergence of a specialist on such an instrument as the horn may affect live performances in subtle ways can be illustrated in the instance of Tuckwell, a native of Melbourne, Australia. After qualifying as a member of the Sydney Symphony Orchestra at the age of sixteen in 1947 (the conductor at the time was Eugene Goossens), Tuckwell went to England. He joined the Hallé Orchestra in Manchester. Here, he has said, he found life much as he had known it in Australia. Would he settle for the lot of a section man in England? He might as well go back home.

The records show that his decision took a different turn. Five years later, after hard work and single-minded application, he became first horn of the London Symphony (1955). The expansion of opportunity for the best wind players, as recording specialists and chamber music performers, found Tuckwell the most qualified hornist for the widest range of opportunities.

To round out the consequences of what evolved from Tuckwell's emergence as "the best" on his instrument, I may mention the program of a concert in Vienna in the spring of 1980 performed by the Wiener Kammerorchester under the direction of the English conductor Steuart Bedford. The music was all British, and began with a suite from Henry Purcell's *The Fairy Queen*, followed by two works of Benjamin Britten. This, too, is in order, but rather than calling upon such possibilities as the Prelude and

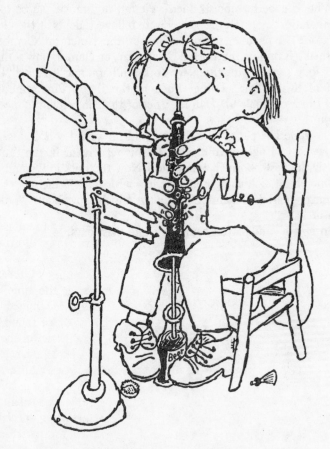

Fugue for String Orchestra, or the *Variations on a Theme of Frank Bridge* (similarly scored), Bedford's choice was the *Serenade for Tenor, Horn, and Strings*. Robert Tear was the tenor, and Tuckwell performed his now well-known speciality (he has also recorded it with the composer). Would that choice have been possible without a soloist of Tuckwell's known capacity and experience? The probability is that the Viennese would not have heard a work which represents Britten at his most poetic best.

Who is a better oboist? Pierre Pierlot, of France, whose long collaboration with Rampal (they were fellow students at the Conservatoire) I have mentioned? One of the American Gomberg brothers (Ralph of the Boston Symphony, or Harold, now retired after long service with the New York Philharmonic)? Heinz Holliger of Switzerland? Lothar Koch of the Berlin Philharmonic? Neil Black of England? Han de Vries of the Amsterdam Concertgebouw?

The time has passed when one could say of a Leon Goossens, renowned in England from 1913 till his retirement in the fifties, "He is the best oboist in the world." Now the question would be not merely Which composer? Handel or Mozart? Which work of Mozart? Quartet or quintet? But also Which movement? Which measure?

Criteria in wind players come very high these days.

* * *

AN ALPHABET (ALMOST) OF EXQUISITES

NAME	SPECIALITY	COMMENT
ANDRÉ, MAURICE	Baroque trumpet	*Ne plus ultra*
BOBO, ROGER	Tuba	Master in search of a repertory
CARLOS, WALTER	Synthesizer	Plugged in, but no Bach
DE PEYER, GERVASE	Clarinetist	Beyond (practical) compare
ESKDALE, GEORGE	Trumpet	First of Haydnites
GOMBERG, HAROLD	Oboe	Orchestral player supreme
HOFFNUNG, GERARD	Master of garden hose	Left his mark in pen and ink
JONES, MASON	Horn	See Gomberg, Harold
KARR, GARY	Double bass	See Bobo, Roger
LORIOD, YVONNE	Ondes Martenot	More than Mme. Messiaen
MANHEIM, MAGNE	"Hardengar" fiddle	To be heard only beside a fjord in Norway
NIXON, MARNI	Other people's voices	Also sings Schoenberg well
OBERLIN, RUSSELL	Countertenor	King of the high register
PIERLOT, PIERRE	Oboe	Reedy and ready
RAMPAL, JEAN-PIERRE	Flute	Bach, Baroque, and Bolling
STACEY, THOMAS	English horn	See Karr, Gary
TUCKWELL, BARRY	Horn	No known counterpart

UNDERWOOD, DALE	Saxophones	Clear, clean, and correct (size of no consequence)
VENUTI, JOE	Jazz violin	Inventor of the four-string bow
WOBISCH, HELMUT	Post horn	From Mozart to Mahler
YAMASH'TA, STOMU	Percussion	See Hans Werner Henze's *Cimarron*
ZABALETA, NICANOR	Harp	The Casals of his instrument

DECORATIONS BY HOFFNUNG

* * *

And so we arrive, all unexpectedly, back at Edith Grove, 19-19A, SC 2 A.E., with spiritual descendants of some who gathered there and waited for the others to arrive, in a spirit of *Music at Midnight*. But for a wrong turn at high speed in a small car, the gathering could very well have included a lineal descendant of the great hornist of those gatherings, Aubrey Brain. That would be his son Dennis, who died in a driving accident at the age of thirty-six on September 1, 1957, already rated the greatest in the world on his instrument.

And, given the chance for a reprise, the group in the music room could—if I were doing the inviting—include some new successors to those celebrities of the past: Arthur Grumiaux, violin, Alicia de Larrocha (what a superb chamber music player she must be), the rising cellist Eugene Moyse, Pinchas Zukerman on viola, perhaps Isaac Stern as alternate first and second violinist to Grumiaux. And, if all the string players were amenable, Rampal might be indulged to join in his favorite pastime: playing the first violin part of one of Beethoven's "Rasumovsky" quartets (opus 59) on the flute.

However, there would be one change. No longer would these stars have to wait for their prized satellites to join them after finishing their evening chores at Royal Festival Hall or "the Garden." Such players as Barry Tuckwell, horn, Gervase de Peyer, clarinet, or Neil Black, oboe, don't do that kind of work these days. That's a consequence of that other era A.E. After Edison.

Index